Alexander Bakshy on Film, 1913-1935

Alexander Bakshy on Film, 1913-1935

Edited by R. J. Cardullo

BearManor Media.com

Published in the USA by
BearManor Media
1317 Edgewater Dr. #110
Orlando, FL 32804
www.BearManorMedia.com

Softcover Edition
ISBN-10:
ISBN-13: 979-8-88771-119-5

Printed in the United States of America

Table of Contents

Permissions

The Berne Convention stipulates that the duration of the term for copyright protection is the life of the author plus at least fifty years after his death. A number of countries, including the European Union and the United States, have extended that to seventy years after the author's death. Since Alexander Bakshy died in 1949, his written work is now in the public domain and no longer covered by copyright law. Moreover, except for *The Nation* and the *New York Times* (with which publications Bakshy has no surviving written agreement, as expressly required by U.S. copyright law), all the magazines in which Bakshy's essays and reviews were originally published have long been defunct. Bakshy, for his part, left no estate, nor did he have any heirs.

Foreword

Harry Alan Potamkin, "Alexander Bakshy," *National Board of Review Magazine*, 11, no. 9 (September 1927): pp. 4, 6.

*Harry Alan Potamkin (1900-33) began publishing film criticism in 1927. From then until his premature death (from stomach ulcers), his work appeared regularly in a broad range of film journals (*Close Up, Movie Makers, American Cinematographer*), liberal periodicals (*New Freeman, Hound and Horn*), and organs of the Left (*The New Masses, Workers' Theatre*). The Compound Cinema: The Film Writings of Harry Alan Potamkin *was published posthumously, in 1977.*

No American has captured in writing the qualities of film so well as Alexander Bakshy, a Russian/Anglo-American critic. Bakshy's brief essay "The Cinema as Art"—written in 1913, published in 1916 in *The Drama* (Chicago), and reprinted in the same year in his volume *The Path of the Modern Russian Stage*—is an amazing statement about the movies and an anticipation of its present and imminent problems. Bakshy almost fifteen years ago recognized the cinema as an art form, but in doing so he did not speak vaguely or too broadly. Bakshy more than a decade ago indicated the folly of literary intrusion on the cinema. He was not carried away by the adaptation of *Cabiria* [1914, dir. Giovanni Pastrone], as was Vachel Lindsay. From his point of view, not even Gabriele D'Annunzio belonged in the cinema.

Yet Bakshy kept his poise when he touched upon these intrusions. Unlike numerous other commentators, he was not shunted into an abuse of the inherent or self-contained film. He recognized that the usual attack is not the cinema's particular concern, that it is really an attack upon evils not peculiarly the cinema's. He understood that there is a quarrel, not between the mechanical and the non-mechanical, but between the artistic and the non-artistic. He remarks upon the need for independent film artists; he realizes that the problem of commercial concentration was present in the movies ten years ago.

But the importance of Bakshy's contribution does not lie in his pointing to the negative aspects of cinematic procedure. It consists of an immediate recognition of the character of filmic pantomime that is almost prophetic. Filmic pantomime, he said more than a decade ago, "is the most abstract form of pantomime," and should be left "to the dancers, clowns, and acrobats, who do know something about the laws of movement" ["The Cinema as Art," *The Drama* (Chicago), 6, no. 22 (May 1916): p. 274]. This is a recognition manifested in the success of the greatest of the movie pantomimists, the low comics. Bakshy saw in the ballet itself the rudiments of cinematic rhythm. As if to confirm his judgment, a few years later the Fernand Léger/DudleyMurphy film *Ballet Mécanique* [1924] appeared.

Bakshy resolved the optical problems of film into simple terms of the camera—which, a decade ago, was an amazing apprehension. What director today knows that the camera and not the picture is the medium? Bakshy anticipated by more than ten years the silhouette film; Germany produced the first multiple-reel movie of silhouette cutouts in 1926 [*The Adventures of Prince Achmed*, dir. Lotte Reiniger; it was also the first feature-length animated film]. Since its origins the cinema has been overrun with investors and inventors: the talking picture, the colored picture, the stereoscopic picture. Bakshy anticipated another "problem" soon to threaten us, the natural-vision film. Yet he met the problem of the natural depth, three-dimensional motion picture, not by opposing it, but by separating the cinema into two kind of pictures: the one-plane, flat film—which would be our present one—and the stereoscopic, in-depth film; a moving picture and a moving sculpture, as it were. This moving sculpture is quite different from Vachel Lindsay's sculpture-in-motion. Lindsay's is based on an analogy with sculpture; it is, in fact, only that sculpture in motion. Bakshy's conception is of three dimensions interrelated by motion, interrelated so as to create a rhythm, preconceived by the *régisseur* and then sustained and exploited by the camera.

The art training of a Lindsay is not such as would be very helpful to cinema, even were cinema only an extension of the graphic. And it is certainly evident that his understanding of art does not include a familiarity with its divisions, together with their circumscriptions and particular concerns. Bakshy is intimately cognizant of what belongs to each of the different plastic arts. He sees the confusion of plastics in futurism, which wanted to give cinematographic value to sculpture and painting. Time, of course, has been included as an element in painting by every important painter. But futurism wanted to *realize* time, not *visualize* it. It is to the cinema that the realization of time pictorially belongs—in other words, actual rhythmic motion. In his recognition of divisions, of categories, Bakshy emphasized the fact that the cinema is a medium, not of colors, but of tones or color-values. The French critics understand this, although French movies are full of color impurities. American journalistic critics, however, are unable to make the distinction. Someone like Quinn Martin [of the *World* newspaper] therefore waxes eloquent on the adventurousness of Douglas Fairbanks in furthering Technicolor.

The work of Bakshy indicates what movie critics should be doing. He has extended the artistic consideration of the cinema. Last year he advocated the exploitation of the screen as the receptive medium— one receptive to new ideas. An elementary use of this notion was made in the enlarged film *Chang: A Drama of the Wilderness* [1927, dir. Ernest B. Schoedsack & Merian C. Cooper; this picture made use of the Magnascope, an optical device used to get a close-up of small objects, and thus to temporarily increase the size of the image on the screen] and *Old Ironsides* [1926, dir. James Cruze; this picture also made use of the Magnascope]. But Bakshy advocated a *multiple* screen for purposes of rhythm, relationship of minor to major actions, and climax. Any one filmic unit could thus be separated into its elements, before having them fused. Undoubtedly, someone will make use of this idea, too. And that is the point of Bakshy's importance. He is not a weathercock but a prophet.

Criticism is altogether too redundant nowadays. No one thinks it important to do anything else but repeat what has been said many times before. Criticism must save its wind, to be sure. It must also have something to do with the generating of that wind. Its prophecy, however, must not be concerned with presentiments so as to appear miraculous, but must subject itself to the discipline of its category. It must be criticism in terms of the intrinsic qualities of the thing criticized: in this instance, the cinema. From a scrutiny of the cinema and what criticism of pertinence it has called forth, certain tenets can be drawn. These tenets must be qualified, extended, and applied, both by the film practitioner and the film critic. In fact, the critic must be a practitioner as well. That is, his criticism must be such as to be immediately convertible into practice. Bakshy's criticism is of that kind.

Introduction

Alexander Bakshy (1885-1949) wrestled with major problems of the drama and the motion picture at significant moments of their evolutions, and he had a sound understanding of general aesthetics as well. Very little is known about him as a personality—the prominent New York drama critics Eric Bentley and Joseph Wood Krutch remembered him only as a name. Born in Kerch, Russia, on the Black Sea, he immigrated to England sometime before 1912 and subsequently became the corresponding art critic in London for several Russian periodicals. Bakshy's confessed lack of scholarly credentials or practical knowledge of the stage did not prevent him from writing perceptive essays, in addition, on the drama; they are collected in his two major books (as well as, posthumously, in *Drama According to Alexander Bakshy, 1916-1946* [2022]), both published in London: *The Path of the Modern Russian Stage* (1916) and *The Theatre Unbound* (1923). Between these two publications, in 1919, he tried unsuccessfully to establish a journal in English for the serious study of the theater, but, as he lamented, his tiny craft titled *Proscenium* "foundered immediately it came out into the open sea" (*Theatre Unbound*, 9).

Applications on file in the U.S. Copyright Office indicate that Bakshy was a citizen of the United States as early as April 7, 1938 (having come to America sometime between 1923 and 1927), and as late as February 25, 1949, and that he maintained a New York City address. But even before this he contributed sixty-six articles as film critic for the *Nation* from 1927 to 1933, in addition to writing theoretical essays for John Cohen's film page in the *New York Sun* (collected in *Scrapbook*, Volumes I-III, which is housed in the Herman G. Weinberg Collection at the New York Public Library). From 1913 to 1945 he free-lanced for other periodicals and newspapers on the subjects of film, drama, painting, even history and ballet—in such publications as *American Mercury, Current History, The Dial, The Drama, English Review, Poet Lore, Saturday Review, Theatre Arts Monthly*, and *The New York Times*.

At the same time, Bakshy was translating the works of Russians like Bunin, Ehrenburg, Gogol, Gorky, Kuprin, Lopatin, Solovyov, and Meyerhold.

When he wrote about film, Bakshy lent a voice of maturity to the current of enthusiasm for the new art among the intelligentsia. In his first American essay, written for *Theatre Arts Monthly* in April 1927, he cautioned the youthful enthusiasts against too readily shouting "masterpiece!" Only in the past few years, he maintained, had the moving picture realized its potential as an art form. Bakshy spoke from experience. His essay "The Cinema as Art," written in England in 1913 (and first published in the United States in 1916 in *The Drama*), was one of the earliest perceptive critical pieces written on the nature of the cinema. In this essay Bakshy called for an end to vulgar realism, to the mechanical reproduction of the stage play. The moving picture must overcome the grotesque gestures and facial distortions of the filmed stage play. To assume a more graceful naturalness was the responsibility of a different corps of actors; the cinematograph must replace the stilted performers from the traditional drama with harlequins, mimes, and ballet dancers who made a living as "students of motion" (Jacobs, 63).

Writing in 1928, in a prefatory note to the reprinting of "The Artistic Possibilities of the Cinema," Bakshy expressed embarrassment at the immaturity of these earlier remarks, for the film medium had evolved far beyond pantomime as the sole method of cinematic acting (3). In spite of his altered view of pantomime, Bakshy's critical theory remained distinctly opposed to the moving picture viewed as a realistic art. He inveighed against the obsession with realism, against those who imagined the cinema as a conglomeration of irrelevant details without emphasis or unity ("Road to Art," 457-458). For Bakshy, the essentials of aesthetic appreciation would always remain the same:

> The work of art is something that is endowed with a peculiar life of its own, and that asserts its identity against our effort to grasp and absorb it into the complex whole which constitutes

our own identity. This life is a form of functioning of the material in which the work of art finds its expression, and the keener our appreciation is of the nature of the material, the more attuned we are to its inner resonance—the more profound and exhilarating is the aesthetic thrill we experience in the presence of genuine works of art. ("New Art," 279)

If the moving picture had progressed beyond the natural gracefulness of pantomime, what was the unique nature of the film medium? For Bakshy, the cinema might be classified into three distinct types of drama. First, there was the "realist drama," which ignored the necessity of form and which proceeded without spectator involvement, limiting the audience to the role of observer. Secondly, the "semi-independent drama," which remained unrelated to the medium's dynamics, but did appeal to the spectator's imagination by selection and style within the individual frame. Thirdly, there existed the "dependent drama," which daringly neglected to disguise the nature of the medium, placing complete emphasis on the presence of the audience ("Road to Art," 455).

Alone among the important contributors to American film literature, Bakshy most consistently advocated, in "dependent drama," direct contact with the audience. While other critics discussed the art of masking art, Bakshy described an aesthetic future where the visible mechanics of the film would provide sensual thrills. In his more theoretical pieces, he objected that the screen itself had not been utilized as an arena of dramatic movement ("Future of the Movies," 362). He imagined a vast screen where images might "leap" from one corner of the theater to another, "flitting" laterally before the viewer ("New Dimensions in the Talkies," 703), or where separate pictures might be flashed onto the screen to reveal a simultaneous number of subjects ("Road to Art," 460). In other words, the cinema might exhibit the thrill of personality once thought to be the province of the vaudeville stage. Only in this instance the personality would derive, not from the delightful antics of an individual actor, but rather from the continuous play of dynamically related images ("Movie Scene," 102).

Bakshy's remarks provide the most radical statement of an assumption underlying much of the theoretical writing of the late 1920s: that technique, based upon a sophisticated knowledge of the medium, might provide aesthetic pleasure divorced from any considerations of theme or subject matter. And filmic technique, for him, included acting—specifically, presentational acting, which acknowledges the audience, whether directly by addressing them or indirectly through the use of words, looks, gestures, or other signs that indicate that the character/actor is aware of the audience's presence. When Bakshy began seriously to examine the cinema, he was in a state of excitement about a possible presentational revival for all of the arts, not just for drama, which for centuries (until the advent of realism in the nineteenth century) had been the natural home of presentationalism.

Because he was bruiting the virtues of presentationalism, he considered the silent film (which he thought of as presentational) more promising than the early "talkies" (which appeared to him ludicrous attempts to imitate stage representationalism). For a number of years sound appeared to be merely a gratuitous intrusion on the purely visual experimentation of the silent picture, with such techniques as double exposure (to round out the presentation of character more imaginatively than flashback) and the split screen (to present simultaneous actions), to mention only two of the formal innovations that Bakshy encouraged during his tenure as film critic for the *Nation*. From his point of view, representational films and realistic theatrical productions were two heads of the same ogre, which only popular audiences could keep alive in their obeisance to Hollywood and Broadway.

Representational films, however, appeared less menacing when photographic and sound technology improved. Bakshy then conceded that, if the controlling producers and directors allow, sound cinema could develop its own potentialities as a representational medium distinct from silent film—which could then be given more freedom to explore presentational expressiveness—and also distinct from its counterpart of representational drama, since the "material on screen [unlike the kind found in the theater] is not actual objects but images fixed on the screen" and thus "has properties that are never found in the actual objects" ("Talkies," 236). If these differences of form are observed, representational sound pictures would have the capacity of dealing directly with the real world, provided they become as truly representational in sound as they can be in visual imagery. Moreover, the visual images that penetrate into the visual substance of the human world can attain greater realism through natural colors and stereoscopic effects ("Talkies and Dummies," 562-563). Such a cinema would outdo and even instruct the drama in representational possibilities, since movies have "greater technical resources for creating that very illusion of life existing outside the theater" ("Future of the Movies," 360).

Bakshy's tendency to think of talkies as representational and silent films as presentational was halted when he began to see presentational possibilities in the use of sound, such as fade-outs and "separating the voice from the image of its owner" ("Year of Talkies," 773). Speech, sound, and image, he then suggested, could be inflected in an infinite number of ways, and the form of the cinema might combine presentational with representational devices, even if (as he suspected) representationalism was going to predominate in the new industry. That Bakshy's optimism about the cinema waned, however, becomes increasingly clear in his movie reviews for the *Nation*. His last one was a virulent attack against Hollywood for its failure to develop either presentational or representational cinema effectively ("More Celluloid," 76).

But before he became disillusioned with traditional moviemaking, Bakshy intelligently probed the evolving techniques of the new medium. For him the most distinctive attribute of the camera, the most formative component, is its freedom of movement in time and space, since these dimensions are relative in cinema and not absolute, as they tend to be in the theater. Motion pictures can mold time by "rearranging its natural sequences, compressing it into a single moment, or expanding it into an infinity" ("New Art," 280). Some of the possibilities of emancipated spatial movement, in Bakshy's loving elaboration, are: movement in the position of photographed objects, through a change in the position of the camera (as in close-ups or high-angle shots), or movement in perception through a change in lighting and coloring of these objects; movement of images through acceleration or retardation; and movement through "the joint functioning of the projector and the screen—the movement of a small picture growing large, or of a picture traversing the screen from one end to another" ("New Art," 281). It is the responsibility of the director to integrate all movement and all sound into a single dramatic pattern whose rhythm creates "an independent ideal world, entirely self-sustained and coherently compact, which has its own life and its own emotional logic" ("Miracle of *Arsenal*," 640).

That the screen (as well as the camera) is a mechanical device does not preclude its development for artistic expression, since "all mechanisms must be controlled by human power at one moment or another" ("Cinema as Art," 272). The screen, if used representationally, "is merely an inert surface playing no part in molding the form of the picture" ("New Dimensions in the Talkies," 703). But a presentational cinema could have the performance emanate from the godlike presence of the screen, which "must become a physical reality in the eyes of the audience, a part of the theater building that provides the graphic frame of reference for the very being of characters in space, as well as for the form in which they are presented to view" ("Screen Musical Comedy," 160). The presentational screen of the future, therefore, should "be the most important part of the building. It will occupy the largest area architecturally possible in the theater, and it will be used for the effects of movement obtained by changing the position of the picture, by changing its size, and, finally, by employing simultaneously a number of separate [visual] subjects that are organized to form a single dramatically dynamic pattern" ("Future of the Movies," 362). Then a "direct physical contact" of screen with spectator could be established ("Movie Scene," 107).

Bakshy's changing ideas about the film actor show his attempts to adjust his thinking about the cinema as it evolved. At first, in silent movies, the actor, was an image presented through moving form and color (if only the colors black and white)—and because of this presentational status, according to Bakshy, he considered it "irrelevant whether the acting . . . is performed by living persons, by dolls, or by cinematographic shadows" ("Cinema as Art," 275). The genius of Charlie Chaplin, for example, lay in his ability to adjust what he had learned from the presentational art of vaudeville to the nature of cinematic art—hence his ability to convey an emotion by "a movement of the body, a twist of the head, or a doll-like fixedness of expression" ("Knight-Errant," 413; "Charlie Chaplin," 247-248); and his sense of dramatic composition in "the use of emphasis in a portrait-like portrayal, the appreciation of rhythmic pattern, the knowledge of the exact location for the dramatic accent" ("Knight-Errant," 413; "Charlie Chaplin," 247-248).

But with the coming of sound and the introduction of dialogue, the actor ceased to be a shadow and became a person. As a result, the movie spectator's aesthetic distance became more difficult to maintain than was the case in the theater auditorium; the inevitable intimacy and realism of the human voice at close range induce the film audience to see the actor as a character. And as the actor becomes character, character becomes bound to a setting of natural surroundings, thus making representationalism an important mode for the cinema. Representational dialogue, however, is different in the cinema from what it is in the drama, where dialogue must perform a duty "for a great deal of human conduct that is essentially wordless" and that in a movie can simply be conveyed visually, photographically ("Hollywood Tries 'Ideas,'" 708). For this reason, "unlike the stage actor, the film actor appears best when he acts least. All he needs is personality, character, for this is enough to make his acting both natural and convincing" ("The Shrinking of Personality," 590).

In spite of his recognition of how congenial the film is to representational acting, Bakshy occasionally ventured the hope (before giving up on Hollywood) that presentational acting and non-realistic speech could be employed in the cinema; but the movie actor in either mode, representational or presentational, would never be the active agent he is in the drama ("Talkies and Dummies," 562-563), in part because of the reduced role of the spectator. That is to say, though the presence of a spectator is assumed in the cinema in order to justify the joint efforts of actor and camera, his role is less indispensable than it is in the theater because of the ultimate impersonality of the newer medium. No frankly or self-consciously acknowledged screen in a presentational picture could create the intimacy of a presentational actor playing to his viewers in the theater; and no representational movie could evidence an awareness of an audience as does the theater performer as he paces his lines, in a representational drama, in response to audience laughter. Nonetheless, Bakshy once suggested that the movie spectator, in surrendering himself to the rhythmic pattern of a film and its impact upon his emotional sensibility, would not only experience the freedom of transcending worldly time and space but could also undergo a sort of Aristotelian catharsis ("Future of the Movies," 360).

Because of the commonalities between the stage and screen—as discussed above, both feature people acting (whether presentationally or representationally) a story within a frame before your eyes—most early movie critics made little distinction between the two art forms. But not Bakshy. "Analogies between the stage and the screen assume that they deal with the same material. But they don't," he wrote in the *Nation* in 1929:

> The material of the screen is not actual objects but images fixed on the film. And the very fact that they have their being on film endows these images with properties that are never found in actual objects. For instance, on the stage the actor moves in real space and time. He cannot even cross the room without performing a definite number of movements. On the screen an action may be shown only in terminal points with all its intervening moments left out.

In watching a performance on the stage, the spectator is likewise governed by the actual conditions of space and time. Not so in the case of the movie spectator. Thanks to the moving camera he is able to view the scene from all kinds of angles, leaping from a long-distance view to a close-range inspection of every detail. It is obvious that with this extraordinary power of handling space and time—by elimination and emphasis, according to its dramatic needs— the motion picture can never be content with modeling itself after the stage. ("The Talkies," 238)

Bakshy's importance as a critic wasn't lost on Harry Alan Potamkin, another early film critic. Pointing to Bakshy's early writings about movie pantomime as a kind of cinematic rhythm and the medium's use of color *tones* before the appearance of flashy color processes, Potamkin declared the following in 1927: "No American has captured in writing the qualities of cinema so well as has Alexander Bakshy" (Potamkin, 4). Bakshy, then, was one of the more progressive cultural critics of the years between the world wars, one who did his part in easing the movies toward acceptance as an art form. In his application to cinema of the discourse of self-reflexive modernism (prizing anti-illusionist medium-awareness)—a discourse that had emerged in theater criticism in the early 1900s—he was also an innovative theorist.

Nonetheless, Alexander Bakshy quit film criticism in 1933, fed up with the low quality of the movies. As he wrote in his final column for the *Nation*:

Not only are there woefully few [films] that are worthy of serious consideration, but if you happen to be a film critic you are obliged to stop and analyze the incessant flow of bilge issuing from the film factories of Hollywood and elsewhere as if it were really to be measured by the standards of intellectual and artistic achievement. The whole procedure becomes unspeakably grotesque, resembling in a way what the Russians describe as shooting sparrows with cannon balls. Worse still, it becomes wearisomely repetitious, for in the films originality is found in virtues, not, as in real life, in sins. ("More Celluloid," 76)

Bakshy managed to deal with the bilge by approaching each piece of film criticism as the occasion for some larger essayistic rumination, say, on the subject of theater vs. cinema. But no reviews of bilge are reprinted in *Alexander Bakshy on Film, 1913-1935*; instead, the reader gets thoughtful commentary on such important films as Chaplin's *City Lights*, Eisenstein's *Ten Days That Shook the World*, Dreyer's *The Passion of Joan of Arc*, Clair's *Sous les toits de Paris*, Pabst's *Kameradschaft*, Kinugasa's *Slums of Tokyo*, Lubitsch's *Trouble in Paradise*, and Milestone's *All Quiet on the Western Front*. The reader is also treated to evidence of Bakshy's penchant for "theoretizing," in essays on film acting, experimental or art-house movie theaters, and sound vs. silent cinema.

In sum, not only was Alexander Bakshy one of America's first full-time professional film critics (and perhaps the best of this incipient lot), he was also one of the nation's first film theorists and was even hailed, in his own lifetime, as "the father of film aesthetics" (Stern, 19). His work now again receives some of the attention it richly deserves—attention heretofore reserved for the work of other significant early American critics such as James Agee, who himself began writing movie reviews for the *Nation* in 1942; Otis Ferguson, the film critic of the *New Republic* during the mid-1930s and early 1940s; Robert Warshow, who wrote about cinema for the *Partisan Review* and *Commentary* in the late 1940s and early 1950s; and Bakshy's admirer Harry Alan Potamkin, the film critic of the *New Masses* during the same years Bakshy was writing for the *Nation*: 1927 to 1933. Gentlemen, move over.

Works Cited

Bakshy, Alexander. "The Cinema as Art." *The Drama* (Chicago), 6, no. 22 (May 1916): pp. 267-284.

----------. "The New Art of the Moving Picture." *Theatre Arts Monthly*, 11, no. 4 (April 1927): pp. 277-282.

----------. "The Road to Art in the Motion Picture." *Theatre Arts Monthly*, 11, no. 6 (June 1927): pp. 455-462.

----------. "Charlie Chaplin." *The Nation*, February 29, 1928, pp. 247-248.

----------. "A Knight-Errant." *The Dial*, 84, no. 5 (May 1928): pp. 413-414.

----------. "The Future of the Movies." *The Nation*, October 10, 1928, pp. 360, 362, 364.

----------. "The Artistic Possibilities of the Cinema." Originally published in *Kinematograph and Lantern Weekly* (August 1913). Reprinted in *National Board of Review Magazine*, 3, no. 11 (November 1928): pp. 3-5.

----------. "The Movie Scene: Notes on Sound and Silence." *Theatre Arts Monthly*, 13, no. 2 (February 1929): pp. 97-107.

----------. "The Talkies." *The Nation*, February 20, 1929, pp. 236, 238.

----------. "A Year of Talkies." *The Nation*, June 26, 1929, pp. 772-773.

----------. "Talkies and Dummies." *The Nation*, November 13, 1929, pp. 562-563.

----------. "A Miracle: *Arsenal.*" *The Nation*, November 27, 1929, p. 640.

----------. "Screen Musical Comedy." *The Nation*, February 5, 1930, pp. 159-160.

----------. "New Dimensions in the Talkies." *The Nation*, December 24, 1930, pp. 702-703.

----------. "The Shrinking of Personality." *The Nation*, May 27, 1931, p. 590.

----------. "More Celluloid." *The Nation*, January 18, 1933, p. 76.

Jacobs, Lewis, ed. *The Art of the Movies: An Anthology of Ideas on the Nature of Movie Art.* New York: Noonday Press, 1960. ("The Cinema as Art," pp. 57-70)

Potamkin, Harry Alan. "Alexander Bakshy." *National Board of Review Magazine*, 11, no. 9 (September 1927): pp. 4, 6.

Stern, Seymour. "Principles of the New World-Cinema, Part I." *Experimental Cinema*, 1, no. 1 (February 1930), pp. 15-24.

1. The Artistic Possibilities of the Cinema (1913)

Prefatory Note (1928) to "The Artistic Possibilities of the Cinema"

Fifteen years ago is a recent but already distant past. My article "The Artistic Possibilities of the Cinema," published in 1913 in the *Kinematograph and Lantern Weekly*, was one of my first literary efforts in English. Hence its ponderous phraseology and awkwardness of expression, as well as its somewhat naïve and confused reasoning. At the time this essay was written—1912—it was to me something in the nature of a manifesto in defense of the movies as an independent medium of art. I hoped it would instantly convert all intelligent people to my ideas. My first disappointment came when the editor of the paper, taking little notice of my repeated appeals, published the article almost a year after he had accepted it. However, I was rewarded for my labors and waiting with the munificent fee of one guinea.

In 1912 and 1913 it was still necessary to argue with artists that the "cinema" was an art. The only artist of standing in England known then to take an interest, and even to experiment, in the movies was Hubert Herkomer [1849-1914], famous in his day as the painter of *The Chelsea Pensioners* [a.k.a. *The Last Muster*, 1875] and of numerous portraits of members of the English and German royal families. Though not an admirer of Herkomer's work as a painter, I was anxious to see his films. A request for an opportunity to view them, accompanied by my article in the *Kinematograph and Lantern Weekly*, brought the answer that he would be glad to show me his work in his studio in Bushey [Hertfordshire]. I remember that my request for an interview was edited for me by a friend, an English journalist, as I was anxious to avoid mistakes. But I addressed the envelope myself, and on it I wrote "Sir Hubert Herkomer, Esquire"—an excess of politeness that, probably, was the reason for Herkomer's greeting me with the question, "Are you Dutch?" The nickname "Dutchman" was then popularly applied to all who spoke funny English.

Herkomer's magnificent castle, built in the German style and decorated inside with mural paintings by the artist, was an interesting, even amusing place to visit. But of his films [at least five shorts made between 1913 and 1914] I remember only that they completely failed to impress me, while in the matter of theories, though he had read my article, Herkomer did not seem to appreciate its unique importance to the world.

What of the views expressed in this article? Today their immaturity is so apparent that I am embarrassed to see it exposed to public gaze. And yet, there are ideas in the essay that are still ahead of the accepted standard. For instance, I advocate there pantomimic, i.e., wordless acting, and only a few months ago I read something by George Jean Nathan [American drama critic] in which he laid down the rule that pantomime was the only artistic form of acting in the movies. Of course, today the conception and, to an extent, even the practice of cinematic art have advanced far beyond pure pantomime, but pantomimic acting still remains an unrealized ideal for the majority of film directors in Hollywood.

My defense in the article of cinematic photography as a field for "original pictorial development" has been borne out by a series of magnificent pieces, from *The Cabinet of Dr. Caligari* [1920, dir. Robert Wiene] to *The End of St. Petersburg* [1927, dir. Vsevolod Pudovkin]. Only now we must aim beyond the pictorial effects of static pictures. The ideal today is pictorial and dramatic dynamism.

I also note with satisfaction the distinction made in this early article between two-dimensional and three-dimensional pictures, as bearing on their aesthetic significance. Equally important is the difference made between the illusory nature of the movies and the actuality achieved, on occasion, in the legitimate stage drama. These problems are still among those marked for solution by the critics, though they are still being persistently ignored by those who now make films.

The Artistic Possibilities of the Cinema

That the cinema has come to stay goes without saying. Little more than six or seven years have passed since it started its sweeping march over the world, but its victory is now complete, and among the different fields in which film has permanently established itself, it stands prominent as the most popular with the public in one—the field of dramatic entertainment. Some people doubt whether the latter really has any future. For instance, in a recent article in *Everyman* ["The Cinema," 25 Apr. 1913, p. 46], Percy Dearmer [Anglican priest, 1867-1936] declares most emphatically that the cinema will not take the place of art—it can never be a theater, and the great work that lies before the stage drama of the future will be just as much needed as ever.

Now it is obvious to me that, however great the confusion in the prevailing notions of art, verdicts on the artistic future of the cinema like the one just cited are simply based on a certain conservatism of thought that satisfies itself with the awkward features of the phenomenon under review, reluctant to take the trouble of looking at the root of the matter. With a phenomenon so new as the cinema, examining elements and bases is the only safe way of arriving at correct conclusions. And in this way I propose to deal with the question in the present article.

To compare cinematic productions with legitimate stage drama, we shall for a time have to leave out of consideration the problems pertaining to the mechanical process of filmmaking and the peculiar optical effect it creates. The chief question we are concerned with now is what constitutes the specific character of filmic drama as compared with the ordinary theatrical production. The answer to this is simple: the cinema is wordless pantomime (as opposed to gramophone talking). This self-evident fact cannot be sufficiently emphasized, as it has been generally overlooked and never fully appreciated. Thus the problem of the cinema resolves itself into the problem of artistic pantomime.

Dearmer believes that many present-day cinematic productions are entirely outside art. I quite agree with him in this belief. But what is wrong with them? Again the answer is apparent: the filmic drama of today is a pantomime in which the performers conscientiously neglect the very essence of its peculiar medium—*motion*. On the other hand, the essence of film acting, as these performers understand it, consists of only one thing—emphasizing and exaggerating actual, everyday gesture and mimicry. "Roll your eyes" is what I should call the emblem of the present-day cinema. The principle of mimic motion is entirely different. It throws aside all the conventional restrictions of motion as set by daily life and finds its peculiar means of expression in the language of movement, infinite in its variety and capable of the highest form of artistic rhythm.

It can be seen from this that artistic pantomime is absolutely inconsistent with "realism" as it is usually understood, and the more so with the realism of cinematic drama. Progress would be made in the latter by mere recognition of the principle of pantomime, thus doing away with its horrible "realism." But now I might be asked, what is there in pantomime? And what future does it possess? To answer this I must point to history—to John Rich's Covent Garden and Colley Cibber's Drury Lane. The pantomime was ousted only by the advent of the modern music hall. But it is already being revived now in new and still more fascinating forms. Take the modern ballet. What is it but a higher form of pantomime? And what are the theatrical productions of Max Reinhardt but magnificent pantomimes? Why, even in the legitimate stage drama, is the new spirit manifesting itself in the eminence ascribed—by Gordon Craig and others—to pure motion? These facts, I think, sufficiently justify me in saying that the only artistic possibilities for the cinema lie in the direction of pantomime in all its various forms. It is already developing in this way, and the time is not far distant when we shall routinely see film ballet as we now see in *The Miracle* [1912, dir. Michel-Antoine Carré].

But the possibilities of the cinema are even more numerous. I shall mention only two forms of pantomime, the artistic possibilities of which in the cinema have not yet been fully realized. These are the silhouette and marionette plays. Of the latter, Maurice Maeterlinck is a known advocate [in such plays as *Interior* (1895), *The Death of Tintagiles* (1894), and *Alladine and Palomides* (1894)], and of both forms it may be equally said that they possess quite a peculiarly quaint charm. It is sometimes argued that an artistic cinema could not and need not exist; that it is popular now just because it is *not* artistic, appealing to the masses by its crude realism, its simplicity and commonplaceness, and that, on the other hand, a really artistic cinema, appealing to select and refined audiences, is simply not wanted, as the ordinary stage can satisfy these circles much better and more fully. For an argument like this one can find only one justification—the belief that no real art can ever be made popular, and that every attempt to popularize it with the masses is predestined to failure.

Without going into a general discussion of this contention, it is sufficient to say that such arts as music and painting do find their way to the masses and with every year extend their influence more and more. The only means by which this was achieved was that of making works of art more accessible to the masses. To make more accessible to the masses the art of pantomime is the mission of the cinema, and there is no doubt for one moment that it is capable of carrying out this mission.

I turn now to that side of cinematic pantomime which distinguishes it from ordinary pantomime, i.e., to its mechanical process. What is its artistic value and significance? The principal component of the process is photography, and the reputation of the latter among people of refined taste is undoubtedly bad. Yet this does not destroy the case for the cinema. In the first place much of the lack of taste apparent in modern photographic art is accounted for by the fact that very few real artists go in for photography. (As to the so-called "artistic" photography, it is quite on a par with the multitude of "artistic" paintings.) What wonderful results can be achieved by photography as a pictorial art are to be seen only in some reproductions in print, which infinitely surpass ordinary photos. The same result would be attained in the cinema were the matter taken in hand by real artists. Even more than this: the artist would then find, in the cinema, a province of quite original pictorial development.

There is still another difference between an ordinary photograph and a cinematic picture. The latter may set as its object only a facsimile reproduction of the model, yet the film director, with the assistance of the lighting cameraman, is more able to make the model look artistic than the ordinary photographer. Saying this I presume such improvements in cinematography as would allow for perfect color and stereoscopic effects (in both these respects we are already not far from the object), and would place the cinema at least on a level with the best modern print.

I have just mentioned the stereoscopic effect. This problem technically has been already solved on the screen in the first place, and without a screen by means of an invention styled the "Kinoplastikon" [which featured three-dimensional pictures in motion on a real stage]. But these achievements raise another problem—the difference between staging plays in two dimensions and three dimensions. The present-day cinema is flat and practically two-dimensional. In this respect it closely approaches paintings, in which flat treatment, with its decorative effects, is considered by some great artists as the very essence of this art. On the other hand, such flat-plane treatment as applied to staging achieves most peculiar psychological effects quite distinct from the effects of an ordinary, three-dimensional staging. For a philosophically inclined mind, this distinction opens up a realm of most fascinating speculation. But here, suffice it to say that for a conscientious and consequential carrying out of the principle of two-dimensional staging, the cinema affords even greater advantages than the ordinary stage.

There is one more aspect of the cinematic play that must present exceptional interest for every student of art. Since Nietzsche, we have been accustomed to speak of Dionysian and Apollonian art. Those who see in the nature of art the spirit of Dionysus believe that art is active life, raised to that state of emotionalism when it reveals in itself its irrational, mystic nature. In drama these believers in the Dionysian art see a means of shaping human life, a form of religious service, a liturgy in which the distinction between actors and spectators disappears and the latter actively participate in the play. The Apollonian art is distinctly different. It is passive and reflective in its nature. Among our different forms of perception, that one is considered artistic which perceives the rhythm, the harmony, the "measure" of the outside world as reflected in our mind. In drama this conception leads to separating the spectator from the stage, to emphasizing the illusionary character of the latter.

Now the establishing of the cinema in the popular estimation and its future development along artistic lines will have a momentous effect upon these two conceptions of art. It is obvious that in the cinema there will never be anything like an active union between the audience and the actor. The illusionary character of the cinematic play is too apparent to allow for it. On the other hand, the screen will develop that reflective attitude toward the play which, though now so lacking in intelligence, is in entire conformity with the trend of feelings in our time. We are too much children of a "decadent" age and consequently too lazy to move and act. If only for this, we may be sure, the cinema will find more sympathy with the public than all the attempts to re-create a liturgical, participatory drama. (*Kinematograph and Lantern Weekly*, August 1913. Reprinted in *National Board of Review Magazine*, November 1928)

2. The Cinema as Art (1916)

A thoughtful exposition of the movies in their social relation to the culture of the masses, which was recently published in the *Atlantic Monthly* [Walter Prichard Eaton, "Class-Consciousness and the 'Movies,'" Jan. 1915, pp. 49–51], is essentially sound, provided that the reader assumes the impossibility of development in the art of the cinema. Judging the cinema by what it is today, the outlook is discouraging. But a little acquaintance with the ideals of the cinema as it *might* be, and as certain Continental *régisseurs* dream of transforming it, will reveal the wildest possibilities of artistic expression in the medium's future development, and a democratic extension of its noble, imaginative influence that is most difficult to measure.

The wonderful popularity enjoyed by the cinema during the last decade has for a long time been a subject of eager discussion in those circles that have the interests of the theater at heart. The various groups of art-workers connected with the theater—the dramatists, the actors, and the designers—are directly involved in this discussion, and it is interesting to note how different has been the attitude revealed toward it by each of these sections. The designers, perhaps the most cultured of the three groups from the standpoint of art, have simply ignored the new medium, regarding it as something so crude and inartistic as to be unworthy of serious notice. It is true that a few genuine experiments have been made in the direction of the cinema, but for several reasons, chiefly because the designers failed to comprehend the real nature of the nascent form, they have all proved a complete failure.

The attitude of most actors has been much more condescending. Those actors who generally concern themselves very little with matters of art have accepted the cinema with the docile humility accorded to all things in the natural order. They have transferred to the new invention whatever knowledge of drama they gained on the legitimate stage, and have supplied only one new feature: extreme exaggeration in mimicry and action, which they hold to be the chief peculiarity of moving pictures. On the other hand, the more advanced members of the theatrical profession, who have been truly anxious to establish on the stage the principles of vital art, however much they may have differed in their interpretation of them, at once realized the danger that threatened the drama from the encroachment of modern movie theaters, and did not hesitate to proclaim a most resolute opposition in an attempt to protect their art from being contaminated by this vulgar, "mechanical" device. Thus we see large sections of the community, for whom art is an object of vital faith, rejecting the cinema as a medium devoid of any artistic qualities.

But it would be wrong to infer that the cinema has always lacked faithful champions. Strange as it may seem, these have come from the group that is furthest removed from the actual everyday problems of the theater—the dramatists. As might be expected, the only fault that the *littérateurs* were able to detect in moving pictures was in the plot, and so they set themselves the task of remedying it. With enviable ease, they began to pour out elaborate philosophical dramas, mystery plays, tragedies, "literary" melodramas, and what not, in order to demonstrate those artistic possibilities that have been lying dormant in the neglected and abused cinema. Once they found that the theater was no longer held in popular esteem, they had no compunction about erecting their rostrum on the picture screen, the more so as they perceived in it the fulfillment of two objects: the popularization of the drama and the elevation of moving pictures to a higher artistic level.

We need only mention such names as Gabriele D'Annunzio and Leonid Andreyev to show what resolute and self-confident archpriests of literature have undertaken the task of reforming the moving-picture play. But though their attempts have raised a host of arguments and controversies among all who are interested in the theater, there can be little doubt that failure must be the inevitable result of their efforts. Their defense of motion pictures is as inherently fallacious as the opposition of designers and actors, since it is the outcome of a complete failure to understand the peculiar nature of the cinema as a medium of art. If the dramatists' defense leaves us entirely unmoved, since it comes from virtual outsiders, we cannot but deplore the opposition of those, such as actors and designers, who should be the first and foremost exponents of the new art. For there is an artistic future for the cinema, a future as great as any form of artistic drama can hope to attain.

We may ignore, then, the criticisms of those who condemn as utterly vulgar all moving pictures, photographs, and gramophones, as well as most other products of our resourceful mechanical genius. These well-intentioned dilettantes are only victims of prevailing artistic conventions, and have no standard of their own by which they may discriminate between what is art and what is not. The future of the cinema does not rest with them. It depends upon those enlightened and liberal lovers of art who can see beyond the conventions of the moment, who possess a range of sympathies that is already wide enough to embrace such divergent revelations as we find in the static art of Egypt, the decorativeness of Eastern art, and the "primitive" work of Cézanne and Matisse, or, to refer strictly to the domain of drama, the medieval booth, the puppet show, and the productions of Edward Gordon Craig. Theirs is the task of creating the canons and standards, of shaping the conventions of cinematographic art, and of building up a tradition that will pass, in due course, through the period when it is merely fashionable and attain, finally, the position of an acknowledged medium for artistic expression.

It is with the object of securing a more sympathetic attitude for this discredited medium that I now venture, however conscious of the heresy, to advance a plea for the cinema as a vehicle of genuine artistic expression.

II

Much has been said in the press about the issues involved in the growth of moving pictures: their special appeal to the masses; their competition with the theater; whether they are to supersede the latter, or whether they are doomed to be merely a transient fashion and eventually disappear; their artistic crudity: that is to say, whether they are a reversion to the methods of the medieval booth; whether they indicate the birth of a new democratic art; and many other, similar issues. With these we shall not concern ourselves at present. Without underrating their interest and importance, we hold that they overlook the most essential factor: the peculiar nature of the medium, which alone should form the basis of its possible artistic application. Before we are able to enter upon a discussion of this factor, a number of deep-rooted, popular misconceptions must be cleared away. I almost despair of my task, for in the sphere of ideas, as in that of biology, the lowest forms of life are the most tenacious.

One of the critic's first duties is discrimination. Yet the criticisms hurled so liberally from all sides at the cinema have been little distinguished by this character. Two things that are entirely distinct have been persistently confused by all critics: the cinema as a medium, and the movie theater as we know it at present. That the second is below criticism—indeed, something coarse, crude, and altogether ugly—can be easily and unreservedly admitted. But to deduce from this fact the impossibility of an artistic cinema betrays an absence of logic and imagination. It is evident, in the first place, that the many drawbacks of the modern moving-picture play are in no way connected with the cinema as a peculiar medium of dramatic expression. For example, take the vulgar realism of motion pictures, about which we hear so many complaints. Is it a peculiar feature of the cinema? Students of theater will agree that naturalism as vulgar as this ruled the legitimate stage long before the cinema became a competitor. Motion pictures simply followed along the beaten track, bringing to logical absurdity what the legitimate drama, not endowed with the infinite resources of its competitor, could only pursue halfway.

It is unnecessary to dwell upon the many similar drawbacks of the cinema. We are not so much concerned with what it actually is as with what it might be. The question that really matters may be stated in the following words: Is the cinema a medium capable of artistic achievement in the two fields that make up its rival, the art of the stage—the dramatic field and the pictorial one? The answer necessarily involves discussing another question: the vexed one of mechanical art. However reluctant I may be to touch upon this controversy, I am unable to avoid it altogether. So I bow before the inevitable and shall try to dispose of it in the briefest manner possible.

It is often contended that an automatic mechanism can never attain to anything like artistic perfection, and that consequently there is no artistic future for the cinema. It is obvious that the whole argument here stands or falls with the definition of "mechanism." But such a definition is never stated in anything like exact terms. That there are no absolutely automatic mechanisms hardly needs to be pointed out. All mechanisms must be controlled by human power at one moment or another, and, what is more important, they are all products of human intelligence. Whatever forces may be involved in their operation are brought together by the action of human thought compressed and wound up like a spring, and constituting their actual prime mover throughout the whole process of their operation. Thus the problem is reduced to defining the degree of independence from immediate human control and power that a mechanism can possess. This is so indeterminate that we see similar kinds of action styled mechanical in one case and personal in another. Who will doubt, for instance, that the action of an organ played at a concert is personal, and that of a locomotive engine mechanical? Yet it cannot be disputed that the second requires as much skill and individual control as the first. The point is not whether these operations are art or are not art, but whether they are mechanical or non-mechanical. I maintain that there is no real distinction between the one and the other, and that both may serve artistic ends if properly utilized.

One more example of the prevailing confusion of thought on this subject: the gramophone is admittedly a mechanical contrivance and so is the telephone; yet no one listening to the opera through the telephone ever says that the music he hears is a mechanical production. The sole difference that exists between this music and its record on the gramophone is that the gramophone fixes only one stage of the process—the vibrations of the telephonic membrane—and allows one to switch on the flow of sound at will, whereas the telephone receives and transmits the sound in one continuous process.

These two illustrations show not only the vague, popular use of the term "mechanical," but also the elements that go to make up the significance of this term. They are three: complexity of mechanism; the number of intermediate stages; and the extent of time between the application of human agency and the appearance of its effect. It is necessary only to rid the mind of prejudice for a moment to be able to see that not a single one of these elements is in any way incompatible with artistic work and achievement. And if, at the current moment, mechanical methods of production under the capitalistic system have served to destroy whatever artistic feeling the creator may originally have had, this situation militates not against the mechanical methods as such, but rather against the way they are used in our time.

III

Now let us endeavor to realize the peculiar nature of filmic drama itself, and then we shall be able to see how far this "mechanical" medium lends itself to artistic expression.

One of the most startling facts about cinematic productions is that the actors who play in such pictures are all members of the legitimate theatrical profession. Their attainments on the stage need not be discussed in this instance, but it seems quite apparent that of film acting they understand very little indeed. The filmic drama raises some of the most fundamental problems of art. But what do these performers know about them? Are they aware that the moving-picture play is the most abstract form of pantomime? Do they realize that if there is any stage on which the laws of movement should reign supreme, it is the cinematographic stage? If they did, they would not have monopolized the moving-picture play as they have done, but would have left it to the dancers, clowns, and acrobats, who do know something about the laws of movement. By no means do I presume to say that dancers, clowns, and acrobats are necessarily artists. But movement is their natural element, and it is also movement that constitutes the real nature of the cinema.

The patron and devotee of present-day pictures may boast of their "wonderful realistic effects," but this popular conception only betrays a complete failure to grasp one salient fact: viewed from the standpoint of the drama, just as from many other standpoints of which more will be said later on, the cinema is essentially and preeminently *dynamic*. It is necessary at this point to realize what the effect of motion-picture scripts would be if this principle of pure movement were recognized throughout. Rolling eyes and wild gesticulation would be abolished. Sham "natural" talking would give place to mimicry and gesture, free and eloquent. The movements of the actors would no longer imitate actual life but would, instead, synthetically express life through the peculiar laws of rhythmic motion. Pantomimes, harlequinades, and ballets would take the place of the current melodramatic and comic films, thus giving adequate expression to the wordless nature of the medium. It be possible to argue, then, that there is no art in the cinema as presently construed. So far as the dramatic aspect is concerned, however, a recognition of the principle of pure movement would constitute a most decisive step in the direction of film art. Other advances would immediately follow, once this fundamental principle was firmly established.

It is often contended that the presence in bodily form of the actor in the stage play is the *sine qua non* of artistic drama. This view is held alike by those who believe in realism on the stage and by those who do not. The attitude of the latter is particularly droll. After disposing of all the realistic mummery, they cling to the last citadel of the "true-to-nature" gospel of art, the bodily shell of the actor. Why is it not his personality or character that really matters? And is that expressed only through the frail physical body of the actor? To the spectator of some artistic works, though, it is in a sense irrelevant whether the acting on the stage is performed by living persons, by plastic dolls, or by cinematic shadows. The effect in each case must necessarily be different, but only insofar as the artistic properties of each of these vehicles of drama differs from the other two. Their absolute artistic value remains unaffected by their being animate or inanimate. In fact, it is open to argument whether the human form is at all suitable as a medium of dramatic art, as readers of Gordon Craig already know.

Yet we need not go so far. In the case of filmic drama, we do not dispense with the actor. We dispense only with his literal body. Perhaps those who cannot reconcile themselves to this fact will find comfort in reflecting upon the time when poets were gradually led to recognize that singing a poem in person is not the only way of rendering the artistic beauties of a lyric composition. In our age of reduplication or reproduction, to the list of arts that already resort to this process (poetry, music, lithography, etching) we can now add the sacred art of the theater. This is a process of natural development, and it would be sheer stupidity on our part if we continued to ignore such a development or notice only its outward features. Just as it did not degrade the profession of the painter when he realized the artistic possibilities of lithography, so will it not degrade the modern actor if he makes full use of the new medium that human ingenuity has placed at his command. The real and only problem for him is to find out what actually constitutes the peculiar properties of cinematic form and how these properties should be managed to achieve the highest artistic effect. The fact that the problem can be solved only by practice and experiment, and that, artistically speaking, present-day filmic practice has produced some appalling results, must not be taken as proof of the inartistic nature of the medium itself. The truth of this statement has been shown above, as applied to the playing of actors. It is equally true when applied to the pictorial element of stage production, as will be shown below.

IV

The peculiar optical effects of the cinema are a result of two processes: the photographic process of making a film, and the visual process of projecting that film on the screen. What artistic possibilities do these processes possess?

There is no need to enter in this instance upon a discussion of photography itself as art. Its shortcomings as a medium and the triteness of the average photographic work can hardly be disputed. But only narrow prejudice can deny photography any artistic quality whatever. The magnificent work so often found at various exhibitions proves most conclusively that photography and art are not so incompatible as some of our purists would like us to believe.

The same is the case with cinematography. So long as it remains in the hands of mere operators and chemists, just as long will its pictorial value be on a par with the aesthetic conceptions held by such craftsmen. And this can hardly be wondered at, given that the nature of the new medium, properly understood, requires such a culture of mind seldom found even among professional exponents of art.

The greatest question all this raises is that of the psychological significance pertaining to the cinema's various dramatic and pictorial forms. One important fact must be stated at the outset. Film has at its command two distinct ways of producing screenplays: the two-dimensional production on the ordinary screen, and the three-dimensional production by means of various stereoscopic devices as well as the "Kineplastikon" [which featured three-dimensional pictures in motion on a real stage]. Too much emphasis cannot be placed upon this distinction. Its importance is enormous, since in the two forms of space—of two dimensions and of three—we obtain dual aspects of the world that are opposed to each other in their very elements. Without going deeply into the philosophical and psychological nature of these forms of space, it may be said that the first symbolizes and incarnates the principles of continuity, cosmic unity, spontaneity, pure sentiment, and kindred psychic experiences, while the second stands for differentiation, individuality, clear-consciousness, and the like. They thus form two distinct worlds: one monistic, fused into a single integral whole, and the other atomistic, broken into innumerable mutually opposed units.

The same two principles obtain in the theater. Staging in one plane produces the effect of dissolving the world, as reproduced in the mind of the audience. It destroys the barrier between the stage and the spectator, turning the play from a mere spectacle into an actual incident in the life of the audience, an incident that, though experienced passively, enters into the soul of the individual viewer as an integral element of his being. Such, for instance, is the effect of some of Maurice Maeterlinck's religious plays [*The Miracle of Saint Anthony* (1904), *Mary Magdalene* (1910)] when staged in one plane. This method may be called subjective-monistic. Its counterpart is the objective-monistic method, which again destroys the barrier between the stage and the audience, but this time by transporting the spectator onto the stage and making him actively participate in the play. The early forms of Greek drama and of the medieval mystery plays may be cited here as examples of this method, though the first also contains considerable elements of subjectivity.

The other way of apprehending the universe is based on the consciousness of all its component parts—on the opposition of self and non-self. The world acquires an atomistic aspect, and the self-affirming personality always feels its aloofness from such an ambience. By a process of active contemplation it may embrace and absorb this encompassing world, but it never becomes fused with the world. In the theater this sovereignty of self-affirming personality finds its expression in the abstractly sculpturesque stagings of Gordon Craig, which we may rightly call subjective-atomistic. These definitions may appear somewhat obscure, but they show the problems of staging that obtrude in the cinema, determining the very nature of pictorial representation.

That is to say, the cinema possesses a greater command of space than the legitimate stage or painting on flat surfaces. It is able, and therefore is obliged, to discriminate between the different methods of pictorial presentation. Unlike the others, it can afford to be logical. But it would only gain in effect and reveal the inner monistic nature of the two-dimensional space if it were more consistent and eliminated every atom of natural relief. The play of lines and colors is all that is required on the flat screen, and if, as everybody believes nowadays, the properties of the medium have any importance in the achievement of artistic effect, then it is obvious that the cinema can only prosper by consistent application of the principle of two-dimensional space to pictures on the ordinary screen.

By contrast, to represent the atomistic world as distinct from the self-conscious personality, the method of three-dimensional staging affords both the actor and the pictorial artist unlimited scope for new and altogether artistic achievements. The productions of Gordon Craig, for instance, unfetter and expand the stage. They are not theatrical in the narrow sense of the word. They purport to create on the boards a world of their own, one entirely distinct from the stage world however far it may be removed from the realistic one. But the stage is only a stage, and the space on it has well-known limitations. The case with the stereoscopic cinema is different. Its command of space is practically boundless. It can create another world and place it before the eyes of the audience to watch with admiration, sympathy, or disdain. The stereoscopic cinema in the hands of real artists could raise even realistic drama (in its wordless form, of course) to its proper position, representing the world as stated objectively and watched from the outside.

As for the pictorial artist, both the single-plane and the stereoscopic moving picture open before him a new field of artistic development. It would be impossible at the present stage of the cinema's evolution to discuss in detail the multifarious problems arising from the application of this new process. Only practical experience could give satisfactory answers to many of the questions raised. But there are some general features of the cinematographic process that already allow for analysis and discussion. The most important of them is the dynamic character of the cinema. In addition to the third dimension that the cinema provides through stereoscopic projection, it possesses yet another coordinate—time.

How does the element of time enter into the pictorial and plastic arts? We know that the Egyptians answered this question by discarding the notion of time itself. Instead of transient time they imparted to their immovable, frigid creations a spirit of eternity. In contrast, the

Greeks, the artists of the Renaissance, and most modern artists try to give the impression of temporal movement by arranging the elements of a picture or a statue in such a way that the eye must travel over the composition or object. The cinema, however, is the first medium in which one can deal with time fairly and squarely—moreover, without recourse to the tricks of the cubist or futurist. Is that not in itself a sufficient reason why artists should seize this unique opportunity?

Following the distinction stated above, we shall have two branches of this mobile art form: the flat-screen cinema (the realm of the flat-surface artist) and the stereoscopic cinema (the realm of the sculptor, who thinks in terms of mass and color). At present, the only indications for this future mobile art are found in the best theatrical productions. I may point out as examples the exquisite stagings of Russian ballet by Léon Bakst, Boris Anisfeld, and Aleksandr Golovin, and their designs for costumes in particular, since in the varying combinations of line and color against the background of the scenery may be found, implicitly, the basis for a mobile art.

V

It is necessary at this point, in light of the foregoing theories, to consider what position the artist will occupy in future cinematographic productions. In the stereoscopic cinema he has already at his command nearly all that he can desire. It is true that the colors of life are yet wanting, but an artist can obtain a genuine shading from black and white, toning the film just as he pleases so that in the end he is not entirely deprived of color. Otherwise, stereoscopic cinematography leaves hardly anything to be desired. It gives a facsimile reproduction, color excepted, of the actual scene. If the legitimate stage itself affords scope for the application of artistic talents, the stereoscopic cinema has the additional advantage of a much greater command of space than the stage.

The problems of photography in the one-plane cinema are somewhat different. These problems are akin to those encountered in other arts dealing with a flat surface; on the other hand, such problems are naturally different insofar as they depend on the mobile conditions of cinematographic production. The influence of these conditions on other artistic effects can be deduced from the fact that in moving pictures, we are seldom able to fix our attention on one given position for any considerable length of time. This being so, the criteria of art as applied to moving pictures must obviously be distinguished from those applied to paintings or lithographs. The laws of composition cannot possibly be the same. What they are, I shall not attempt to define here, but an artist who took up the cinema would find that such laws do exist and, gradually, by experiment and practice, he would subject them to his control. At present, our ideas on mobile composition are so undeveloped and crude that posterity will hardly be able to believe that they were ever held. It is necessary only to remind ourselves of the revolution started in this field by Jacques Dalcroze with his rhythmic gymnastics. It is still open to an artist to give such dance-like routines a worthy counterpart by fixing them on the film. In this connection the attempts made by Alexander Wallace Rimington in England and Alexander Scriabin in Russia to create a new art of color-music are of some interest. Rimington has already given us a detailed exposition of his theory and a description of the color-organ, the instrument he specially invented for this purpose. There can be little doubt that this new form of art will have a great future, and that in one way or another it will become one of the most essential components of the artistic cinema.

Yet another cinematic problem is akin to the one encountered in ordinary photographic prints. Line drawing being excluded by the nature of photography as we know it at present, the problem is how to achieve the best results with a medium similar in character to the wash. The problem lies not so much with the lighting of models as with the production of the film and its projection on the screen. Greater artistic effect would probably be achieved on screens of more solid consistency than those now in vogue—for example, on screens of a grained surface such as that provided by a white plastered wall. Then the lighting and shading on the film would give more concentrated, solid, and flat masses, thus obviating unnecessary details, which are often annoyingly conspicuous. The silhouette motion picture, which is practically unknown, possesses wonderful possibilities. For fairy tales or grotesque (yet sentimental) stories, hardly any medium could be more fitting.

VI

In conclusion, let me recapitulate my principal points. The artistic failure of the modern cinema is due solely to a lack of understanding of this medium's peculiar properties. It is dynamic throughout. Expression of the rhythmically moving body must be the only law of the actor, expression of rhythmically moving form and color the only law of the pictorial artist.

The actor, moreover, must cease to ignore the silent nature of the cinema in performing "realistic" plays. Pantomime and ballet are the only forms open to him. He can achieve greatly varying psychological effects by performing his parts in two or three dimensions. The silhouette, however, is the form of acting in which the one-plane principle of staging finds its most complete expression.

The pictorial artist must discriminate between flat-screen film projection and the stereoscopic kind. With the first, he must try to eliminate all "sculptural" relief, so as to concentrate on evolving the color-value of light and shade, and to make the screen as good an artistic medium as paper is. With the second kind of projection, he must solve the complicated problem of planes and volumes that the stereoscopic form of projection places before him. In the application of both methods, the artist must develop formulas for mobile composition and mobile color.

So much for the actor and the designer. Above all, the cinema needs men of great genius, deep insight, and spiritual culture. More than the theater, it is a synthetic form of art, as both the dramatic *and* the pictorial arts constitute the basic elements of its nature. To be raised from its present state of degradation, the cinema requires men who combine a talent for dramatic and pictorial presentation with the wisdom of sages. It requires that clear-consciousness without which there can be no real character in the world, nor any individual feeling toward it.

Art is the revelation of the human spirit in every form capable of expressing it, conditioned only by the nature of the medium used. So the cinema will rise to the level of art when men of high intelligence and thought express themselves in forms determined by the natural properties of this new medium. Everything seems to indicate that we shall not have long to wait for such a fulfillment. (*The Drama* [Chicago], May 1916)

3. The Problem of the Artistic Cinema (1919)

What is to be done with the cinema? It is impossible to destroy it, though at least three-quarters of its productions fully deserve to be burned, and it is equally impossible to ignore it, because of the shrieking hideousness of these same three-quarters. It remains, therefore, to try to improve it. Only a few years ago suggestions of this kind used to arouse skeptical smiles among all who considered themselves guardians of pure art. Now, I notice, the idea begins to find favor even in these circles. So far, so good. The next step is to conceive clearly what *can* be done with this prostituted medium.

Let us examine the problem.

The most obvious defect of present-day films is their subject matter. Not only are the sentimental, detective, and comic stories that form the greater part of the modern cinematic repertoire crude and puerile in themselves, but the way they are told seems to be even more absurd. Two or three episodes, supposed to be happening concurrently in the story, are let loose upon the screen to play a sort of leap-frog. Then, at the most critical moment of the script, one or another character is suddenly torn out of his surroundings and shown separately on an enlarged scale. The result of this piecemeal rendering of the story is the complete destruction of all unity in acting. In addition to this, the story is narrated with innumerable details that serve to connect one episode with another, thus still further diluting the drama of acting. If, this notwithstanding, such films yet succeed in impressing the not particularly exacting audiences of our time, they are able to do so only thanks to the entanglements of their plots and the forced melodramatic situations that are thus obtained.

It may seem strange that film directors, however ignorant of art, should display so much independence in departing from the well-established methods of building up dramatic effect. Is the reason for this the ease with which such independence can be indulged in the cinema, or is it the difficulty of following the methods of legitimate drama? Both explanations are right, though the second is perhaps more important.

The difficulty to which I refer is to be found in the limitations of mimic acting. When an actor on the ordinary stage plays a love-scene, his command of speech enables him to give vent to his feelings and express an extensive gamut of emotions, even when the scene occupies a considerable length of time. A film actor, deprived of his speech and depending only on his movements and facial expression, can sustain himself in such a scene no longer than a few minutes. A change of situation, or the breaking up of the scene into fragments, becomes for him absolutely imperative as a refuge from complete failure. Hence the preference of film directors for complicated plots with unlimited opportunities for incessant changes of scene.

May it then be concluded from this that plots for the cinema can never be properly dramatized? Not at all. If mimic acting cannot sustain a consistent dramatic development, obviously it must either be supplemented by other methods of acting or be abandoned entirely in their favor. And here we find that the wordless drama, which seems so utterly beyond the power of the modern cinema, has been realized with the most conspicuous success by choreographic acting. With the assistance of music, or even without it—and I can see nothing to prevent choreographic performance from developing to a stage where it would become an art complete in itself—this form of acting is entirely free from the limitations that time imposes on mimic acting. It is capable of infinite variety of movement and can build up a dramatic climax unhindered by consideration of time and independent of incident. Thus, it provides a vehicle for purely dramatic acting, and, consequently, a means for dramatizing cinematic plots.

But its substitution for mimic acting will, naturally, involve considerable changes in the character of screenplays. Choreographic performance is obviously conventional or stylized and, therefore, excludes realistic drama. In this, however, it is not so far removed from mimic acting as it would appear at first glance. For mimic acting is also essentially conventional, and if, in the usual type of scenario, we do not find that its conventionality clashes with the realism of the story, the reason is that we see only a little of real acting—but a great deal of realistic incident and environment. A realistic drama based on the psychology of characters is equally impossible for both mimic acting and choreographic acting. On the other hand, the latter can go as far in the world of stylized artistic forms as the human body—the only realistic element it still preserves—will allow.

The claims of art have now been considered with regard to the plot and acting of cinematic plays. It remains to discover what changes may thus be called for in methods of production and general visual effects. Generally speaking, staging depends upon the character of the performance. It is of one kind when the effect aimed at is in the nature of choral drama, another when presentational drama is the object, and another again when the aim is to produce an illusion of the world portrayed in the script. The obviously unreal character of the picture on screen excludes the possibility of choral drama in the cinema, since in the latter the essential condition of unity between the actor and the spectator would be entirely missing. But the other two kinds of staging are fully within the scope of the cinema, though their actual forms must necessarily differ from the forms used in the theater.

To take representational productions first, it will be seen that the methods of creating illusion can be either realistic or stylized, given that the illusion sought is either one or the other. There is no need to dwell on the use of the realistic method in the cinema, as it is already the stock-in-trade of present-day films. Moreover, the place of realism in the artistic cinema should be strictly limited, confined only to such forms of choreographic acting as can be treated in realistic fashion, such as a pure display of dance in natural surroundings. But conventional choreographic acting requires a stylized setting. And here we come to the problem—that of realism vs. stylization—that has given rise to the most popular expressions of skepticism with regard to the artistic possibilities of the cinema.

"The painter," runs the stock criticism, "can do little in the cinema in the way of artistic setting, as he is deprived of the use of color." To begin with, the painter can do something at least truly artistic, if not fully realistic, even when using only pure monochrome. What is far more important, however, is that painting is not the only art that can be applied to scenery. There is, for instance, the art of architecture, which does not depend on color at all, and which can treat its material with a freedom fully equal to that of painting. For this, of course, architecture must transcend the limits of practical utility, and become a general art of purely formal relations between shapes and volumes. Thus it will enter upon a path pregnant with the most tremendous artistic possibilities, and, insofar as cinematic production is concerned, will create a method that will not only take the place of painted scenery, but far surpass it in the wealth and originality of its forms.

In fact, these extraordinary possibilities may even conceal a danger for the dramatic side of the cinema, against which, however premature it may appear at this juncture, a word of warning is necessary. To wit: we have had abundant evidence of dangerously abnormal development in the case of pictorial scenery on the ordinary stage, and of realistic setting in the modern cinema. It is not only the actor and acting that suffer there, but also the drama as a whole. And this raises the question of whether the cinema can create a form of drama that would be emancipated from all elements that are not essentially dramatic. Numerous examples of how this problem has been solved in the theater are supplied to us by classical Greek drama, the medieval pageant play, the Italian *commedia dell'arte*, the Elizabethan theater, the Japanese Noh, and so forth.

In the examples mentioned above, the solution was found by creating the dramatic form through means that proclaimed their theatrical nature, i.e., by means whose purpose was not to create an illusion of some world existing outside the theater, but to serve only for the presentation of the drama to the audience. In the theater these means are the actor and the platform on which he acts, which is merely a part of the playhouse as a whole and not an extraneous appendage to it. By analogy, in the cinema the presentational drama must be based on the three elements that make up this medium, i.e., the actor, the camera, and the screen. On these three the whole burden of presenting the dramatic script must rest, and their presence must proclaim itself in a clear and unmistakable voice.

As for the choreographic actor, his art is so essentially presentational that there should be no difficulty in discarding whatever illusionistic garb he still wears. The camera, for its part, can also contribute to the effect of the drama, without pretending to be merely an inert and neuter medium whose duty it is to give a faithful record of the original scenario. In fact, the camera already proclaims itself too loudly— because at the most inappropriate moments—in realistic screenplays, and it will merely have to learn how to express itself in presentational cinematic drama. The greatest difficulty we can foresee will be in the case of the literal screen itself. To make that blank square on the wall as clearly a part of the movie house as was the proscenium in the Greek theater, as well as the apron stage in the Elizabethan theater, presents a problem whose the solution will require much ingenuity on the part of future practitioners of cinematic art. For all that, this problem does not seem to be insoluble, as experience, I am confident, will prove in a short time.

While discussing all these possible developments, I am not losing sight of the fact that the ordinary movie camera and projector are far from being technically perfect. They are incapable of producing a stereoscopic effect that creates pictures of a real, though not necessarily realistic, world—which is of tremendous importance as an aesthetic factor—and they fail to faithfully record rapid movement, without which dancing on the screen is impossible. But these defects are not inherent in the camera and the projector. Technically, they can be removed, and in some cases they actually have been removed. If such defects still persist in present-day movie houses, the reason is neither technical nor artistic, but rather solely commercial.

I will leave for another day the discussion of other important aspects of the cinema, as I believe that a new form of art cannot reach its highest expression in a single leap, but instead has to proceed from stage to stage, leaving behind what retards and encumbers it, and accumulating and carrying forward what has stood the test of experience and of ever strengthening aesthetic judgment. In sum, the first task for the cinema of today is to rid itself of the crudities and vulgarities of its "realistic" pictures, and to intelligently start creating a representative, filmic drama by dramatizing plots through the substitution of choreographic for mimic acting, and through the development of architectural methods of motion-picture production. (*Proscenium*, no. 1 [1919])

4. The New Art of the Moving Picture (1927)

Our age knows a great number of mechanical inventions that have completely altered our mode of living. Mechanization of the sources of energy, of manufacturing processes, and of means of transport have enabled us to increase our comforts and conveniences in a million different ways. Yet few of these inventions can claim the distinction of having created something that had never existed. Practically all of them are directed either to the multiplication of things or to their reproduction and transmission. In particular inventions have always been used in this way in the sphere of art, where their own creative power has accounted for not more than an infinitesimal fraction of the artistic qualities of the thing produced. Neither the piano-player nor the gramophone, nor broadcasting, nor photography, nor machine-printing can yet be regarded as a new medium of artistic expression, possessing newly created qualities of aesthetic appeal.

There is only one mechanical invention that *has* created an entirely new medium, with forms of expression unlike anything in the other arts—and this invention is, of course, the motion picture. Its very singularity among all other emanations of mechanical genius explains a great deal about the history of the motion picture as a branch of purely commercial activity and a vehicle for the making of art. It was natural that film should have been fastened upon by men to whom the mechanical nature of the medium was its strongest appeal: these men knew the commercial value of mechanical processes, and they could appreciate the particular market value of this novelty. It was equally natural that people of artistic culture should have failed to see the essential difference between the motion picture and other mechanical devices. For whatever creative powers this new medium possessed, they certainly were not very conspicuous in the manufactured productions of its early sponsors. To believe in their existence required more than an effort of imagination: one had to forget the sorry results of the innumerable other attempts at producing works of art by mechanical means. Hence, the prejudice against the motion picture was natural, the contempt for its puerile artistic efforts inevitable.

It is only within the last few years that evidence has begun to accumulate that points, beyond all possibility of doubt, to the emergence of a new art form. The old skeptics are gradually relenting in their indifference, while young enthusiasts, with the zeal of all neophytes, are only too ready to discover a masterpiece in this or that picture—particularly when it is of German or Russian origin. It is not for the writer of this article, who for fifteen years has preached the principles of art in application to this new medium, to quarrel with such a suddenly developed enthusiasm. It is necessary, however, to preserve a sense of proportion. The time to shout "Hosanna!" is coming, but it has not yet arrived.

How, then, are we to know when it will come? How are we to tell the true masterpieces from those that pass under this name today? Perhaps the best way of tackling this problem is to begin by defining the salient characteristics of the motion picture.

The motion picture is a means of creating *visual* impressions (thus differentiating it from devices that aim at the reproduction of *sound*, like the gramophone). The visual impressions it creates consist of *movement* (thus differentiating the motion picture from the magic lantern [an early form of optical projector of still pictures using a transparent slide]). The movement the picture shows arises either from the *change in the position of objects* (in this it differs from such devices as Alexander Wallace Rimington's color-organ [on which colored keys were arranged above a conventional keyboard and connected to a lens-and-filters system, allowing colors to be "played"] and Thomas Wilfred's Clavilux [which means "light played by key," and which permitted the creation and performance of *lumia*, or light art], which can show only the movement of color, or of abstract form), or from the *change in the lighting of objects* (in this the motion picture resembles Rimington's and Wilfred's devices). This movement is one *recorded on a film* by means of a cinematographic *camera* (in this it differs from the movement produced by the color-organ and the Clavilux, which is brought about by manipulating the projector). The record of movement on the film is *thrown onto the screen* by means of a *projector* (in this the motion picture resembles the magic lantern and other light-projecting devices).

In other words, the motion picture is a close relative of the magic lantern and various other light-projecting mechanisms, sharing with them the use of the screen and the projector, but differing from them fundamentally in the use of film as a vehicle for photographically recorded movement. Such is, then, the medium that has been placed at the command of the artist (so far, alas, only figuratively speaking) . How is he to treat it in order to produce the best results—in other words, to achieve art?

Reduced to its fundamentals, the work of art is something endowed with a peculiar life of its own, asserting its identity against our effort to grasp and absorb it into the complex whole that constitutes our own, individual identity. This life is a form of functioning of the very material through which the work of art finds its expression, and the keener our appreciation of the nature of the material, the more attuned we are to its inner resonance—the more profound and exhilarating is the aesthetic thrill we experience in the presence of genuine works of art, just as, by contrast, the keener is our resentment when confronted with imperfect or utterly false ones.

The essentials of aesthetic appreciation are the same whether it be appreciation of painting, music, literature, or drama. It is the material that differs and that, consequently, functions differently, shaping itself into resonant or, some would say, "significant" forms in accordance with the peculiar nature of each medium. The motion picture, insofar as it attempts to create works of art, is like other arts: it must find forms that will be fully expressive of the effortless functioning of its material.

This admitted, it will be easy to indicate, in broad outlines, the forms of functioning that are natural to the material of the motion picture. There is in the first place the whole world of objects visible to the camera eye. These objects may be human beings, animals, or still life, but they have one characteristic in common: they are mute as far as the camera is concerned. This is therefore a purely visual world, and moreover a world seen not by the human eye but by the camera: a much more powerful instrument—for seeing detail, magnifying the image, and bringing distant objects into view—than mankind itself has been endowed with. At present the camera still lacks the capacity of the human eye for seeing things stereoscopically, but this deficiency is bound to disappear as soon as any of the existing stereoscopic devices becomes commercially viable.

But if the camera lens is different from, and in many ways superior to, the crystalline humour of the eye, the film that receives and fixes the images differs still more from the human retina. While the retina enables us to see a single but complete image covering a certain field of vision, the cinema, thanks to the mechanism by means of which it receives its impressions and afterwards displays them before us, can split one image into a number of parts, can join a number of different images into one, and can also group together and show simultaneously—but independently—a variety of images entirely unconnected with one another except on the film itself. The retentive power of the retina is very insignificant, indeed, when compared with this marvelous ability of the cinema to bring together, within the same space and for all practical purposes, at one and the same moment, images that originally may have been separated by great gaps in space as well as in time.

As regards the contents of the vision that is placed before us by the motion picture, we are therefore faced with a peculiar world that is both more restricted and more expanded than the one we habitually confront in our daily life. It is as if we were suddenly to lose our sense of hearing while at the same time acquiring a more powerful sense of vision, as well as a new sense of hovering in time in any direction we may wish, in fact, of molding time—rearranging its natural sequences, compressing it into a single moment, or expanding it into infinity. Even

H. G. Wells's "time machine" could not perform such miracles. This is not to say, though, that those who rule the destinies of the motion picture today have grasped and realized to the fullest the power over space and time that is inherent in their medium.

The ability of the motion picture to "hover in time" must not be understood in the sense of "annihilating time." On the contrary, time is the very soul of the motion picture: it is the governing condition of movement—of changes in the visual aspect of things. Accordingly, from the standpoint of art, the world of images created by the motion picture must function in movement: i.e., through movement in time it must reveal its form and significance.

It is important to note here that this movement is not merely the change in the position or lighting of objects in relation to one another. The objects may be perfectly immovable in this latter sense, and yet the effect of movement will be obtained merely by moving the camera, just as by the same means they could be shown to be stationary, though they might actually be moving. Close-ups and various camera angles are also elements of movement as produced by the camera.

Another form of movement arises from the peculiar nature of film. By a quick succession of scenes the cinema makes the whole world dance to its tune—mountains, rivers, buildings, human beings. It can retard movement or accelerate it, and film can also give it rhythm. Finally, there is the movement that is the result of the joint functioning of the projector and the screen—the movement of a small picture as it grows large, or of a picture's traversing the screen from one end to another.

At present, the screen and the projector play only the perfectly neutral role of intermediate agents for stimulating visual impressions. They have no lot or part in shaping the general effect of movement as produced by the motion picture. But there are immense possibilities latent in both of them, and it is to be hoped that as soon as our omniscient technicians of the movie trade learn a little more about the nature of their medium, we shall witness some very startling developments in the pictorial and dramatic powers of motion pictures.

All these various forms of movement are the natural modes of functioning for the world of images that the motion picture lets loose before our eyes. Such images are indeed "let loose" by the present-day manufacturers of movies, whereas it is the purpose and meaning of all art to bring order into chaos by revealing what is the natural, and therefore the inevitable, mode of functioning for the material that forms the resources of this or that particular medium. Unfortunately, a discussion of the specific way in which the motion picture uses its material today, and of the possibilities of artistic treatment that still remain unexploited, cannot be undertaken in the present article. (*Theatre Arts Monthly*, April 1927)

5. The Road to Art in the Motion Picture (1927)

There are obvious points of difference between the drama of the stage and the drama of the motion picture. There is also a close analogy between them when considered in their relation to the spectator. Realistic drama, for instance, whether on the stage or the screen, aims at placing before the spectator a picture of life as it would appear to one invisibly present during the events portrayed. In this case, the drama is largely independent of the spectator. And to fully achieve the effect of faithful representation, realistic drama must be equally independent of the forms that its medium—the stage or the movie screen—is apt to force on it.

Then there is the case of the drama independent of the medium through which it is expressed, but semi-dependent on the spectator. In such a drama, the life represented is treated so that it will appeal not only to the spectator's power of observation but also to his imagination, by means of selection, simplification, and style. Films like *The Cabinet of Dr. Caligari* [1920, dir. Robert Wiene] and *Siegfried* [1924, dir. Fritz Lang] may be quoted as good examples of this form of drama.

One more step in the recognition of the spectator occurs when the very working of a play or a picture becomes dependent on the fact that it is a dramatic performance displayed before an audience. The nature of the medium is no longer disguised. Instead of being represented as it is, life is translated into the terms of the stage or the movie screen, with the full emphasis laid not only on the self-referential medium, but also on the presence of the spectator for whose special benefit the show has been produced. It cannot be said yet that the motion picture has its equivalent of this form of drama, although it is undoubtedly moving toward this end.

If such, roughly, are the main forms of drama, one may perhaps conclude that the same criticisms would apply in the case of the motion picture as in the case of the theater. Thus, realism might be condemned in the cinema only because it has been condemned on the stage. Such a procedure would hardly be justified, however. The motion picture, much as it has been influenced by the theater, is an independent medium of art. It should certainly be held answerable for its sins, but these can be only its own sins and only such as violate the nature of its own art.

Indeed, realism in the motion picture is an entirely different problem from realism on the stage. The latter strives to produce an illusion of real life by means of real actors acting in a natural manner, and of real-looking but mostly counterfeit sets and properties. The former uses, or can use, real nature and real people, but its people are deprived of speech and its nature has neither volume nor color—nor do its people. The only real thing in the motion picture is movement, without which all its objects would appear as lifeless shadows. The sea, for example, would look utterly dead and unreal on the screen if there were no light playing on its surface, or if it had no ripples or waves. Mountains, trees, and buildings would loom phantom-like if we could not see them continuously changing their shapes. And living creatures, if denied movement, would look scarcely better than the masks of wax figures. There are, therefore, clearly defined limits for the illusionist effects of real life and nature in the cinema: the motion picture can be realistic only when its shadowy world is set in motion.

Nor is this all. In life and in the stage drama, action and emotion are expressed not only through movement but also through the spoken word. The speechless motion picture is denied this means of expression and, as a result, is compelled to resort to captions and exaggerated miming. But unsatisfactory and unrealistic as these substitutes are, they do not dispose of the whole difficulty. There remains the important difference that compared with a spoken scene that may last for thirty minutes without a change in the situation, not to speak of the setting, a scene in the cinema can be sustained by mime alone for no more than a minute, and, with captions, perhaps for another minute or two. From this arises the necessity of continually changing the perspective of the scene by introducing close-ups and different camera angles, and by breaking up the scene into fragments interlaced with fragments of other scenes. Thus again movement is introduced to keep the motion-picture drama alive. But though it succeeds in saving the drama, movement also succeeds in effectively destroying its realism.

The spectator, it must be remembered, observes the motion-picture world by proxy, as his intermediary is the camera-eye of the film. Through the deployment of the camera, the spectator acquires the ability to be invisibly present in the very midst of the events he observes, and of following them from place to place. This unquestionably carries realistic illusion much farther than is possible in the theater—where, from his fixed position in the auditorium, the spectator can see the stage only from the outside, and where he is also obliged, owing to the limitations of stage technique, to use his own imagination in following the change of action from one scene to another. In this respect the motion picture certainly surpasses the stage. But it immediately oversteps all bounds of realism when it begins to use its camera lens, as in the case of the close-up, to enlarge an object beyond all proportions of normal vision; and film completely transcends the realistic formula when it resorts to its recording power to bring into almost simultaneous view a variety of scenes, widely separated in space and time, which no human being could similarly observe under natural conditions.

It may truly be said of the motion picture, then, that, so far as realism is concerned, it is the very bed of Procrustes. Sound, volume, and color are the first limbs to go. Still-life goes next when it yields itself to a moving camera, or to movement of any kind. Scenes of human action lose everything beyond the power of miming, and are cut up, in any event, even if they ultimately find a place in the picture. And, finally, normal vision gets tossed out with the close-up, as does any normal sense of space with the shuffling of images by the cinema.

In the face of all these limitations, there can be no excuse for speaking of realism with regard to the motion picture. Life and nature are not reproduced faithfully, but are shown in a new aspect determined by the peculiar properties of the medium in their relation to the spectator. Only moving objects and the form of these objects when they are moving can be said to belong to the real world proper. The rest of the cinema is supplied by its own natural functions, for the special purpose of appealing to the spectator.

It is the failure to appraise the true value of the part played in the motion picture by movement that has been responsible for the obsession with realistic effects that has dominated the work of the greater number of directors since the early days of cinematic art. This failure had its origin in the still-life realism of the picture-frame stage and the easel painting. Seldom completely successful in its illusionistic aims, and rarer still in the achievement of aesthetic significance, such realism was at least able to give a fair imitation of the real thing. Its trees and buildings did look like real trees and buildings. But in the motion picture the still-life is very nearly a "still-death," and therefore its being realistic or not is a matter of small consequence. On the other hand, life in motion is "life" because it is in motion, and therefore, again, its being realistic or not is only of secondary importance as compared with the fact that it is in motion. In actual practice, much of the realistic detail is obliterated by the natural working of film technique. But where it does obtrude itself, it is just so much clutter that only holds back the dynamic progress of the moving picture.

From the point of view of the still-life, realism means a conglomeration of casual and even irrelevant details and facts. It carries no emphasis, no unity of design, no organization of elements. Its utter lack of form militates against every precept of the modern conception of pictorial and scenic art. To replace its impersonal drabness with a treatment that is free and imaginative, to get away from its trite subjects to the colorful visions of fancy and creative imagination, would seem to be the duty of every genuine artist who would attempt to instill the principles of art into the motion-picture drama. And in a sense it is.

Obviously, a setting designed to appeal to the eye is preferable to one that lacks such appeal. It is the essence of art to organize all its material, to give it a form that carries significance. The only question is whether the pictorial effects of an easel painting or a drawing retain the same power of appeal when used in the motion picture. Obviously, yet again, they do not. One can even go so far as to assert here that a deliberate emphasis on the pictorial beauty of single subjects breaks up the unity of the picture and presents the spectator with a number of loose ends that he can neither pick out nor tie into a knot.

Assuredly, the material of the motion picture must be organized, but its organization should be in the nature of a dynamic pattern where each separate pictorial subject is balanced in relation to all other subjects, while the component parts of each remain fluid in relation to one another. To enter as an element into a mobile form, the static picture, first of all, has to break down its equilibrium. It therefore ceases to be a "picture," and, consequently, has no further use for the principles of design and composition as these are employed in the easel painting.

This very failure to appreciate the relative unimportance of still-life effects in comparison with the effects of movement characterizes the work of several directors who represent what may be described as the German school of the motion picture. It would be unfair in criticizing the pictorial emphasis of such films as *The Cabinet of Dr. Caligari, Waxworks* [1924, dir. Paul Leni], *Siegfried, The Last Laugh* [1924, dir. F. W. Murnau], *Variety* [1925, dir. E. A. Dupont], and (the weakest among them) *Metropolis* [1927, dir. Fritz Lang] not to give credit to their originality of conception, their thoughtful and very sensitive use of material, and their excellent photography, though one is inclined to resent the quasi-profundity of these pictures' solemn mysticism and their peculiar relish of paste-board tableaux. It is remarkable, however, how completely the dynamic nature of the motion picture has escaped the notice of the German directors.

The picture that claims credit for being the first to organize its sequences in a mobile form was made, not in Germany, but in Russia. It is *Battleship Potemkin* [1925, dir. Sergei Eisenstein]—an unpretentious, "realistic" film and no masterpiece in any sense of the word (particularly in its mutilated version as shown in America), but decidedly a pioneer work of far-reaching importance. In *Potemkin* one sees a deliberate attempt to base the emotional appeal of the film on variations in the tempo of its moving objects. The carrying out of the idea is still very crude, but it is sufficiently effective to show what potentialities lie dormant in this method.

Incidentally, *Battleship Potemkin* illustrates that a perfectly realistic detail, when shown in close-up, may sometimes assume a wholly symbolic aspect. Such, for instance, is the effect produced by the slow swinging of a gun on the *Potemkin* as it is being trained on the approaching enemy. One sees only a part of the gun clearly silhouetted against the sky, with no human beings around it. Yet, realistic representation that it is, it looks like the very incarnation of a watchful and tremendously destructive power ready to spit fire at anything that may venture a challenge. No such impression, one feels sure, could be produced by the real gun in its actual setting.

This remarkable power of transforming ordinary objects, of endowing them with a new significance and a new power of appeal, places the motion picture in a class by itself. It is much more independent of the forms of the material world as they are seen by the human eye than is the theater or painting. This independence, however, implies dependence on the fact that the motion picture rests entirely on the use of movement as a means of appeal to the aesthetic consciousness of the spectator. Even when realistic or pictorial effects are the principal concern of the director, movement reveals itself as the determining artistic factor. It will gain immeasurably in its constructive and dramatic powers when once its peculiar role in the cinema is frankly admitted and movement's different forms, at present mostly overlooked or ignored, are put to their proper uses.

In a previous article on this subject [in *Theatre Arts Monthly*, April 1927], I classified the visual effects of movement in groups corresponding to the constituent elements of the motion-picture medium. Of these effects of movement, the most obvious—those arising from moving figures and objects—have received the greatest attention. Since the naturalistic convention dominates the minds of the majority of movie directors, the natural forms of movement have thus inevitably become the most readily exploited. Indeed, ancient and modern races (the latter in the form of speeding motor cars) as a means to dramatic climax are the stock in trade-of-most contemporary films.

The possibility of further progress for this form of movement lies in two directions. There is in the first place the unexplored field of conventionalized movement as we see it in modern ballet. The obstacle to this development is the difficulty of carrying a strict rhythmic pattern through the whole length of a picture. But this is not an unsurmountable obstacle, as it is possible through a special treatment of film form to provide a rhythmic basis not only for moving objects but even for stationary ones. The other direction of progress suggests itself along the lines already indicated by *Battleship Potemkin*. A variation in dynamic pattern is obtained by relating and contrasting scenes of differing speeds of movement, as the momentum of the whole scene rather than the movement of single figures provides the primary element of structural form.

The movement produced by the camera lens in the form of close-ups and changing camera angles has so far been exploited mostly as effects of still-life, helping to draw the attention of the spectator to this or that particular detail or serving merely for pictorial purposes. It is obvious that such shots and angles should also be brought within the dynamic scheme of the motion picture, where their very considerable power of dramatic and symbolic suggestion would receive added dynamic emphasis.

Perhaps the most important form of movement from an artistic point of view is that contributed by the motion picture as the carrier of successive, recorded images. A reference has already been made to the effect of rhythm that can be obtained in the context of a full-length film. Many attempts in this direction have been made by various directors (notably Abel Gance in France)—without, however, achieving any positive results. Though unable to disclose the details of a process that is awaiting patent specifications, the present writer is bold enough to claim that the problem admits of a very simple solution. Whether his faith in this case is warranted or not, it is hardly open to doubt that the rhythmic movement of a picture would provide a powerful means for bringing continuously changing scenes into a structural unity, and for giving dramatic moments the accumulated force of dynamic accent. In addition to this, rhythm makes possible the use of the pause—a measured suspension of movement, the absence of which in today's films deprives them of one of the most effective elements of dramatic narrative.

Yet rhythm is not the only unexplored resource of the cinema. Considered, for simplicity and brevity's sake, as functioning in conjunction with the projector and the screen, film can be seen to possess another form of movement of exceptional interest. It has been a long-standing conviction of the present writer that the current practice of confining the projected picture to a small and uniformly-sized section of the screen constitutes an arbitrary convention that is both undramatic and inartistic. The recently produced *Old Ironsides* [1926, dir. James Cruze] bears out the author's view to the fullest. By means of a special optical device, this picture, in reaching its climax, is suddenly enlarged on the screen to almost twice the size of its normal projection—with an effect of startling dramatic power.

The principle having thus been vindicated, one is led to ask why its application should not be extended to more scenes. It is clear that some incidents require less prominence than others. It would be reasonable, therefore, to give them a smaller frame. On the other hand, where the story demands a dramatic accent, a larger frame, up to and including the largest size, the scene in question should get the prominence it requires. One might even suggest that incidents of secondary importance, which are shown largely for the sake of continuity, should all be confined within a single frame. Treated in this manner, one scene would be brought into view by the side of a second scene, and would remain before the spectator's eyes while the action otherwise proceeded from one section of the frame to another.

The use of enlarged projection opens up another possibility—perhaps the most important of all. In an art like the motion picture, which bases itself on the organization of dynamic objectives, the pliability of its material is an essential condition of success. The stringing of all scenes into a single line of sequence is therefore an unnecessary limitation on the resources of the medium. At present we see diverse subjects broken up into fragments, which are afterwards shuffled together to form a continuous procession of images. An infinitely better effect would be obtained if a number of subjects were treated simultaneously within the same frame with an enlarged projection. The position of the subject on the screen would thus not be restricted to one, fixed section. It would be determined by the relative function of the scene in the general dramatic and dynamic scheme. The subject would grow large or small, sometimes dwindling into nothingness, and it could move from one end of the screen to the other, while other subjects would be passing through similar evolutions.

Let me emphasize that a simultaneous demonstration on screen of several subjects does not necessarily mean a division of interest. The contrary of this has been proved on the stage, and the screen, in this respect, has the added advantage of being able to stress one subject against the others by giving it, at any required moment, the prominence of a larger size. Simultaneous treatment is not suggested as an aim in itself, however. Rather, it is proposed as a means of achieving a balanced interweaving of several dynamic objectives, the total effect of which would be to create a pictorial and dramatic progression governed by the principles of counterpoint and orchestral harmonization. By this means—one can assert with confidence—the art of the motion picture would make an appreciable advance toward the goal it shares with all arts, which is the greatest power of appeal charged with the utmost aesthetic significance. (*Theatre Arts Monthly*, June 1927)

6. Drama and the Screen (1927)

Moving-picture drama is not moving pictures plus drama. It is drama in the moving pictures. Wherefore something must be found in the movies that, under proper treatment, will result in drama. Curiously enough, drama to be drama must move the audience, and moving pictures to be moving pictures must move themselves. Thus the problem of the motion-picture drama is nothing more than finding a way of making the motion pictures move themselves in a manner that will also move the audience.

Now to move anything is to carry, convey, or draw it from one place, position, or state to another place, position, or state. Drama carries, and sometimes draws, people from one state of mind to another. In doing so, however, it follows a definite and well-tried system that makes the moving from one mental state to another like the moving from one house to another, an adventure that grows in interest and excitement as one experience succeeds another. The better the drama is, the more interesting the adventure, and, therefore, the greater the variety of sensations as well as the subtler their arrangement in contrast and juxtaposition, so that the "moving" as a whole forms a balanced, mentally satisfying cycle of experiences.

What can the moving picture do to achieve this effect of dramatic development? Obviously, it can achieve such an effect only by moving itself in a manner that will produce a variety of sensations while at the same time coordinating them all in a single, inwardly balanced visual progressivism. This is far from being the case in the vast majority of motion-picture dramas as we know them today. A few of the present-day movies do make an attempt at coordinating their material, but they fail miserably in their effort, and for no other reason than this: they have not yet learned the meaning and uses of variety.

The moving picture lives on the screen so long as it moves, and the variety in the moving picture is the variety of movement. Yet the principal movement relied upon by most contemporary directors for their so-called dramatic effects is the natural movement of figures and objects within the frame itself. They seem to forget that it is not only the actors but the picture as a whole that is continuously moving. It is moving when the camera is brought from a long shot to a medium shot or a close-up, or when the camera shoots a scene from one angle and then from another. The picture is moving when one scene gives place to another scene—as rapidly or as slowly as the speed at which the change of scene takes place on the screen. The picture is moving, or rather it can be moving, when the entire image is enlarged or reduced in size, or when its position on the screen changes from side to side or from top to bottom.

Such are the different movements that, together with the movement of figures and objects, must all be woven into a single pattern, albeit a pattern that is unfolded before the audience as a mobile form and that has its dramatic accents, suspenseful moments, and climactic events all properly distributed and effectively arranged. Take, for instance, the conventional use of the close-up. No matter what the position of a given episode in relation to other episodes, it is the common practice to use a close-up when the characters are speaking to each other, in shot/reverse-shot fashion. Need it be said that this method is absurd? That the movement from a long or medium shot to a close-up, and subsequently to another close-up, should not carry a greater justification than the simple desire of showing the characters as they speak? And yet, when used in its proper place, the close-up can have an extraordinarily telling effect. It acquires a symbolic significance that can lift an episode above all others, and thus give the picture the very emphasis it needs to be appreciated as drama.

To take another example of the failure of the movie director to grasp the importance of movement, consider the jumble of scenes that are thrown onto the screen in telling a story. Does one ever see scenes, as scenes, contrasted with each other? Do they ever come as a surprise? There may be surprises in the story itself, but one never sees them welded to the surprises that could be effected by the mere change of visual impressions.

To the same movement-group one should also add the effects of tempo and rhythm. Though attracting more attention now than formerly, these effects are still far from being thoroughly understood. The matter is too complicated to be discussed in this instance, but I can hardly restrain myself from giving expression to at least one ardent longing that no picture has yet been able to satisfy: when, oh when, will some director give me a picture that expresses suspense by means of an absolute pause—a complete blank between one scene and another? And, if he can add to this the sprightly humor that would make him start the picture from the top corner of the screen and bring it down to the bottom corner, or that would make the picture appear on a section of the screen where it is least expected, changing its size, shape, and position in accordance with the dramatic demands of the story— well, if any director will give me this, I shall not hesitate to proclaim to the world: "Hosanna! The master has come and the kingdom of the movie drama is with us!" (*New York Times*, August 7, 1927)

7. Vaudeville on Screen (1927)

The ways of glorification are strange and devious. Heroes get monuments raised to their memory. Saints get their halos. The humble motion picture, born in a shed, rose quickly to be honored in "palaces." [For example, the Palace Theatre in Syracuse, New York, 1924; Albany, New York, 1931; Cleveland, Ohio, 1922; Canton, Ohio, 1926; Columbus, Ohio, 1927; Marion, Ohio, 1928; Lorain, Ohio 1928; and in Louisville, Kentucky, 1928.] Today, with the royalties much more in supply than in demand and palaces almost as common as coffee pots, no edifice is regarded grand enough to house the movies. The grandest of them all, opened a few months ago, is no less a place than a "cathedral." [New York's Roxy Theatre, billed as the "Cathedral of the Motion Picture," opened on March 11, 1927.]

A cathedral—the seat of a bishop! To have a bishop officiate at a cinematic ritual: what greater glory could be desired for the movies? I remember how, thrilled by this thought, I attended the first service in this "cathedral." I was anxious to see the bishop, and eagerly waited for him to come and give his benediction to *The Love of Sunya* [1927, dir. Albert Parker; the Roxy Theatre's first presentation, starring Gloria Swanson]. But he did not. In fact, he never does in this cathedral. I should not be surprised to hear that he is never there at all, and that somebody else does the bishoping in his absence. "Bishoping"—this is precisely the word, for does it not mean "using the arts to make an old horse look young, or giving a good appearance to a bad one"? *Now* I understand why this particular edifice is called a cathedral. A case of unconscious humor, I suppose.

There must be something in glorifying the cinema that makes it particularly conducive to this kind of humor. Who would think, for instance, that the name "a temple of the movies," so proudly borne by some of the most imposing-looking movie theaters, is really a joke, or in any event a play on words? To a simple person, of course, a temple is merely an edifice erected in honor, and for the worship, of some deity—the deity of motion pictures in this case. But the people who own "movie temples" can hardly be described as simple.

Though not all theater owners are descendants of ancient Athenians, some of them seem to be conversant with ancient Greek. (They are even known to take their own utterances with a measurable grain of Attic salt.) It is thus that they have discovered the true meaning of the word "temple." That it derives from the Latin *templum* is a matter of common knowledge. But that *templum* derives from the Greek *tempo* has been a secret revealed only to the owners of movie temples. And it is not surprising that they have been guarding this secret so jealously, since their temples are places in which the motion picture is "tempo-ed" down, or reduced to the humble position of handmaid in a household of gaudily dressed young damsels known professionally as variety acts.

I have no quarrel with these gentlemen on this score. Most of them are good showmen, and it is the showman's business to pull our leg when he has a chance to do so. After all, a "temple" is the last place I should care to go if I were bent on cinematic pleasure. The further away the movies—and, for that matter, all dramas—are from "temples" or "cathedrals" of any kind, the healthier it will be for all concerned. But there is another side to this question. The practice of honoring motion pictures by prefacing them with vaudeville entertainment is not confined to a few big "temples." There are innumerable other tabernacles, palaces, or whatever else you may choose to call them, in which the larger part of the ceremony is given over to variety turns, with the motion picture slipped in at the end almost as if it were a sort of conscience-money.

This fact has been frequently noted and commented upon. The young enthusiasts of the motion picture have been particularly loud in condemning the practice, bewailing it as a slight on their newly enshrined idol. Alas! As has been proven time and time again, enthusiasm is the lesser part of discretion. It is futile to denounce vaudeville acts in movie houses unless something is suggested that will not only replace them, but will also carry the same appeal to the audience as they do. That vaudeville acts are popular with the public is a truism needing no further testimony. But they are popular not because of any superiority of art as compared with the average feature film. Indeed, it is sometimes a problem to decide which of the two comedies—the one on the stage or the one on the screen—deserves the award for sheer ineptitude. A feature film, therefore, is no substitute for vaudeville. The true substitute can be only one: and that is a vaudeville motion picture.

A vaudeville motion picture! The words seem to suggest a sequence of one- or two-reel comedies interspersed with acrobatics, camera tricks, cartoons, and the like. God forbid that any such creation should exist! Short subjects of every kind, comic or otherwise, could all be in vaudeville form, but it would not be they that make the vaudeville, any more than the show-business item in any newsreel would make one. The appeal of vaudeville comes from a different source, and it is a source that can be tapped in the motion picture even as it is tapped on the ordinary stage.

Why is the vaudeville form of entertainment so popular with the public? Why is it, of all forms of theatrical art, the least susceptible to fads and fashions? Because it is direct and personal in its appeal and because, to be so direct and personal, it is obliged to keep strictly within its natural means of expression. In vaudeville there is no place for shams. Everything in it helps to reveal its nature. Vaudeville's audience feels at home because it is always conscious of being an audience; it does not sneak its laughs and does not hide its moments of thrill, but rather voices them openly, as if exercising its natural right. The performer, too, assumes no disguises. He is always a performer, an entertainer, a showman. Between him and the audience there is a frank understanding that the business of one is to entertain those in the auditorium of the theater, while the business of the other is to watch and appraise those on the stage. What could be more natural, more direct, and more personal?

The secret of vaudeville's perpetual youth and of its appeal to the public is therefore nothing other than its making no secret of being an entertainment. Its actors, dancers, acrobats, and magicians are just actors, dancers, acrobats, and magicians, who are there on the stage for the special purpose of pleasing the audience through the display of their art and skill.

Now, can the motion picture do this, as well? Can it also be a *frank* entertainment designed to please the audience by the display of its art and skill? I am convinced it can. Seeing the actor in the flesh does not in itself make for a vaudeville; seeing him serve his act across the footlights does. Hence the motion picture, to catch the true spirit of vaudeville, must also serve its entertainment direct to the audience. At present, in its dramas and comedies, it packs the spectator inside the camera and sends him on a dizzying voyage into known or unknown lands, spying on the lives of people in their homes and offices, on their fields, mountains, rivers, and seas.

Yet there is no denying it: looking through the camera, like looking through a keyhole, is on occasion a very exciting pastime. But is this the kind of pastime that can be enjoyed with real facility and comfort? Would we rather not sit in our chairs and have the other fellow, the cameraman, do the spying for himself—and then perhaps show us what he deems worthy of our attention? It makes all the difference in the world, where entertainment is concerned, to feel that somebody is up there in front of you, manifestly trying to make you happy.

With this knowledge of what is needed to make the spectator feel thoroughly at home and at perfect ease when at a motion-picture show, we shall have no difficulty in coming to a friendly understanding with our entertainers of the modern screen. One of the first items to be stipulated in our agreement will have to do with our mutual diplomatic recognition:

> We the audience, of one part, and we the movie entertainers, of the other part, hereby solemnly declare that we recognize one another as independent, autonomous, and sovereign powers exercising our authority in, for, and on behalf of our respective territories—to wit, we the audience, in the territory

known as the front of the movie house; and we the entertainers, in the territory known as the screen of the movie house.

This recognition will be followed by a treaty of amity: "And whereas it has been felt by both parties to this instrument that it would be to their mutual benefit to maintain and encourage a friendly intercourse between their respective territories, it is hereby agreed

(1) That in consideration of various tokens of appreciation to be supplied by the audience, the entertainers shall use their best endeavors to ensure to the audience a full and unobstructed view of their, the entertainers', territory—to wit, the screen—so that under no circumstance shall the audience be led into a belief that the entertainers had abandoned their territory within the movie house for some other land outside the latter's boundaries.

(2) That in the exercise of their professional duties, inasmuch as they intend it for the appreciation of the audience, the entertainers shall conform to the code of etiquette current among civilized communities, and shall conduct themselves in a manner befitting a friendly intercourse and expressive of their interest in the reciprocal sentiments of the audience.

(3) That . . ."

Perhaps it is unnecessary to quote further from this proposed document. Enough has been said to indicate the principles of the proposed understanding. The rest will be a matter of talent, imagination, and enlightened showmanship. (*New York Times*, September 11, 1927)

8. Hollywood Speaks (1928)

Three new mechanical marvels—television, color cinematography, and talking pictures—broke into the headlines almost simultaneously. Ultimately each may figure as conspicuously in the everyday life of the American citizen as the radio has come to do; the last already has its place on Broadway, if you will, in the form of the radio play. We should have learned before now, however, that invention is not always an unmixed blessing, and there are good reasons for doubting that either the motion-picture industry or the general public has cause to be glad that the irrepressible technician has at last succeeded in teaching shadows to talk. Edison let us in for a good deal when he made the movies possible by bringing the perforated film and the star-and-cam sprocket wheel together, but his ingenious contrivance assaulted only one of the five senses; only the imagination can guess what the ear may henceforward be compelled to endure.

The stock if not the earnings of Warner Brothers corporation (owners of the Vitaphone sound-system patents) has gone soaring, but Hollywood sees only trouble ahead for an industry that was doing very nicely, indeed, before the new invention threatened complications that cannot possibly be solved for a long time to come. If the movies should actually be replaced by the talkies, it would mean, first, that the international market—upon whose existence the real prosperity of the industry depends—would of necessity be destroyed, and, second, that an entirely new technique of production would have to be evolved.

The stars of the screen do not know how to speak, and the scenarists do not know how to write dialogue. Nor can the latter difficulty be overcome by the purchase of successful dramas. Plays intended for the stage cannot be photographed as written for the simple reason that the narrative form of the movies, with its rapid changes of scene, is entirely different from that of the stage, where events are revealed in a different order and where everything that is represented to the eye takes place in only two or three places. Adaptation involves a retelling of the story in such a way that, for instance, many things merely reported on the stage are acted out in the cinema, and this means that the stage dialogue is unsuitable for a talking movie. Actually, to prepare a play for the talking pictures requires a rewriting almost as complete as that involved in the dramatization of a novel, and even after the technique for doing so has been perfected, the mere time required will be very much greater than is now needed for the preparation of a simple narrative sequence without words.

Nor is it, on the other hand, pleasant to imagine what the public will be called upon to endure. Silence imposed certain definite and very fortunate limitations upon the silliness of cinematographic dramas. The infantile sentimentality and abysmal vulgarity of those who make such dramas expressed themselves only through gesture, and they suffered from a blessed inability to suit the word to the action. Occasional subtitles gave us a hint of what the performers would have said had they been able, and the memory of this hint is far from reassuring. Moderately literate people shuddered, and even the most naïve of audiences frequently tittered, when the level of intelligence and taste behind a silent drama was suddenly revealed in the words of a caption. What will the movies be like when every gesture is accompanied by some audible "came the dawn"?

It is a notorious fact that ninety-nine out of a hundred of all the original stories written for the movies are artistically at the level of the cheapest magazine fiction, and that an equal number of those based on other works are reduced to the same level in the course of the process of adaptation. The mechanical perfection of the cinema already furnishes the most violent contrast to its artistic immaturity, and the makers of the photoplay can say today—more completely than they ought to be able—that they know nothing that is worth the saying. The last ten or fifteen years have shown so little improvement in any important direction that there was no good reason for hoping that any such improvement would ever take place, but at least it may reasonably be maintained that under the circumstances every limitation was an advantage. To accord the movies a new means of expression now, before they had begun to make any good use of those that they had, is to curse the motion picture with a new curse.

Each new mechanical contrivance is greeted in the newspapers by some editorial writer who recalls the first message sent across telegraphic wires: "What hath God wrought?" Each time it is used, however, this question seems less and less a rhetorical one. (*The Nation*, September 26, 1928)

9. The Future of the Movies (1928)

The movies of today are a vast industry supplying the nations of the world with a standardized, machine-made entertainment. The standards are those demanded by the world market that the industry serves. Consequently, they are inevitably determined by the lowest common denominator of the movie-consuming intelligence of the moment. It is said that the American "hick" is the arbiter of taste who dictates the fashions of Hollywood, because today his appreciation of a picture spells its success or failure.

Indeed, the time does not seem to be far off when this proud position will be held, probably, by the humble Kaffir or Hottentot of the kraals of Africa, whose intellectual and moral reactions to the unhappy ending, for instance, will then be carefully studied, with the help of charts and diagrams, in the selling and producing offices of Hollywood. If the future Napoleons and Genghis Khans of Hollywood, to spread their world dominion, do develop respect for the Hottentot ideal of a vamp, or perfect lover, or man-about-town, it is certain that their efforts will have as little influence on the production of worthwhile movies as they have today, when only a few valiant gentlemen attempt to realize their lifelong ambition of putting this or that classic on the popular screen.

It is one of the gratifying signs of the present situation that leadership in the art of the movies definitely seems to be passing into the hands of smaller producers, who meet with the ever-growing and already ample support of cultured people all over the world because the standards of quality, and not those demanded by global "boobery," are the standards governing their work. In this respect it is difficult to exaggerate the importance of the so-called "little-theater movement," and particularly of home movies, both of which promise an assured outlet for the work of the independent artist. Judging by the trend of the present development, it is quite likely that the future movie will be largely an entertainment at home obtainable either through a broadcasting station or, for the more discriminating, through a film library supplying films, probably by means of the collotype or photogravure process, and at prices only a little higher than those at which books are purchased today.

More, however, than in the question from whom and how we shall be getting our movies, we are interested in the mystery of the future movie itself. What is it likely to be? Will it be all talking, or all silent, or mixed? And what will be its forms, and how will it affect the theater of the live actor?

Insofar as the talking picture is concerned, there cannot be the slightest hesitation in saying that, in the field of popular entertainment, it is bound to oust and supplant both the silent picture and the theater of living actors. The silent picture will give up its present position of dominance simply because the talking one has a more obvious and more easily workable means of carrying dramatic appeal to the audience. And the theater of live actors will have to go into retirement because the talking movies, technically developed as they are sure to become in time under the stimulus of competition in the same field of entertainment, will outdo the theater in all those effects of representation, whether naturalistic or "artistic," that stand for so much in the eyes of the average playgoer.

There is no need to shed tears over the coming substitution of a machine for the live actor. The machine does not dispense with the actor, and is entirely subservient to the will of the artist. But the danger of the machine is that it is just as subservient to the will of any boob who may have enough money to buy it. And when it comes to money, it is seldom the artist who has enough of it, as one observes from the condition of things in Hollywood. The danger of the talkies, therefore, is merely the danger that the Hollywood methods will completely submerge even the not particularly inspired methods of Broadway.

There is one consolation left to those genuinely concerned for the future of dramatic art, whether on the stage or on the screen. The industrialization of the popular forms of drama will leave the artist free to concentrate on those qualities of his medium that contribute most to the creative potency of his work. In the theater the artist will emphasize the direct contact between the actor and the audience, and the fact that the play is actually performed on the stage in front of a number of spectators who have gathered there for that special purpose. In the talking movie, insofar as the independent artist has the opportunity of handling the matter, the artist will develop that combination of speech and picture in which the dramatic effect will depend on the unique and complementary qualities of both. And, finally, there will be the silent movie—*the* movie in the strict sense of the word—in which the artist will continue to express himself through the various forms of visual movement, the wealth and significance of which are still but dimly realized even by the most venturesome among artists.

How greatly underestimated the resources of the silent movies are—this is revealed in the present stampede of Hollywood producers in the direction of talking movies. Through sheer technical as well as artistic incompetence, in spite of all the big talk that comes from Hollywood, American film producers have suffered an inglorious defeat in their previous effort to sustain the drawing power of the silent picture. With the growing popularity of the new system of presentation, the motion-picture houses have been more and more changing into regular vaudeville theaters. The talking picture has now delivered the *coup de grâce*, and the Hollywood silent movie can be seen taking the full count, with its seconds shouting "foul" and swaggering in the usual manner about its hidden prowess. Nobody will put any trust in the ability of Hollywood to come back, though attempts, and well-intentioned ones at that, will undoubtedly be made here and there. But it is Hollywood and not the silent picture that has suffered defeat The silent picture is perfectly able to stand up for itself, provided it is allowed to use its full force and to fight in its own way.

The metaphors of the boxing ring are more appropriate here than they may seem at first glance. The photoplay, after all, is a form of drama, and dramatic effects are essentially impacts on the emotional sensibility of the spectator, with the dramatic climax playing the part of the knock-out blow that, in the popular phrase, "brings the house down" (nothing less than the whole house, be it observed). The cold sweat that follows this experience must be that consummation of dramatic thrill which Aristotle calls "catharsis " All this seems pretty elementary and obvious. And yet even these axioms of dramatic art are persistently ignored by the producers of movie drama.

The classic example of such blindness one finds in the case of William Randolph Hearst, the gentleman who, according to his recent biographer [John K. Winkler, *W. R. Hearst: An American Phenomenon* (1928)], lost $7,000,000 in furthering the art of the motion picture. Of course, anybody who can lose $7,000,000 can afford to lose $7,000,000. But for Hearst to have done so in making screen drama seems hardly believable. We know how he made his great fortune. He did so by *dramatizing* information in his newspapers. He bent his every effort on one main purpose, which was to attract the reader's attention, to strike his imagination, to rouse his emotions. He knew that the appeal had to be made to the senses, so he applied "sensationalism" in the form of lurid stories and shrieking headlines. There may be some who still believe that information should be supplied pure, or at least with not more than 1½ percent of intoxicating dramatic content. That is, of course, a matter of personal preference. The fact remains that as a dramatizer of news Hearst was supreme.

Now observe Hearst as a producer of screen drama. According to his biographer,

> everything had to be *real* with Hearst. If the script called for the ladies of the ensemble to wear Irish lace, Belfast was asked to send entire bolts of its best and most costly hand-woven product. The result often was that . . . screenplays that should have cost two or three hundred thousand dollars actually required two or three million! [Winkler, 255-256]

This was the extent of Hearst's sensationalism in the movies: real Irish lace, and, one assumes, real silks and velvets and emeralds and pearls. Was this used to attract the attention of the spectator, to strike his eye, to rouse his emotions? No, it was just "art," which in Hearst's understanding obviously did not mean drama.

Ah, what an irony of fate! Here was a man, perhaps the greatest master of our age in the art of playing on human emotions (whether base or noble is a separate question), a man who not only knew all the old tricks of the game but who enriched them with a thousand of his own—and this man, when he came to deal with the screen drama, forgot all about his sensational stunts, his banner headlines, his four-inch type, and the innumerable other devices with which he assailed the public. Instead he spent a goodly fortune in providing real Irish lace and real this and that, as if it mattered two pins whether they were real or not. If ever there was a case of genius misapplied and wasted, Hearst's was one.

The silent motion picture must now adopt Hearst's methods of sensationalism. Since it cannot really shriek and cannot bang, it must learn to shriek and to bang with silent images. It must learn the uses of emphatic statement, of dramatic accent—but not of statements or accents produced with the help of music and sound devices, which would be like pasting miniature rattles in the places in newspapers where bold-faced headlines should be. The silent film, instead, must give dramatic accent by changing the form and position of the visual image on the screen: the very way of sensational make-up in the newspaper, and the way forward for drama on the screen.

To demand this from the movie artist is to demand an emotional or dramatic progression represented by a combination of all the basic movements of the medium into a single, dynamic pattern. Some of these movements have already been fairly thoroughly explored and effectively turned to dramatic uses. The principal one is that of independently moving objects. Human beings, animals, automobiles, trains, rivers, and waves all have movements that can be manipulated and organized to fit a certain pattern. Here one finds effects of tempo and rhythm in the actual movement of objects. In *The Big Parade* [1925, dir. King Vidor] and *Battleship Potemkin* [1925, dir. Sergei Eisenstein], we see these effects very skillfully and forcibly exploited for dramatic purposes. *Contrast* in the direction of moving objects is effectively brought out in the abstract picture *Ballet Mécanique* [1924, dir. Fernand Léger & Dudley Murphy], and even more so in the German film *Berlin: Symphony of a City* [1927, dir. Walter Ruttmann]—in both cases, however, without much dramatic significance.

Another important form of movement is contributed by the combined movement of the camera and the film. It may result either in merely elective camera angles, as in *The End of St. Petersburg* [1927, dir. Vsevolod Pudovkin], or in a certain fluidity of the visual world that, as in *The Last Laugh* [1924, dir. F. W. Murnau] and especially *Sunrise* [1927, dir. F. W. Murnau], renders it more malleable to dramatic effect. The so-called close-up, which is a special type of camera position said to have been introduced by D. W. Griffith, is extensively used in Hollywood, though without, alas, any reference to its dynamic or dramatic significance. There is an important problem here that will be solved only when the relationship between the scale of the object, its absolute size in relation to the size of the image, is thoroughly studied.

But perhaps the most revolutionary change in the form of the movie will be brought about by treating the screen itself as an arena of dramatic movement. Considered at present so devoid of merit that it is usually hidden behind a curtain, the screen in the movie theaters of the future will be the most important part of the building. It will occupy the largest area architecturally possible in the theater, and it will be used for effects of movement obtained by changing the position of the picture, by changing its size, and, finally, by employing simultaneously a number of separate subjects that are organized to form a single, dramatically dynamic pattern.

There is already much evidence pointing in this direction. The device called the Magnascope, demonstrated in *Old Ironsides* [1926, dir. James Cruze] and *Chang: A Drama of the Wilderness* [1927, dir. Merian C. Cooper & Ernest B. Schoedsack], indicates the dramatic possibilities of mere visual enlargement. Abel Gance in France, in his picture *Napoléon* [1927], obtains the effect of overwhelming grandeur by using a triptych screen with the simultaneous projection of three separate films. In *The Crowd* [1928], King Vidor puts one picture inside the other to give a realistic representation of the thoughts passing through someone's head. And, finally, F. W. Murnau in *Sunrise* combines a number of different sequences within a single frame in order to convey a symbolic meaning

We are thus on the threshold of a new development, one suggested for both practical and artistic reasons. Most narrative subjects viewed in single file, so to speak, have to be ruthlessly pruned to conform to the requirements of time. On the other hand, there are stories that cannot be properly appreciated unless they are unfolded simultaneously along several interweaving channels. For such material, contrapuntal or symphonic treatment seems to suggest the only effective dramatic form.

There is yet another possible development of the motion-picture drama, in which the screen in its bodily form is likely to play an important part. Like the theater artist of today, the movie artist is confronted with the problem of pure cinematic entertainment. So far this problem has been attacked, with considerable though incomplete success, only in the pictures of Charlie Chaplin, where it finds a partial solution in the superb and purely conventional acting of Chaplin himself. But Chaplin is an exception. Nor are his pictures quite consistent, since his method of frank entertainment extends only to his own acting. To be completely cinematic and at the same time theatrical, the motion picture must appear as nothing but a motion picture that is exhibited on the screen to provide a narrative entertainment for an audience. It will be able to do so only if it treats the screen not merely as an inert canvas but as the actual bearer—in fact, as the very locale—of the dramatic development portrayed in the picture.

When the motion picture reaches this stage of complete liberation from the effects of illusionistic representation, and proclaims itself openly as a means of dramatic entertainment, it will stand revealed before the admiring spectator as a wonderful mechanism in which profound experiences are given almost tangible form through the magical combination of camera, film, projector—all three combining to light objects, and people, on the screen. Such will be the final glory of the silent movie drama, unless the latter be killed in its coming fight for existence by its quickly growing and rapaciously inclined little brother: the talking picture. (*The Nation*, October 10, 1928)

10. Introducing the Dramatic Accent (1928)

There are many features in the movies of today that are apt to rouse the ire of the artist. Fortunately, there is also one feature that makes, or at least should make, the artist thank his stars for living and working in our time. This feature is the youth of the movies—their limitless possibilities, and the creative stage of development through which they are still passing. In fifty or a hundred years the movies will be an old art with established traditions and a whole pantheon of famous names. Today the cinema has no traditions, and though some names are famous enough, one feels it is more tactful not to examine their achievements too closely.

It is this freedom from the necessity of following in the footsteps of other people, side by side with the never-ceasing incentive to experiment with new methods and to search for new forms in order to find expression for one's creative impulse, that gives the modern movie artist the glorious feeling of having a world to conquer, as well as the power to accomplish the task. Indeed, there is scarcely a direction in the motion picture as a medium that does not open a vista of new, hitherto unexplored resources. The novelty and the multiplication of resources, however, cannot in themselves be the object. They are a means to an end, and in the movies as a form of dramatic art (using the term in its general sense and not as applying to the stage), there can be no other end than that of dramatizing motion-picture material. It is from the point of view of the ultimate dramatic effect, then, that one has to consider both the methods in current use and such innovations as may be made or suggested by the more venturesome spirits in this new art.

At the outset it is well to remember that all drama is merely a means of conducting the spectator through a balanced series of emotional and intellectual experiences. Drama's special method of appealing to the spectator is to place before his sympathetic observation a number of conflicting forces, which gradually reach their greatest stress, or climax, and thereafter either completely cancel each other out or, in the form of those that remain, combine in a resultant. Drama, therefore, in the first place is a dynamic pattern. But the forces that go to make this pattern in the motion-picture drama are not real human beings or objects, but mere visual images, and very incomplete and fragmentary images at that. Hence, as compared with the ordinary drama onstage, the screen drama is faced with a special problem of its own—the problem of conveying the correct relative value of each separate force in the dynamic pattern, and of giving the required accent to this or that particular scene.

One quickly realizes that very little effort is made to tackle this problem of structural, dynamic design in the commercial practice of today's screen dramatists. All the more reason, therefore, why it should attract the special attention of the non-commercial moviemaker—the experimentalist *par excellence*.

What does it actually mean to give a value or accent to a scene or character? Obviously this means giving a scene or character a certain amount of prominence. The problem sometimes arises on the ordinary stage when, for greater emphasis, assistance is sought in visual effects. The spotlight is the solution resorted to on such occasions. In the motion picture, however, with its prevailing naturalistic settings, the spotlight is hardly practicable, though it might make an interesting experiment to apply such a prominent device consistently to a fantastic subject. To find a method of a more general application, one has to turn to a different factor, namely, the factor of size. Here one may be surprised to find that the problem is not nearly as simple as it looks. To begin with, one has to differentiate between two dissimilar factors: the relative size of objects within each separate image, and the relative size of the images themselves over the course of a full sequence.

Where we deal with the relative size of objects, it is obvious that the larger the objects look, the more prominent they are. Thus, by using various shots, from long shot to close-up, one may develop a fixed scale of dramatic accents, with the close-up as the most emphatic of all. This would certainly constitute a great advance on the present, very indiscriminate use of the close-up, particularly in speaking scenes. But it would also somewhat restrict the use of the close-up to the particular function of dramatic emphasis, whereas the close-up also serves the important function of informing the spectator of facts and details that would otherwise remain unobserved. To preserve and make effective use of both functions of the close-up, i.e., the dramatic as well as the informative one, would require a very careful and subtle adjustment, but it should be possible to achieve and therefore should be a tempting goal for an artist.

Turning to the other possible variant—the relative size of images within a full sequence—we find at least four avenues of approach. It is possible, for instance, to vary the size of images within the same frame, so that the full area of the frame would be used for the accented scenes—i.e., the most prominent ones, dramatically speaking—while the frame masked to various sizes would be used for the less important incidents. Another method of obtaining accent may be found in varying the throw of the projector: for instance, by means of the Magnascope, in which case the scene needing emphasis, though of ordinary size on the film strip itself, will appear on the screen perhaps twice as large as it normally would be. By combining the Magnascope and the masking of the frame, a third method is obtained that has the advantage of a greater range of sizes than would be secured by using each method separately.

Finally, whether with the help of enlarged projection by means of the Magnascope or some other optical adjustment, or without such enlarged projection, there is the possibility of combining a number of reduced subjects within a single frame. The dramatic use of this method would reserve the full size of the frame for all the important scenes, whereas the less important episodes, particularly those used merely for continuity, would be reduced to perhaps one-sixth of their usual size and placed within the same frame, side by side. Thus half a dozen scenes showing a character leaving one house and arriving at another would appear like a series of illustrations on the same page, with the difference that the characters would be coming and going in each separate picture, and that one of the sections—for instance, the central one—could be used for a sort of reduced close-up showing the changing expressions of the principal character throughout the whole set of scenes.

There are other, clearly visible possibilities in this method of combining a number of subjects within the same frame. The opening scenes in F. W. Murnau's *Sunrise* [1927], and the use of a triple screen in Abel Gance's *Napoléon* [1927], are the first, and still very rudimentary, indications of a treatment that will find its complete realization in building a dynamic pattern along the lines of counterpoint, and in combining the movement within the image with the movement of the image over the surface of the screen—including the surface of the entire motion picture.

Insofar as the dramatic accent as such is concerned, it is important to point out that the two principal methods described, i.e., varying the relative size of the objects and varying the relative size of the images, stand in relation to each another in inverted ratio. However paradoxical it may sound, an image with small objects appears larger than a close-up. For this reason, the combined use of both methods represents a problem whose solution can be found only by experimentation. The whole problem of dramatic accent on film, then, is largely a matter of size, as would be far less the case on the stage—and therein lies its fascination. (*Movie Makers*, December 1928)

11. The Movie Scene: Notes on Sound and Silence (1929)

In literature the distinction between art and bilge—to use the terminology of H. L. Mencken—is so generally recognized that no critic in his right mind ever dreams of addressing his encomiums or strictures to the whole of the publishing trade, as if all books, magazines, and newspapers were art or even some kind of literature. In the movies, although scarcely 5% of all films made have anything to do with art, and the remaining 95% (outside of news and scientific films) are image-soaked pulp designed to feed the undiscriminating mind, the respective provinces of art and bilge are not yet recognized. The result is that every day one sees a mass of devastating critical fire, from the biggest aesthetic guns, concentrated on what is actually no more than the movie equivalent of a dime novel.

The ineffectiveness of this criticism need cause no worry, since the interest in the average Hollywood picture is no more open to aesthetic influence than the interest in cheap magazine stories and comic strips. Here one is up against a social rather than an artistic problem. On the other hand, such lumping together of all photoplays, as if the difference between them was one of degree, has had its corrupting effect. Standards of value have become extremely flexible, not to say loose; the least display of originality immediately raises a motion picture to a state of eminence that in other arts is attained only by acknowledged masterpieces. It is gratifying, no doubt, to see a picture that does not specifically assume, and address, a moronic intelligence on the part of its audience. But it is a far cry from this to art. Therefore, as the first step in the true appreciation of the movie scene today, let the gods keep apart for us what ignorant men have joined—Princess Art and King Bilge of the Empire of Moving Shadows.

There is only one thing that need be said here about the dominant section of this Empire. The Hollywood manufacturers of movies, who are both its servants and its rulers, should be reckoned as one of the wonders of our age. It staggers the imagination to see this huge industry—one of the greatest in the United States—resting on the lack of vision and technical competence that provides its foundation. The great fortunes, and the acumen and pertinacity shown in amassing them, should deceive no one. It is doubtful whether any of their possessors could competently direct a single picture. Yet the thing that the movie industry needs most is such technical competence. And what "new ideas" Hollywood accepts are mere variations on well-worn themes. For a really novel idea it has neither time nor intelligence, neither sufficient imagination nor the necessary daring—the daring of a Henry Ford, who did not hesitate to stop production and scrap an old plant in order to produce a better car. Still, if one could lay a charge against Hollywood, it would be not that it doesn't know how to produce art, but that it knows almost as little about how to make good, satisfying bilge.

The emergence of the talkies has somewhat complicated the situation. As soon as the picture houses over the length and breadth of America are equipped with the sound mechanism (and the high cost of this equipment is likely to extend the process over a considerable number of years), the film manufacturers will once again be faced with the problem of production on a uniform and regular basis. By that time, they will not only be able to overcome the competition of vaudeville acts by the simple process of providing a talking vaudeville on the screen (as they are already doing), but they will also engage in successful rivalry with the legitimate stage, thus extending even further their present audience.

The above obviously takes for granted that the talking picture has come to stay. There are many who are doubtful of this prospect. The weight of the evidence, however, is entirely against them. The fact that establishes the talking picture as assured of a prominent future is a very trivial one—the thing works. Its performance today may be primitive and crude (which is hardly to be wondered at considering the infancy of the process), but it has already proved its ability to convey its material to the audience. A medium that can do that—and do it with the extraordinary ease and effectiveness of the talking picture in its shorter subjects—need not worry about its future.

How far and widely the cinema has ranged in search of effective form, talking or silent, is told by two films at opposite poles as mediums of expression—though released within four years of each other. *The Last Laugh* [1924, dir. F. W. Murnau], which starred Emil Jannings at his early best, told its compassionate story entirely in pantomime, without even one written caption. *The Singing Fool* [1928, dir. Lloyd Bacon] is foremost among talking pictures, in the transition from silence to sound, for the warmth with which it successfully brings a theater personality—Al Jolson—to the screen. The only point in common between these two movies is that they are "one-man shows."

To the visual quality that formerly was the entire art of the screen, synchronized sound effects, as substantially displayed in *The Singing Fool*, have brought new possibilities of artistic value. Deftly selected, such effects are of particular aid in the symphonic rounding out of a picture, as in the part-talkie film version of Kenyon Nicholson's 1927 play *The Barker* [1928, dir. George Fitzmaurice]. Here, in the opening sequences, the babble and stir of the carnival crowds suggest their presence rather more by sound than sight. Circus noises—the strident barkers, shrieking calliopes, and twanging instruments—create atmosphere without the loss of dramatic force, a problem that the all-talking pictures have not yet been able to solve.

Nonetheless, fate has been kinder to Hollywood manufacturers than they themselves realize or are willing to admit. A year ago the industry, undermined as it was by its incompetence and fear of outside competition, was moving rapidly toward a crisis. Today, with the talking picture thrust upon it, the film industry can envisage a future that is greater than anything it has ever known. The heads of the movie-manufacturing business are capable of strangling any promising idea, but what may save the talking picture, as it would probably have saved the silent one, is the inevitable competition, on the one hand, with the little-cinema movement (which is sure to develop into a very powerful force), and, on the other, the equally inevitable rivalry with the stage.

But here again it is important not to mix any questions of aesthetic evaluation with the appreciation of the general output of the film industry. The talking picture is a medium of expression like the printed book or the gramophone record. Its mechanical nature makes it particularly suitable for industrial production. This does not imply that the part played by the mechanical and industrial factors in its origin disqualifies sound cinema as a medium of art. But it does unfortunately mean that because of these two factors, film lends itself readily to commercial exploitation, with the resultant loss of quality that comes from standardization of form and moronization of content. It is therefore a foregone conclusion that the victory of the talking picture over the legitimate stage, which seems to be inescapable, will result in a general loss of quality—not a very great one considering the present condition of the stage, but withal appreciable enough to be felt by the more sensitive among us.

It may be interesting now to subject the talking picture to a more technical scrutiny. If it is going to have different types of screenplay, what are they? One of these types, which is already taking shape, is obviously the "canned drama." The term carries a derisive connotation, but this is hardly warranted. At its worst, "canned drama" may mean a faithful copy—a reproduction of a play as produced on the stage. It is difficult to follow the reasoning that pours so much aesthetic scorn on the idea of "copy." A great work of art will retain some of its greatness even in a poor copy, as, in fact, it does every time a dramatic masterpiece is seen on the stage in an interpretation by indifferent actors. In the case of a talking picture, it is not so much the quality of acting that is at issue as the quality of its reproduction.

It is relevant here to note that in the experience of the present writer, the crudeness of the actual reproduction detracted very little from the thrill that he received when watching on screen the antics of Fuzzy Knight as he sings and dances in *Fuzzy Knight and His Little Piano* [1928], or when listening to the patter of Eddie Cantor during *A*

Ziegfeld Midnight Frolic [1929]. If the talking picture could do no better than "can" the *real* masterpieces of theatrical presentation, it would still deserve every praise for making these masterpieces accessible to large masses of people. Fortunately for the talking picture, though less so for these masterpieces, its own powers of expression are so superior to those of the stage that, before long, it will ignore the various forms of stage presentation as resolutely as the silent picture does today.

Let it be said that our dramatic literature has grown out of the physical peculiarities of the theater building as these have changed throughout the ages. A stage play, however great the scope it may give to the imagination, is forced to conform to two components of its theatrical being: it has to deal with actual space, and it has to deal with actual time. No such physical restrictions exist for the motion picture, whose space and time are not actual but merely relative. On the stage no part of the actor's body may be hidden from the audience unless it is supposed to be hidden from the other characters. In fact, theatrical convention allows the audience to see no more than the characters themselves are supposed to be seeing. In the motion picture the position may be entirely reversed. By showing only the character's feet the audience may be kept in ignorance as to the identity of the character, while dramatic suspense is being worked up and a situation developed where the disclosure of the character's identity supplies the climax.

In the matter of entrances and exits, the stage demands that while the action is proceeding, no character may come into the view of the audience, or withdraw therefrom, without complying with the natural laws of movement (provided the play be realistic). The motion picture need not concern itself with these requirements at all. It can start, interrupt, or end a scene at any moment it may choose, without bothering in the least by what means it shall bring the characters on or take them off. Something similar can be said about the matter of time. The duration of a scene on the stage is a definite fact that is related to the whole course of events portrayed in the play. On the screen, by contrast, the actual duration of a scene is hardly of any consequence, since it can be pulled out or drawn in like an accordion. The way of achieving this is through the by-now familiar parallel action obtained through alternating short sections of two or more different sequences. The dramatic force created by this method is overwhelming, and is best shown in the work of the master who discovered and made the most effective use of it—D. W. Griffith, in such films as *Intolerance* [1916], *Orphans of the Storm* [1921], and *Way Down East* [1920].

Griffith was also a master director of crowd scenes, a technical skill he first exhibited in *The Birth of a Nation* [1915], and since then has exhibited in almost every film he has produced, including *Orphans of the Storm* [1921]. The importance of alternating long and close shots during a sequence, especially one featuring crowds—a method that gives the screen its greatest physical advantage over the stage—was an early principle in Griffith's film directing. (Clear-cut action and continuity, sometimes obviously theatrical, have nevertheless always been features of visual narratives told with a camera.)

To the merely spectacular handling of crowd scenes and mob-like effects in most movies, the Russian directors have added a type of naturalism inherent in their performers and therefore peculiarly their country's own. In Sergei Eisenstein's *Battleship Potemkin* [1925] and *Ten Days That Shook the World* [a.k.a. *October*, 1927], as well as Vsevolod Pudovkin's *The End of St. Petersburg* [1927], the drama of the street scenes is intensified by a shadow of real restlessness, an imminent or actual surge of mass human movement that is always believable and ever suspenseful.

Since the talking picture is heir to all these dramatic assets of the silent picture, is it likely, one may ask, that it will continue to confine itself to mere reproduction of stage form? Even the movie manufacturers can be trusted in two or three years' time to rebel against such a lack of imagination. And when this happens, a new cine-dramatic literature will arise to find its expression through the medium of the talking picture. It is not asserted here that this literature will be art. The chances are that 95% of it will be the same as the 95% of the silent picture.

There are other technical developments that may come to fruition in the talking picture if the gods are kind. There is, for instance, the possibility of blending a recited story with the action on screen in a way that will make the reciter's voice and the screen images continuously supplement one another (not merely duplicate one another), with the result of enhanced effectiveness and greater dramatic power. Incidentally, this narrative form could retain the silent actor and, in a manner of speaking, give speech to the animals.

The great future awaiting the talking picture, alas, signifies the doom of the silent variety as a form of popular entertainment. As to this, it is futile to deceive oneself. The popularity of the talkies is not wholly a craze for novelty. Their success is due much more to the warmth and even intimacy that have been given the motion picture by the human voice, and which is so unmistakably missing in the silent picture as it comes out of Hollywood. With this added vocal appeal, and the greater ease with which it lends itself to dramatic treatment, the talking picture cannot possibly fail to displace the silent picture from its present position of dominance. Although it is doubtful whether the big companies that manufacture silent movies today will be making them ten years hence, this does not necessarily mean the death knell of the silent picture. A medium of such extraordinary power of expression cannot die only because it has lost favor with the consumers of bilge. But to survive the blow that is being aimed at it, the silent picture must wake up to the wealth of power now lying dormant within it and not hesitate to use it to the fullest.

Its first point of attack should be that very warmth and intimacy which have been denied it by the omniscient gentlemen of Hollywood. In other words, the silent movie must reveal itself—must acquire a "personality." The problem, fundamentally, is as simple as that of the personality of the theater. It will be recalled that even before the arrival of talkies, the silent picture was losing ground under the steadily growing popularity of vaudeville acts. And vaudeville, of course, is only another name for the theater of personality, of *theatrical* personality—to be precise, of its own undisguised "self." Briefly, the vaudeville is vaudeville: the actors acting, the stage carrying the actors, the audience watching the performance. Everyone is "self" and enjoying himself. That is the whole secret of vaudeville, as well as the formula for its working system.

There can be no theatrical intimacy outside this vaudevillian formula, and the silent movie as "spectacle," in the strict sense of the term, cannot possibly succeed unless it also acknowledges this formula. The motion picture must be "self" and enjoy being "self." In its inner structure it must stress that dynamic quality which makes it a "motion" picture. At the same time it must establish a definite physical relationship with the spectator. It can achieve this in only one way, i.e., by making the screen the frame of reference for both its visually dynamic form and its narratively imagistic content. Once the picture is visually related to the screen and the subject of the picture is seen as being presented unmistakably from the screen (not as seeming to emerge spontaneously from life), a direct physical contact is established with the spectator—a contact that is the condition of all theatrical intimacy.

With the blood of intimacy coursing through its veins, the silent picture will be able to call forth some of its latent and neglected powers. It will dramatize its form by making it more flexible and more susceptible to accent or emphasis. The silent picture will organize its form by making it follow a strict dynamic pattern governed by the rules of counterpoint and rhythm. It will expand and enrich that form by making it combine simultaneously a number of parallel and interrelated subjects, as so many strands woven into a single composition. Having done all this, the silent motion picture will realize that, without any conscious effort, it has been creating something that has an independent aesthetic reality—something called art. (*Theatre Arts Monthly*, February 1929)

12. The Talkies (1929)

It is a sad reflection on the limitations of intellectuals and artists all over the world to see history repeat itself in the contemptuous resentment with which they are greeting the arrival of the talking picture. Just as twenty years ago, when the silent movies began to stir the world, so today the patrons of art and the theater refuse to see in the talking picture anything but another vulgar product of our machine-dominated civilization. But so, too, does history repeat itself in the eagerness of the commercially minded not to miss their share in the windfall of the talking picture, however little they may understand the problems that arise from the use of the new medium, or be able to see where to look for their solution. Thus between the incompetence of the commercial entertainer and the self-righteousness of the superior intellectual, the talking picture is apparently doomed to grope blindly for several years before it reaches anything that may be properly described as an original form of drama. That it will eventually reach this goal does not seem to the present writer in the least doubtful.

In the meantime, let us consider the prospects of the talking picture. So far its greatest successes have been scored in a field that does not quite come under the definition of "talking." Pictures like *The Singing Fool* [1928, dir. Lloyd Bacon] and *My Man* [1928, dir. Archie Mayo] are really "singing pictures." The fact, however, that they succeed in conveying their appeal to the audience is vastly significant. Lacking as they are in color and depth, they still capture something of the personality of the artist. No doubt Al Jolson [in *The Singing Fool*] and Fanny Brice [in *My Man*] are more intimately felt and radiate more genuine warmth when one sees them on the stage. At the same time, even on the screen they are unmistakably their peculiar and likable selves. The movie soundtrack, though still very imperfect, serves them much more loyally than it does the "talking" actors, since singing reproduces better than speech.

With the inevitable technical improvement in the production of the human voice and in the effects of color and stereoscopic depth, the singing picture of today will naturally expand into a full-blown musical comedy. So long as this genre of entertainment rests its appeal on the singing of popular stars and the gyrations of pretty chorus girls, the screen musical comedy will be able to depart little from the orthodox methods of the stage. In this respect it is in the same boat as the screen drama, which would also take the stage for its model. For it has been laid down by our aestheticians that in copying the stage, the talking picture would lose all claim to being regarded as a medium of art. Though why should it? A perfect copy is obviously as good as the original, and it is absurd to claim that no reproduction can be perfect. Besides, in the case of the talking picture, one does not so much copy an original stage production as imitate the stage form—which, if a sin, is certainly not a cardinal one.

At present, the trouble with the talking picture is to be found less in its attempts to imitate the stage than in its numerous technical imperfections. It is safe to predict that within the next ten years these will be removed. And it is only then that the real aesthetic problem of the talking picture will become apparent. The ability to give a perfect imitation of the stage or to create a new and completely original dramatic form means nothing unless it is infused with the genuine spirit of art. It is here that one becomes seriously alarmed. In the coming fight between Hollywood and Broadway, the odds are ten to one that the former will be victorious. But if the defeat of the Broadway journeymen can hardly be regarded as a great loss to art, the victory of the Hollywood robots will undoubtedly endanger the future of drama on the stage as well as on the screen. The talking picture is merely a mechanized tool; but the Hollywood manufacturers of films represent mechanized brains, and what this means to art we have already learned from the experience of the silent movies.

In this rather dismal picture of the future there are two important factors that have yet to be taken into account, and that are likely to counteract if not completely overcome the influence of Hollywood.

The first of these is the remarkable growth in volume and quality of amateur or independent production, together with the rapid spread of little-cinema houses. Before many years are past, these developments will seize artistic leadership in the movies and force Hollywood to accept a different, superior set of standards. The second factor is the inevitable evolution of the talking picture in accordance with the laws of its own nature. This undoubtedly will exercise a far-reaching influence on Hollywood production methods. When the talking-picture mechanism is made perfect, the really important development will be along lines that are already beginning to reveal themselves, and which will definitely direct the talking picture away from the stage and toward a new, authentic motion-picture drama.

Such an evolution is inevitable. It is dictated by the inner logic of the medium. Analogies between the stage and the screen assume that they deal with the same material. But they don't. The material of the screen consists not of actual objects but of images fixed on film. And the very fact that they have their being on film endows these images with properties that are never found in actual objects. For instance, on the stage the actor moves in real space and time. He cannot even cross the room without performing a definite number of movements. On the screen an action may be shown only in its terminal points, with all its intervening moments left out. Similarly, in watching a performance on the stage, the spectator is governed by the actual conditions of space and time. Not so in the case of the movie spectator. Thanks to the moving camera he is able to view any scene from all kinds of angles, leaping from a long-distance view to a close-range inspection of every detail.

It is obvious that with this extraordinary power to handle space and time—by elimination and emphasis according to its dramatic needs—the motion picture can never be content with modeling itself after the stage. The fact that it has now acquired the power of speech will certainly not make it any more willing to sacrifice its freedom and individuality. Nor is there any need for such a sacrifice. Dialogue can be concentrated—reduced to a number of essential statements—as effectively as action, just as it is done now in the subtitles of silent movies. Then, too, the talking picture will develop, from an aural perspective, the specifically cinematic device of the close-up. It will be able to put in focus an individual utterance, and at the same time put out of focus all the other voices—a procedure unquestionably in advance of the method of the realistic stage, which, in order that certain characters may be heard, enforces a most unrealistic silence among all the other characters. Such being its technique, the spoken drama of the screen will obviously and inevitably develop into something original and non-stagy—something that will be completely in sync with the dynamic spirit of the cinema. (*The Nation*, February 20, 1929)

13. Free-Lancers (1929)

Standardized mass production on a world scale has made Hollywood the dominant force in the world of cinema. Thanks to Hollywood, the making of motion pictures has become an industry, and though we may not rejoice in this fact as much as some of our friends in Russia seem to, we must admit that it is in accord with all modern developments. If we have machine-made, standardized homes, clothes, food, newspapers, and radios, why not also movies?

Moreover, Hollywood satisfies a certain social need by providing its entertainment in quantities and qualities that are demanded by the countless numbers of its consumers, and which could not be supplied except by an organized industry. On the other hand, of course, there are the obvious drawbacks of industrial standardization: banned is artistic and intellectual culture; banned, independence of outlook and originality of treatment. The resultant product is inevitably bilge, no matter how glorified or how skillfully decked out in borrowed plumes of a vulgarized and usually outlived artistic fashion.

Thus, among people who resent the effects of Hollywood, there has grown up a demand for motion pictures of superior aesthetic and cerebral appeal. In America, the first attempt to satisfy this demand came with a series of Sunday showings organized by the Film Arts Guild in 1925. This was followed by the establishing of permanent movie theaters in New York such as the Fifth Avenue, the 55th Street, the St. George's in Brooklyn, the Little Carnegie, and the latest of them all, the Film Guild Cinema, besides a number of other, similar little-cinema houses in other parts of the country. This movement is undoubtedly showing signs of rapid progress. But though numerical growth is an important factor in the situation, the success of the movement will depend largely on the artistic policy pursued by its sponsors. In this respect, it must be admitted, not everything is as well as it should be.

To be sure, the little-cinema houses deserve every credit for introducing to the United States a number or foreign pictures of outstanding merit. They have made available such films as *The Cabinet of Dr. Caligari* [1920, dir. Robert Wiene], *Ballet Mécanique* [1924, dir. Fernand Léger & Dudley Murphy], *Battleship Potemkin* [1925, dir. Sergei Eisenstein], and, more recently, *Berlin: Symphony of a City* [1927, dir. Walter Ruttmann], *The End of St. Petersburg* [1927, dir. Vsevolod Pudovkin], *Thérèse Raquin* [1928, dir. Jacques Feyder], and *Ten Days That Shook the World* [a.k.a. *October*; 1927, dir. Sergei Eisenstein]. But, side by side with these truly remarkable achievements in film art, the little-cinema theaters have also tried to foist on the public as genuine masterpieces works puerile and utterly inept.

There is so much that can be done by these experimental theaters in the way of real artistic leadership that one is apt to grow impatient with the lack of vision displayed by the majority of them. An agreeable exception is the Film Guild Cinema, whose director, Symon Gould, showed commendable daring in selecting Frederick Kiesler for his architect. At present it is still too early to pass an opinion on the most original part of Kiesler's design—his use of side-walls for additional projection—for the installation of this feature has not yet been completed. But the very attempt to build "a 100% movie house," whether successfully realized or not, is of tremendous importance. From now on, no film theater making any claim to distinction will be able to content itself with copying the popular, essentially stagy, designs of today. It will have to come to grips with the screen as an architectural feature—one of the most important issues in the art of motion pictures—and for raising this aesthetic issue, as well as introducing several other interesting innovations, Kiesler and Gould deserve the gratitude of all believers in cinematic progress.

Unfortunately, one cannot express similar enthusiasm over Gould's choice of pictures, but at least one item on his first program—*The Fall of the House of Usher* [1928], directed by James Sibley Watson, Jr., and Melville Webber [an adaptation of Edgar Allan Poe's 1839 short story]—was appropriate to the occasion and symptomatic of the future. This extraordinary filmic achievement by two amateurs has settled the question of the vaunted technical superiority of Hollywood. Now we know that, if Hollywood does not do better than it does, the only explanation is its own incompetence. But in the example of Watson and Webber we also see a promise for the future.

Free-lancers like Fernand Léger and Dudley Murphy, the directors of *Ballet Mécanique*, as well as a number of others, have in the past given many a stimulus to the art of the movies. There is also no lack of gifted amateurs today. In our own New York there is Ralph Steiner, the director of H_2O [1929], which is a real masterpiece. There are others. Their principal need is an outlet for their work, an outlet that, in the nature of things, can be provided only by the little cinemas. Thus the more such movie theaters, the more chances for the free-lancers—and the cycle will be complete. Hollywood beware! (*The Nation*, March 13, 1929)

14. The Art of Directing (1929)

There is no lack of books explaining the methods of writing scenarios for the movies. One is shown how to prepare a working continuity and how to use such technical devices as fades, dissolves, vignettes, etc. No doubt the information contained in these books is very useful, particularly for an amateur moviemaker who is obliged to learn his craft from books and his own fledgling experience. And yet none of these books is of much help to the amateur when it comes to the actual making of a picture, since none of them explains how to translate events as they happen in real life—or are described in imaginative literature—into their equivalent cinematic language.

For this reason special interest attaches to a little volume on film directing by Vsevolod Pudovkin [published in English in 1929 as *Film Technique*], the gifted Russian who directed *The End of St. Petersburg* [1927]. The book was originally published in Russia in 1926 and has since appeared in Germany [1928], where it has been acclaimed as one of the most important contributions to the study of the cinematic idiom. The current article is an attempt to present the salient points of Pudovkin's discussion on the nature of filmic material and the methods by which this material can most effectively be used.

It will be recalled that in its early stages of development, the motion picture was regarded primarily as a means of recording and reproducing dramatic action. As far as it lay within its photographic powers, the photoplay aimed only at supplying the closest possible approximation of the stage play. Before long, however, it was discovered that the motion picture was capable of much more than the mere mechanical recording of events and actions as these took place in front of the camera. The latter, it was learned, could not only look at but also react to its impressions—by sorting them out, analyzing them, and then building them up again.

In filming a procession, for instance, the camera could photograph first from the roof of a high building, taking the general view of the marching band; then, stopping at a window on the second floor, it could look more closely at the instruments of the bandmembers, the banners, and other outstanding objects; finally, coming down and plunging into the processionists, it could study them, picking out a man here or a group of men there. The camera, deputizing in this case for the living observer, could thus view the procession from three different vantage points. In doing so, it would obtain not merely a record of the scene but a many-sided picture of it, regarded in full relief and reflecting the camera's own contact with the actual event.

This ability of the camera to guide the spectator through a process of active observation definitely contrasts with the passive contemplation of a set scene as required of the spectator in the theater. Unlike the latter, the spectator in the cinema is no longer confronted with a real event or real objects. Instead, he views a series of aspects of a scene, which his imagination then welds into a single picture. The realization of this difference marked the parting of ways between the stage and the motion picture, and inevitably led to the development of a special technique for presenting events not as they are, but in their cinematic equivalent. To wit: one of the first things the movie director must acknowledge is the fact that the material with which he deals consists of segments of film, or scenes, and that it is the assembling of these scenes, in the so-called cutting, that constitutes the picture on screen.

Let's closely observe this fundamental difference between stage and movie material. On the stage the material is real, consisting of actual objects that have their existence in space and time. When an actor is at one end of the stage, he cannot reach the other end without taking so many steps, i.e., without moving his body through a certain space within a certain time. The movie actor is not bound by these conditions. He can pass from one point to another both in space and time, completely eliminating all the intervening points and moments. In this way, the motion picture achieves a concentration of action impossible on the stage. The utmost the stage can do is to eliminate what happens between acts. The motion picture, by contrast, can condense even a single action, such as the very movement of a man from one end of a room to the other.

But if the intervening moments can be eliminated in the screen image, they can similarly be eliminated in the actual action photographed by the camera. To shoot the fall of a man from the roof of a skyscraper, for example, one need not make the man fall the whole distance from the roof to the ground. All that is necessary is to let the man fall from the roof into a net only a few feet below him—a net invisible to the camera lens—and then fall again onto the ground from a distance only a few feet above it. By joining the two scenes, the cutter or editor creates the impression of a fall from a great height, though no such fall ever happened in real life or as a real event.

Another way of concentrating action may be seen in the following example. In filming the aforementioned procession, one may desire to show the different groups that take part in it. But instead of showing the whole procession as it files past the camera, one need only include a small number of short scenes depicting the bandmembers, the onlookers, children, etc. These few scenes will convey the desired information in only a fraction of the actual time taken by the procession as it passes in front of the camera.

Two peculiar effects follow from this power of the motion picture to arrange its scenes in any way that may be desired. First, screen time becomes quite independent of real time, and is determined only by the number and duration of the individual scenes that have been selected to represent the event filmed. Likewise, screen space—what actually appears on the screen—is only the result of cutting. In 1920 the Russian director Lev Kuleshov proved as much in the following experiment. He made a picture consisting of the following scenes: Scene 1: A young man walks from left to right. Scene 2: A young woman walks from right to left. Scene 3: The two meet and shake hands, after which the man raises his hand as if pointing at something. Scene 4: A large building, with wide steps leading up to it, is seen. Scene 5: The young man and woman are seen walking up the steps.

The story told by this little motion picture is obviously that two young people meet to walk up some steps into a building. In fact, however, the first three scenes were filmed in three different places in Moscow; the fourth scene represented the White House in Washington, D.C.; and the fifth showed the steps of a church in Moscow. By the magic of the motion picture, all these different places were made to merge into one, which had its being only on the screen.

One other important characteristic arises from this power of the film director to arrange his material as he pleases. Such power implies selection and emphasis, which enable the spectator not only to envision the scene as a whole, but also to concentrate his attention on this or that individual detail. One of the most potent advantages of the cinematic medium is that it can so conduct its observation of people and things right into their very heart, penetrating into their innermost secrets. But again, in revealing the significant detail to our view, the motion picture does not repeat the actual process of singling out the detail. It eliminates all the work of finding and presents us, instead, with the final result of the process.

How significant and dramatically expressive a single detail can be is revealed in an episode from the trial scene in *Intolerance* [1916, dir. D. W. Griffith], where Mae Marsh has each of her hands twist the other in an attempt to control her emotion. At one point, only the hands are shown, each one in the act of twisting. Detail is a synonym for authorial penetration, as this example shows. The movie director who searches out detail is a discoverer and a creator, as well as the possessor of a potentially profound vision. The actress's twisting hands and smiling face enabled Griffith to create one of the most memorable images on screen thus far. His genius helped him to choose these two details out of a thousand other possible details. But the same process lies at the basis of every cinematic sequence. Each event or action, before being shown on the screen, must be reduced to its essential elements and then be built up again through these very same.

Take the example of an automobile accident. If one analyzed it, he would find it made up of a hundred different details. Six details, however, would only be necessary to describe the episode. This is how it could be done: Scene 1: A street with moving automobiles. A man with his back to the camera, crossing the street. He is suddenly hidden from view by a car. Scene 2: Close-up of this car's driver, seized with fear and frantically applying the brakes. Scene 3: Close-up of the pedestrian with his mouth open, as if screaming. Scene 4: Close-up of the pedestrian's feet near one of the car's wheels, as seen from the driver's seat. Scene 5: The skidding wheels of the automobile. Scene 6: The body of the pedestrian, near the car.

It will be realized that to be able to create the episode through these six scenes, a director would have had to pick them from a number of other possible moments before he commenced shooting. In other words, he would have had to come to the set with a preconceived idea of how to shoot the sequence, of what it had to look like on the screen. This idea would find its realization in the cutting, which would finally fix the selection and order of the individual scenes. At the same time, although in forming his screen images, the director would be free to select from the photographed action the exact elements that matched his conception, he would not be completely free to arrange these elements, in any way he so desired, by means of the editing process. Their order would be determined by the natural course of the automobile accident and the psychologically justifiable course of human observation. Nor would the director be free to shorten or extend the duration of each scene. For, as independent as screen time is from the time of the real event, it has to conform to a certain temporal scheme of relationship among the various scenes. In the car accident described, for instance, the filmed sequence would have appeared absurd if some of the scenes had been allowed to drag on.

Thus the art of motion pictures lies largely, though not entirely, in preparing the working continuity of a film and in cutting it. That is, the arrangement of scenes must follow a certain order. In fitting a close-up into a series of long and medium shots, the order will have to correspond to the movement or dynamic that runs through the whole sequence. As in the following shooting sequence: Scene 1: Medium shot of a man, putting his hand into his pocket. Scene 2: Close-up of the hand, taking out a revolver. Scene 3: Medium shot of the man, pointing the revolver at his opponent.

Cuts must rhythmically follow the course of events as would an emotionally agitated observer. Above all, however, the arrangement of scenes will serve to express the individual style of the director and his feel for the medium. As an example of such individual style and feel, one may cite the following bit of brilliant cutting from *Battleship Potemkin* [1925, dir. Sergei Eisenstein]: Title 1: "In answer to the savage brutalities of the czar's henchmen, the mutinous warship fires a salvo at the city." Scene 1: The slow turning of a huge, menacing-looking gun. Title 2: "The gun is aimed at the municipal theater." Scene 2: A group of sculptures on the cupola of the theater. Title 3: "One shot for the headquarters of the generals." Scene 3: The gun fires. Scene 4: A view of a marble Cupid above the gates of the theater building. Scene 5: A different view of Cupid. Scene 6: A terrific explosion that makes the gates of the building totter. Scene 7: A stone lion, lying down. Scene 8: The stone lion, with his head raised. Scene 9: The stone lion, rising and roaring. Scene 10: Another explosion, which finally destroys the gates of the theater building.

It may be noted that the stone lion—lying down and then rising—was actually three lions, photographed in the Crimea, hundreds of miles away from the scene of the action in Odessa. Similarly, the gates of the theater building were filmed in Moscow. Such is moviemaking. (*Movie Makers*, April 1929)

15. The Newsreel (1930)

The motion picture was a screen newspaper before it was a screen play: it recorded events before it began to invent them. But there is clearly a marked element of entertainment that distinguishes the motion-picture record from its analogue in the ordinary newspapers. It is a peculiar kind of entertainment, and its presence or absence, as the case may be, does not become apparent until one sees a fairly large number of screen news items presented at one time.

Such an experience has now been made possible by the Newsreel Theater, which has recently opened in New York. The venture is no doubt timely and welcome. There has been a need for it for some time. But just a few visits to this theater are sufficient to make one realize that screen journalism has hardly advanced beyond the rudiments of its art. The material of the new theater is the familiar newsreel of all the movie houses, except that it is reinforced by the addition of sound. Since it has been elevated, however, to the position of an independent show, it immediately forces the question of whether the newsreel in its present form offers both sufficient entertainment and sufficient information.

I feel fairly certain that it does not. The criticism that might be leveled against it and that comes easiest to mind, of course, is its obviously tabloid character. There is no doubt that in its subject matter, the American newsreel fashions itself after the model of the tabloid press. Like the latter, it is anxious to let us see and hear one Peaches Browning [who in 1926, at the age of fifteen, married New York City real estate developer Edward West "Daddy" Browning] discourse learnedly on feminine fashions, or introduce us to the plans and hopes of the boy who has inherited a million-dollar fortune. The newsreel panders to our morbid curiosity, and such "celebrities" are its stock-in-trade.

Being tabloid, however, means something more than mere sensationalism. It stands for compressed and vivid presentation. And the principal characteristic of the motion picture—one of its chief virtues, in fact—is that it deals not with abstract ideas but with vivid, concrete images, even when, as in the talking picture, they are accompanied by words. For this reason the chief fault to be found with the newsreel is not so much that it is a tabloid, but rather that it is not *enough* of a tabloid. Instead of giving us a mere reproduction of an event or a person, it should present a selective picture that would bring out the most characteristic features of its subject; and to do this it must use a more imaginative, more flexible technique.

The connection between this problem of form and the entertainment value of the newsreel will be readily appreciated. It is one thing to see and hear Peaches Browning as she is, and quite another thing to have her presented to us as she would be seen by an observant journalist who is also an artist at his job. A composite portrait of a person could thus be made vastly entertaining where a faithful reproduction would be merely dull. Seeing that so many of the "events" reported in the screen news are specially staged for the benefit of the camera and the microphone—a practice that places the modern newsreel somewhere between the pure record and the invented skit— there should really be no difficulty in enlivening movie newsreel reporting by allowing it more freedom in the way of deliberate arrangement, along with the personal touch of an imaginative journalist. (*The Nation*, January 8, 1930)

16. New Dimensions in the Talkies (1930)

The seeming similarity of the talking picture and the stage in the material they both use and the dramatic effects they produce has been responsible for the present confusion of thought regarding the true province of the movies. It is not merely that the prevalent copying of stage technique reduces motion pictures to the position of a reproducing rather than a creative medium. The far more important fact is that the movies have not yet learned where exactly they stand in relation to the stage; what territory, if any, in the realm of representation in sight and sound they are entitled to share with the stage; and what territory they hold exclusively for their own use.

In one respect both the stage and the cinema are undeniably alike. What they create is a dramatic spectacle before an audience, and there are only two principal forms in which such a spectacle can be created. The history of the theater teaches us that there can be spectacle of the illusionist kind, which is based entirely on the effect of illusion produced by the appropriate acting and setting (as in modern realistic plays). And there can be spectacle of the frankly artificial kind (as in most musical plays), where the self-reflexive nature of theatrical presentation is the basis of dramatic form. The two forms, illusionist and non-illusionist, are fundamentally opposed to each other.

The illusionist stage strives to make the audience feel as if by some miracle it were watching, not a theatrical performance, but the actual life of a group of people in their natural surroundings. By contrast, the non-illusionist stage lays particular stress on those elements of acting and setting that reveal most strikingly the fact that the characters are merely actors performing on a stage in front of an audience. The world of an illusionist play is separated from the world of the audience by an impassable gulf. No contact exists between the actor and the spectator;

they are on two different planes. But when the play is openly a stage performance, its very form depends on the presence of the spectator and the continuous contact maintained between him and the actor. It is because of this difference that the incongruous conduct of characters in a musical play seems in keeping with the style of the performance, whereas similar antics in a realistic play strike the audience as grotesquely absurd and an offense against good taste.

Although it is still hardly recognized, there is a division in the motion picture similar to that existing in the theater. The illusionist film and the non-illusionist film represent two distinct forms of cinematic art. And whether the aim be illusionist or non-illusionist presentation, it is essential that the artist realize the difference between the effect of illusion on the stage and the effect of illusion on the screen, as well as the difference between the specific conventions characteristic of theatrical performance, on the one hand, and of cinematic production, on the other.

A single example will illustrate this point. To stress a particular scene and bring it nearer to the audience so that it may be seen better, the characters on the stage usually take a position close to the footlights. In plays in which illusion is of no importance at all, like musical comedies and revues, the same desire for visual emphasis leads to the use of an even more artificial convention, the spotlight. Now the screen has no footlights, nor can it use a spotlight very effectively. When it has to emphasize a scene or a detail, it resorts to the close-up. But unlike the downstage position of actors, this device does not destroy illusion. The characters shown in close-up remain an integral part of the world of the film. And it is easy to see why. Instead of disturbing the natural movements of the characters, as the stage must through its dependence on spotlights and footlights, the motion picture "disturbs" only the spectator. It is he who is brought nearer to the scene of action, although he never actually leaves his seat. With the help of the ubiquitous camera, which acts as his proxy, the spectator is able to observe events from a variety of vantage points. What he sees retains the effect of illusion, but it is an illusion obtained in continuous movement from a number of viewpoints, and not from a single, fixed point as in the theater.

The moral of this illustration is brief. Stage illusion and film illusion are two distinct things, and so are stage convention and film convention; what is more, in no possible combination do the four mix. However, the elimination of "mixing" still leaves the problem of the true realization on screen of illusionist and the non-illusionist principles, in their pure cinematic forms.

One of the curious effects produced by an illusionist talkie patterned after the stage is the discrepancy in the sensations received by the eye and the ear. Figuratively speaking, the spectator finds himself in the peculiar position of having his eyes forced to rove over all the different people, objects, and places represented in the picture, whereas his ears are bound to his seat. For a sensitive person, the position is decidedly uncomfortable. There is no reason why the spectator should be subjected to such inconsiderate treatment: why shouldn't his ears be as free to survey the world of sound as his eyes are to survey the world of sight? Even as the selection of images in the silent movie is the function of the camera, so should the selection of sounds in the talkie be the function of the microphone.

The cinematic illusion of life is the sum total of innumerable impressions, which are so deftly, though seemingly freely, arranged that a group of consecutive words and images can be welded into a palpable reality, although this may exist only on the screen. It is impossible to exaggerate the importance of this power of the motion picture to create an illusion of reality without really producing something that has an actual existence. The reference here is not to so-called film tricks, but to the routine practice of every film director. Indeed, in the silent pictures the events and even the characters we see on the screen are often largely, if not wholly, imaginary. Shots made in different parts of the world for different purposes are frequently joined in a film, one after another, and give the impression of a single and naturally unfolding event. For instance, now that Richard Byrd's Antarctic expedition has come home with miles of celluloid record, any Hollywood studio could stage a dozen different expeditions to the South Pole, each with a different story and a different set of characters—all of which would look as authentic as Byrd's own documentary images. And it is quite likely that a great deal of that material will yet be used in Hollywood-made pictures, which will show characters who have never been farther south than the Panama Canal having innumerable adventures with Antarctic whales, seals, and penguins.

Similarly, a character looking out of the same hotel window will see the streets of Paris or of New York, of Shanghai or of Sydney, as a result of the simple process of the director's cutting into the film whatever urban views may be required by the story. Now, with the advent of sound, the creative artist in the cinema can extend yet further his power over material. He can pick out his elements of sound and speech from a number of sources, sometimes completely dissimilar and independent, and can bring them together in simultaneous or sequential order to produce the desired effect on the audience. Suggestions of such free treatment of sound are to be found in a few American pictures, notably *Alibi* [1929, dir. Roland West], *Applause* [1929, dir. Rouben Mamoulian], *The Love Parade* [1929, dir. Ernst Lubitsch], and *All Quiet on the Western Front* [1930, dir. Lewis Milestone]. But the acknowledged masters of this technique of assemblage—in the visual sense—are the Russians, and foremost among them is Sergei Eisenstein. His elaborate theory of montage, as the Russians call the assembling or editing of film material, seems to be capable of natural extension to include the selecting and grouping of auditory material, which can act as a stimulus for certain cumulative psycho-physiological reactions.

The direction in which further progress is likely to continue in the illusionist talkies is therefore fairly definitely marked out. The same cannot yet be said of the non-illusionist movie, for this form is still embryonic. When a spectator watches a musical comedy or a vaudeville act on the stage, he is not disturbed by the unreality of the acting and setting he sees. What interests and delights him most is the quality of the performance. There is a kind of tacit understanding between the actor and the spectator that the business of the one is to act, to display his skill as a performer, and the business of the other is to watch and appreciate whatever is presented to him. This understanding is possible because the actor and the spectator are in the same auditorium facing each other as physical entities. There exists between them a unity of space, which the history of the theater tells us has always been emphasized by the architecture of the stage whenever the dramatic form in vogue implied contact with the audience.

The same relationship between the audience and the motion picture characterizes the non-illusionist film. The aesthetic aim is not illusion but performance, meaning not the barring of illusion but only its subordination to the artist's self-conscious presentation of his material; and by the very nature of this aim, its realization presupposes an intimate physical contact between the performer and the audience. The unity of space required is not to be understood in the sense that the events pictured in the film must appear as if they were taking place in the same building as the projection of the film. Although such an effect is not impossible—a recent comic cartoon showed a dog on the screen conducting a real orchestra in the pit in front of the screen— the cinematic form deems it neither important nor necessary. Film's command over screen space, as well as screen time, is one of its priceless possessions, and its abandonment would deprive cinematic art of its main advantage over the stage.

Fortunately there is another means of establishing a direct contact between the audience and the picture. The physical link is provided by that familiar but usually inconspicuous member of the cinematic performance: the bearer of images, the screen itself. In the illusionist film it is merely an inert surface playing no part in molding the form of the picture. In the non-illusionist film, the screen may become an active medium that proclaims its existence through the position occupied by the image on its surface. The image, along with the spatial relations within it, becomes bound to the screen and thereby to the physical unit of space in which it is being seen by the audience.

An approach to this non-illusionist art of the film may be seen in modern sound cartoons, among which the *Silly Symphony* series [starting with *The Skeleton Dance*; 1929, dir. Walt Disney] and the *Micky Mouse* series [starting with *Steamboat Willie*; 1928, dir. Ub Iwerks] are artistic achievements of surpassing excellence. But they are no more than an approach. For ordinary—that is, natural—photographic images, the non-illusionist form demands a different treatment. Instead of a single image, the screen may carry a continuously changing pattern of several interrelated images. A picture could open, for instance, with an image creeping slowly upward from the bottom left corner of the screen, then suddenly leaping to the top, right corner, then moving to the center and swelling to the limits of the screen, where it would fade out and give place to groups of images flitting across the screen now in one direction, now in another, or spacing themselves equally in a pattern of images placed side by side. Separated events, persons, or places may be shown simultaneously.

Technically, all of this can best be accomplished by the use of the entire surface of the screen, which, given the cameras and projectors in use today, still remains an unrealized ideal. But the enlarged projection provided by the Magnascope [an optical device used to get a close-up of small objects, and thus to temporarily increase the size of the image on the screen] and by the widescreen film already supplies the basis for such technical reform. As compared with the prevalent single-image film, the multiple method presents several important advantages. Its ability to give the image a lateral movement on the screen practically provides the cinema with a new dimension. Images can now be assembled not only in time, but also in space. Thanks to this new power, simultaneous, parallel strands of images restore to film the visual continuity of its early days, which has been destroyed by the fragmented assembly inevitable in the single-strand film. From the dramatic standpoint, too, the force of contrast and emphasis obtained through the simultaneous juxtaposition of a number of images is itself beyond anything possible in the typical narrative picture.

In relation to the problem of sound, the advantages of the multiple method are exceptionally great. It solves the problem of non-illusionist singing and dancing, not by the inept copying of the conventions of the stage, but by establishing a purely cinematic convention of performance on the screen. For the screen itself, not the stage boards, becomes the meeting place of images and their accompanying sounds, and no considerations of realistic truth can govern such an assembly of singing-cum-dancing shots (together with shots of more natural dialogue). Finally, and this is perhaps its most important contribution, the method of simultaneously presenting several shots or images diversifies and expands the means of rhythmic organization of sounds and images to a degree hitherto unknown to the screen. So great, indeed, are the possibilities of this form of cinematic art that one hopes Hollywood will have the imaginativeness and daring to tolerate such originality of creation in its more gifted directors. (*The Nation*, December 24, 1930)

17. The Plastic Structure: Dynamic Composition (1930)

Insofar as visual images constitute the basic material of the motion picture, the problem of cinematic composition is nothing else than the organization of these images in a sequential order. It is clear that there is more than one way of carrying out such an organization. The simplest and most obvious way is to arrange the images in an order in which their subject matter is used as so many connected links in the chain of representations that forms the narrative. In this case the actual form of the images plays but a subordinate part, being at best—as in close-up, for instance—only the function of their representational content.

The motion picture as an art of storytelling has been principally concerned with supplying the spectator with such visual *information* as would ensure the desired intellectual and emotional response. At first, when the plots were simple and the technique still elementary, a straightforward stringing together of a series of scenes was all that was considered necessary for unfolding the narrative. Later, more complicated stories and greater complexity in the images helped to bring into use flashbacks and parallel action, the two devices of cutting that introduced the method of simultaneous or juxtaposed composition. In this way the content of images became for the first time a formal element of cinematic composition. This structural treatment of the images, let it be noted, had nothing to do with their visual form; it was merely a means of organizing their content—a means that not only unquestionably has its origin in the peculiar mechanical structure of the motion picture, but that also has its analogues in other, non-visual arts such as fiction and poetry.

During the last few years some very interesting attempts have been made in various countries, particularly Russia, to develop other methods of formal composition on the basis of image-content. The problem has been attacked from two different sides. On the one hand, experiments tried to establish a primary cinematic unit in the form of a group of images constructed somewhat along the lines of a grammatical sentence. Examples of this method are found in Sergei Eisenstein's *Ten Days That Shook the World* [a.k.a. *October*, 1927], in which the use of symbols to construct various "figures of speech" deserves special notice. On the other hand, attempts have been made to base the composition of whole films on such methods of formalized treatment of image-content as the arrangement of "rhymed" sequences—with certain images recurring at definite intervals—or of whole cycles of sequences along the lines of a repeating pattern, somewhat after the manner of certain verse forms. In Russia, Dziga Vertov is considered the leader of this school of cinematic composition.

Side by side with the line of development just described, which is based on the assumption that *the form of a cinematic composition is the function of the sum total of its image-content*, the history of the motion picture reveals another line of development that sometimes merges with the former and sometimes follows an independent course, and which proceeds from the assumption that *the content-material of a film is the function of the overall organization of its visual form.*

Ever since the first motion pictures were made, it has been universally recognized that the cinematic visual image has one fundamental characteristic that distinguished it from the visual images in other arts. This characteristic is movement. Although the term, particularly in the solemn guise of its "dynamic quality," has acquired a sort of mystic halo, it is well to remember that the word "movement" is essentially pragmatic in origin and represents a strictly definable property of the motion-picture mechanism. The men who made movies when the art was still new and unexplored were not theorists. They were concerned exclusively with giving their pictures the semblance of life, and it took them only a short time to discover that a motionless object on the screen was as good as dead. Hence the orgy of recorded motion that distinguished the early movies.

It was at a comparatively early stage, too, that the necessity of movement not only in characters and objects, but also in whole scenes in relation to one another was realized. Two reasons dictated this necessity. In the first place, there was the technique of cutting, which arose from the fragmentary nature of the film record, and which had the effect not only of speeding up movement but also of compressing time. In certain situations this latter effect was found to conflict rather too harshly with the sequence of events in *real* time. For instance, a scene showing a man in front of a door on the street, followed immediately by a scene showing the same man inside the house, is likely to produce the impression of something unreal. An interval of time is clearly demanded between the two scenes, and this is supplied by a third scene, which may be a close-up of the man, a view of the room he is about to enter, or some other related subject. The device of parallel action is but an extended application of the same principle, and achieves the similar effect of expanded time that sometimes, as in the climaxes of D. W. Griffith's pictures, is deliberately prolonged—beyond even the realistic implications of the subject at hand—to achieve a specific emotional end.

The other and perhaps even more important reason for changing scenes, and thus introducing a greater mobility of visual images, is found in the very nature of realistic acting as it is deployed on the screen. In real life or on the stage, speech itself constitutes action. Such speech, in the form of a conversation between two persons, may contain a series of moments pregnant with dramatic significance although the person speaking may engage in little physical movement. On the screen the situation is different. Deprived of his words, even when these are present in the form of subtitles, the screen actor can express himself only by means of gesture and movement. The realistic convention of acting, however, excludes all but a few of these forms of expression. The inevitable result is that, while the stage actor who uses speech can sustain a situation without a change in setting for the length of a whole act, the screen actor finds his resources of expression—his gestures and movements—exhausted within as short a time as a minute.

It was to relieve the screen actor of this predicament and, at the same time, to give greater emphasis and variety to his means of expression that long sequences were reduced to a series of fragmented scenes with full and medium shots, close-ups and different camera angles, thrown in for the sake of variety and emphasis. It is instructive to note that, with the advent of the talkies, long scenes depending entirely on dialogue and showing very little movement made their appearance on the screen. The fact that the latest talkies indicate a return to the technique of the silent picture, with its short and fragmentary scenes, only goes to prove that the handling of dialogue on screen is still far from being efficient and that the old, dynamic form of composition wields a superior power of emotional appeal.

If the movement involved in the change from one scene to another brought to the fore the immediate significance of the form of the visual image, the movement resulting from a series of such changes, organized in a manner conforming to a certain rhythmic scheme, placed the visual form in the position of being the dominant factor in the building of any cinematic composition. At this point it is unnecessary to go into a description of the various methods of the rhythmic organization of images beyond pointing to the work of Abel Gance, Fernand Léger, and Dudley Murphy, F. W. Murnau, Sergei Eisenstein, and Alexander Dovzhenko. The important fact to be borne in mind is that cinematic rhythm is a form of visual composition itself charged with a powerful emotional appeal, and that, while remaining independent of the image-content, at the same time it conveys and shapes the appeal of such content.

The effect of rhythm is to organize sequences into visible beats and accents. It establishes a visual continuity of fragmented images that is a function of time. Rhythm leaves untouched, however, the problem of spatial continuity, of the spatial relationship of images to one another as elements of a total visual composition. No motion picture known to the present writer has thus far suggested a satisfactory solution to this problem. Yet so long as this problem remains unsolved, the cinema as a medium of dynamic visual art will never reach its complete maturity. The continuity of visual form, rhythmically as well as spatially, implies a dynamic composition of which the only existing illustration in other visual arts is found in the moving composition of ballet.

Just like the ballet, the cinematic visual form has to be built in time, and its elements of composition should be, not static images, but lines of force or movement in definite directions. It goes without saying that movement in this sense includes not only the movement of images in time, let alone the mere sight of moving objects, but also the movement of images in space over the entire surface of the screen. The technical obstacles that still stand in the way of such dynamic composition are likely to be removed in the near future by various devices (already announced) for enlarged projection. In these devices, therefore, lies the promise of a mature cinema whose intellectual and emotional appeal will be precisely the function of its dynamic composition. (*Experimental Cinema*, February 1930)

18. The German Invasion (1931)

Five or six years ago, the German cinema was the great sensation. It demonstrated to the general public that films could be made with intelligence and imagination, that there was such a thing as the art of the film. Although the lesson of this demonstration was clear to all who cared to see it, the hopes for a renascence of the cinema in Germany and under the German stimulus in Hollywood were doomed to an early disappointment. The Germans in Germany and the Germans in Hollywood, succumbing to the same system of commercial mass output, lowered their standards to suit the big public almost as quickly as they had sent them rocketing to the heights of *The Last Laugh* [1924, dir. F. W. Murnau], when their main concern had been to express themselves with the utmost power of conviction. To complete their downfall, the Russians displaced the Germans from their leadership, and the talkies delivered the *coup de grâce* by disorganizing their production methods and introducing a new technique.

Thus, for a couple of years we heard very little about German films. Then one German talkie alter anther found its way into the smaller movie houses of New York, and today, if we glance at the list of offerings current in this city, the number of German pictures on it is likely to give us quite a surprise. This week, for example, out of the twenty-one first-run films shown in New York, fifteen are American products and six are German. That does not mean, of course, that a third of the movie audiences of New York patronize German movies. Probably the entire daily audience of the six little theaters exhibiting the German films does not reach a quarter of the number visiting the Roxy alone. The significant fact is not the number of people who go to see the German pictures, but the emergence of the German work by the side of the American and the apparent eagerness with which it is sought by the so-called little theaters.

In the face of such an unmistakable revival of interest in the product of the German and Austrian studios—an interest that is only partly accounted for by the presence of a large German-speaking public in New York City—it is worth inquiring into the quality of this product. Do these new German talkies contain a message or even a promise of an art essentially different from the banalities of Hollywood? Do they suggest a new understanding of the use of sound and dialogue on the screen? Do they place the Germans again in the vanguard of cinematic progress? Without attempting any hasty generalizations and speaking only on the basis of what has been seen thus far in Manhattan, the answers to these three questions must all be no—a provisional "no," but no. So far the German producers have shown us very little that is artistically valuable in itself or significant of future developments in the cinema. (*The Nation*, May 13, 1931)

19. S.O.S. (1931)

On this, the third anniversary of the talking picture (*The Jazz Singer* [1927, dir. Alan Crosland] startled the world in the summer of 1928), I find myself quite unable to offer the usual congratulations. The promise the talking picture held out at its birth of growing into something worthy of public respect and even admiration has not been fulfilled. Today it looks so utterly sick both in body and mind that, unless some drastic change, takes place it seems destined to drag on a miserable existence as a deformed and blabbering half-wit.

In saying this, I do not mean to suggest that I greatly miss its elder brother, the Hollywood silent picture, whom it dispatched into limbo with such childish unconcern. On this point the situation was summed up pointedly about two years ago by Rex Ingram, the well-known director of *The Four Horsemen of the Apocalypse* [1921], who expressed himself as follows:

> Silent films are finished—and a good thing, too. The plain truth is that the motion-picture industry was like a man dying of anemia . . . Everybody had been doing the same old thing. There was nothing fresh to do. You got the same old stories and, with trifling alterations, the same old situations; and you could do nothing more with them. [*London Evening Standard*, April 27, 1929]

Ingram's words need but one qualification. If the motion picture resembled a man dying of anemia, it was not because of the silence of the silent picture, but because of the moronic standards of filmmaking that Hollywood considered the alpha and omega of cinematic wisdom. One notes two significant facts in this regard. In Soviet Russia for the past three or four years, the silent picture has attained a level of artistic expression that has made it the most vital and widely acclaimed contribution to film art. In this country, by contrast, the silent picture had lost favor with the public long before the sensational arrival of the talking picture. It was a fortunate thing for the Hollywood movie lords that the talking picture arrived when it did. It caught the imagination of the public and regained for the movies their lost ascendancy. But Hollywood never learned its lesson. It has treated the talkie as shabbily as its silent predecessor, and today it is reaping the results of its stupid and shortsighted policy in the growing indifference of the public— and the threat that this implies for its financial returns.

Is the situation so utterly hopeless, then? I believe it can still be saved, but this needs an enlightened policy on the part of both the producers and the public. It seems almost incredible that of all the big industries in the United States, the movie industry is practically the only one that conducts no organized artistic and scientific research. A new idea in filmmaking must be presented in a complete and finished form before the producers will condescend even to look at it. And since the cost of making a film is beyond the means of your average worker, this attitude virtually destroys any chance that an original conception—formulated outside the industry—will ever be tried and developed for practical use.

The producers must realize that what is at stake today is the prestige of the cinema itself, and there is no way of maintaining that prestige except by encouraging, if only on a small scale, untrammeled artistic and scientific effort, and by cultivating, even if it does not result in high profits, the support and interest of the discriminating minority of the American public. The latter, for its part, can help to save the movies. All it need do is make its disaffection and demands sufficiently vocal. One of the ways of accomplishing this is to form a genuine public organization along the lines of the Film Society of London. I'm waiting . . . (*The Nation*, August 5, 1931)

20. Concerning Dialogue (1932)

The talking picture has been in existence for four years and is now so firmly established that even the old enthusiasts of the silent picture have lost all hope of ever restoring their favorite to its former glory. And yet criticism of the talking picture as a talking picture goes on unabated. By many of the supposed champions of cinematic art, dialogue is still held to be an abomination.

The stock argument against using dialogue in a film is of course well known. Dialogue, we are told, is the natural medium of the stage; but dialogue is wholly foreign to the screen, whose appeal is directed to the eye and not the ear. It may come as a surprise to the film enthusiasts of this generation, but will hardly be news to those who remember the history of the modern theater, when we recall that barely twenty-five years ago there was a very similar outcry against dialogue. Only then it came from theater reformers such as Gordon Craig and his followers, who voiced the belief that dialogue intellectualized the theater, whereas the true art of the stage expressed itself primarily through visual forms that appeal directly to our senses. Perhaps, after all, the present opposition to screen dialogue is rooted in the same old aesthetic of non-intellectual and "mystic" art, for it certainly cannot be justified on any other grounds. Speech is an integral part of man's being. In a silent film, with its necessary convention of a soundless world, pantomime is appropriate and legitimate. In the sound film, realistic pantomime in a realistic setting is a deliberate artifice condemned by its own internal contradictions.

But, if we must be honest about dialogue, if we must face squarely its particular problem in the sound film, what are we to think of the popular practice that takes dialogue written for the stage and puts it on the screen in its original form, except for some pruning and compression necessitated by considerations of time? Obviously, those who resort to this practice fail to see, or pretend not to see, any important difference between the function of speech on the stage and its function on the screen. To them speech is speech, no matter where it is used, provided they can weld it to physical action and set both tripping along through their allotted number of reels. The result is the Hollywood picture, something that is neither fish nor fowl and that inevitably leaves a rather queer taste in the mouth.

Now we all know that a stage play, no matter how realistic, never reproduces life as it is. It must shape life to fit the mold of the stage. Whatever its material, a play remains a play or, in other words, a version of human existence informed with theatrical pretense and made to unfold itself within the walls of the theater. Speech is the principal handmaid of this theatrical pretense, and the enormous work it does in translating life into the terms of the stage is something to be marvelled at. Indeed, what does speech not do? It informs the audience of events that have taken place offstage. It elaborates and fills out action. It makes thinking habitually loud and explicit. Speech swells and keys up emotion. It bedecks argument with sparkling wit. And sometimes, as in Shakespeare, it comes forward and glories in its own imagery and music.

It is perfectly natural that stage speech should perform all these various duties. For the stage is limited in its means and, moreover, cannot disguise its fundamental artifice and conventionality. But is it equally natural for this theatrically inflated speech to appear in the real world that is the province of the talking picture? After all, the material of the cinema is not an acted life, a life on the stage, but the real, honest-to-goodness life of people as it is lived in natural surroundings. And yet what does Hollywood do? It takes a life that has already been fashioned to fit the stage, transplants it to new soil, and then leaves it there to swell (but not to grow) with all the excess of stage verbiage. No representation of life in a talking picture can ever be convincing so long as it carries the hallmark of the stage battle of words. Even so-called "natural" stage dialogue is too inflated to appear natural on the screen. To be used at all it has to be stripped to the bone and reduced to the normal function of speech, which in nine cases out of ten is only a concomitant of action and not its source or substitute.

And yet even deflated dialogue is not enough. Years of slow development have gained the film a freedom from set scenes, and a power to select and order its primary material, that are peculiarly its own. The stressing of dialogue, however, as the main vehicle of dramatic narrative has thrown the film back on the long scenes of its early youth. To be sure, lately the talking picture has been trying to recover its lost flexibility and freedom of movement. But it is not really in earnest about the matter. It still pays infinitely more attention to the running stream of conversation than to the arrangement of separate units of speech in significant combinations.

More could be said about the use of dialogue as an element of a purely conventional—or convention-conscious—screen art, an art that, without violating the essentially realistic nature of its material, would provide means for establishing an intimate contact with the audience, and would rival the stage in the imaginative interpretation of life. But this would require a radical change in the accepted form of the motion picture, and the prospects of any such revolution in Hollywood are too remote as to call for immediate consideration. (*The Nation*, August 17, 1932)

21. Acting and the Movies (1935)

In his book of memoirs, *My Life in Art* [1924], Konstantin Stanislavsky of Moscow Art Theatre-fame relates the following episode. On one of their tours in the provinces, some members of Stanislavsky's company happened to be walking in a park. They came upon a spot that bore such a striking resemblance to one of their sets for Ivan Turgenev's *A Month in the Country* [1872] that, then and there, they decided to play the scene in question in its natural setting. "It was my turn to make an entrance," relates Stanislavsky:

> As set out in the play, Olga Knipper and I walked down a long alley saying our lines; then we sat on a bench, just as we used to do on the stage; began to talk; and—stopped, for we found ourselves unable to proceed. In the environment provided by living nature, my acting, I felt, was utterly false. Yet people say that we have brought simplicity in acting to the point of complete naturalness. How *conventional* the things we were accustomed to do on the stage proved to be! [383, *My Life in Art*]

We also find this episode related in the book *Film Acting* [published in English in 1933], which came out not so long ago in Russia and whose author is Vsevolod Pudovkin, the distinguished director of *The End of St. Petersburg* [1927], *Mother* [1926], and several other well-known pictures. Pudovkin's comment on Stanislavsky's experience in the park is that, in a similar situation, a film actor would—or at least should— feel perfectly at home.

And, indeed, there is an essential difference between stage and screen acting. The stage actor, no matter how naturalistic he may wish to be, is compelled, in other ways, to mold and even force his voice, his gestures, and his facial expressions so that he may be heard and seen from all points of the theater auditorium. No such necessity exists for the film actor. The subtlest of his facial expressions and the softest of his whispers are conveyed to the audience by the camera and the microphone. Complete naturalness, and not merely stage naturalness, is therefore entirely possible in movie acting. Yet how rarely it is that we observe perfect naturalness on the screen. What are the obstacles that hold the film actor back from reaching his goal? And how can they be overcome? Answers to these questions form the burden of Pudovkin's argument concerning the art of acting in the cinema.

The term "natural" describes the behavior of human beings in real life. Obviously, this behavior is the expression of a person's character. One behaves as one is, even when one tries to appear as someone else. For an actor to act naturally is tantamount to identifying himself with the character he impersonates. It is just there, however, that the film actor finds himself up against a seemingly insurmountable obstacle. To wit: the technique of moviemaking is based on welding a great number of fragmentary scenes into a related narrative. So short are the individual scenes, and so arbitrary is the order in which they come before the camera, that it is a utterly impossible that a film actor can feel consistently immersed in his character. The result is that, instead of finding the response to the enacted situation within himself, the screen actor is obliged to go through a set of mechanical actions dictated to him by the director.

Some Russian film directors have tried to solve this problem by going back to long scenes with as few close-ups (or scene changes, for that matter) as possible. To Pudovkin such a solution is not conceivable. It implies the sacrifice of what is the most important quality of the movies—their power of singling out and emphasizing the significant detail. No, he says, the solution must be sought elsewhere. It is to be found in the method of rehearsal founded not on the actual unrolling of the story, but on the sequence of images as they are to appear on the screen. To the objection that it would be physically impossible to rehearse, in a connected sequence, scenes involving different locations or different natural surroundings, Pudovkin answers that the important thing is to enable the actor to sustain the continuity of his role's emotional tenor. If, for example, the story requires an actor to swim a river, a climb over a wall or a struggle with some other obstacle would be sufficient to produce the same internal or psychological effect, while permitting the actor to pass, uninterrupted, from the emotional state of jumping into water to that of emerging onto land, which are the two significant moments of his experience in this case.

Other methods, such as enlisting the actor in the work of shaping the scenario and editing the film, are suggested by Pudovkin as means to achieve greater familiarity with the character portrayed and, consequently, greater naturalness in acting. It can be assumed that such a procedure is practical in Soviet Russia. In Hollywood, of course, this procedure would express itself, for the most part, in heated arguments over the number of close-ups to be allotted to each star.

Apart from these considerations, it is legitimate to ask how patterning one's acting on the form it will assume on screen can possibly contribute to the greater naturalness of that acting. Does not such acting imply a constant straining for effect, a constant effort to be seen and heard in some way by the audience? Pudovkin answers this question with the statement that all art presumes the existence of the beholder or listener, and that dramatic art in particular, whether on the stage or on the screen, can function properly and fully only in intimate contact with the audience. A man's actions in real life may be perfectly natural, but to become charged with life and reality when seen by a theater audience, they have to pass through a process of conscious selection and arrangement—of rhythmic accent. Hence, convincing naturalness on the screen can be achieved only by "playing up" to the audience. This conclusion may seem paradoxical, but as set forth and illustrated by Pudovkin, it is undoubtedly justified.

The simplest way of reproducing a scene with a number of people talking, for instance, is to record the dialogue just as it is spoken. But such a method would make no allowance for the shifting interest of the audience. Pudovkin therefore rules out this method as false, as depriving the audience of the sensation of naturalness that springs from the ability to focus attention on what arouses the greatest interest at any particular moment. Perhaps the most interesting example bearing on this point is the treatment of dialogue in *The Deserter* [1933], a recent film directed by Pudovkin.

Here is a sample scene from this picture. We see a close-up of a man asking a question. Our interest immediately shifts to the man to whom the question has been addressed. In real life we would instantly turn toward him with an expectant look. Pudovkin permits us to do so as we watch *The Deserter*. He shows the man but does not let him speak until after a lapse of a few seconds. In this instance the image precedes the words; the sound lags. The man continues by answering the question. We are absorbed in his argument or explanation. Suddenly somebody makes a loud remark. We hear the words before we see the interrupter. Pudovkin duplicates the effect. Now he makes the image lag behind the words. The man then resumes his answer to the question. There are more interruptions. He stops talking, listening tensely to his opponents. We watch the drama of his struggling emotions. Pudovkin lets us see the man standing silent while, offscreen, we hear the voices of his attackers. In this case, image and sound have become divorced.

This scheme of treatment is capable of further variations. But enough has been said here to indicate how nicely such treatment dovetails with Pudovkin's concept of naturalness as the total intended effect of assembled images and sounds, on film. (*New York Times*, May 5, 1935)

22. New Paths for the Musical Film (1935)

Speaking generally, the sound picture of today is a swift, supple medium with a range and power of dramatic expression surpassing anything that the old silent picture was ever able to achieve. The one branch of the sound movies in which the advance has been the least noticeable, however, is the musical film, a form of cinema that owes its existence entirely to the advent of sound and that, from the start, has involved a new and wholly different conception of filmic technique.

It is this peculiar nature of the musical film, or the song-and-dance picture, as it is more properly called, that has never been adequately understood, and for this reason has played havoc with the determined efforts of directors to achieve an appropriately natural and convincing form of expression. Ever since the days of *The Jazz Singer* [1927, dir. Alan Crosland], it has been universally assumed that the musical film differs from screen comedy and drama only in the fact that the former has singing and dancing, whereas the latter does not have them. The truth of the matter is that the musical film is not just a straight film embellished with incidental singing and dancing. It is first and foremost a musical entertainment, a display of singing and dancing, while the rest of the picture is only a means of providing plausible excuses for such entertainment.

The crux of the problem lies, of course, in what is accepted as plausible. On the musical-comedy stage a duet, a chorus song, or a chorus dance routine is plausible not because the characters would engage in such antics in real life, but because there is an established convention permitting the audience to regard the stage performer as an entertainer, rather than as a character in the real world of the play. No such convention has been developed in the musical film as we know it today. The screen performer is always a character living in the real world of the screenplay. He can appear as an entertainer, too, but only when he impersonates an entertainer, and even then his audience is not the one watching him in the movie house but the one that is with him on the screen. Hence the difficulty of making singing and dancing realistically plausible in the musical film.

In real life, of course, there is little singing that has dramatic significance, as singing is done mostly on set occasions such as parties, concerts, and stage performances where the singers act as entertainers. The same restriction applies to dancing, as opposed to a dance exhibition. It is only when we view real life through the prism of fantastic romance or grandiose extravaganza that we can accept as plausible characters who burst into song or indulge in the eccentricities of exhibitive dancing.

Some continental directors, notably René Clair and several Germans among the Americans—occasionally Ernst Lubitsch—have taken advantage of such an escape from the limitations of realistic plausibility to give their musical films a freedom of treatment that does no violence to the otherwise natural behavior of their characters. But this solution, clearly, has a limited scope. It cannot apply musical treatment to a picture of life that retains the normal, realistic logic of our everyday experience. With their sure instinct for the living truth, American directors have stuck to realistic subjects. They have confined themselves to stories in which characters can appear as entertainers, preferably professional entertainers, for in this way stage dancing and singing can be credibly incorporated into the body of the film. Nonetheless, despite their ingenuity in devising plausible excuses for song and dance, these directors have been unable to keep strictly within the realistic formula.

On the one hand, the Americans have found no substitute for such an artificial stage device as the duet and therefore have to smuggle it in, as they did recently in *Naughty Marietta* [1935, dir. Robert Z. Leonard & W. S. Van Dyke], for the sake of the musical entertainment it provides. On the other hand, when they employ a theatrical performance as an excuse for singing and dancing, they find it well-nigh impossible to maintain the illusion of the stage without sacrificing the vastly more telling effects that can be produced by the camera and the microphone.

On such occasions, as in *Gold Diggers of 1935* [1935, dir. Busby Berkeley], they pay perfunctory lip service to the realistic formula—here a charity show for the "Milk Fund"—only to quickly throw it overboard and fly off into a display of singing and dancing couched in terms of fantastic trick photography. One can see from this that the realistic formula has not saved the musical film from its share of glaring contradictions. This is not so much the fault of realism, however, as of its interpretation in the hands of American film directors. Seen in its true light, realism can still solve this problem—provided it is fortified with the device of split-screen composition.

Let me explain. The main difficulty of the musical film is the treatment of ensemble singing and dancing. The difficulty, really, is of the directors' own making. For there is no reason why voices and movements should be combined only by bringing the singers and dancers, bodily, into the same physical setting, whether that be a home or a stage. Could not the same effect be produced by taking a number of isolated characters, in their natural backgrounds, and bringing them together into a vocal or dancing ensemble upon the surface of the screen?

In real life occasions for solo singing or dancing are comparatively frequent: a girl may sing a love song in the solitude of her bedroom, and a boy may do the same in his den. Placed side by side on the screen, these two can be made to blend their songs in what will sound like a duet. The effect of ensemble singing will be there, but the singing will be done without forcing the characters into unnatural situations. The only problem to solve will be that of blending the two songs in a well-balanced musical composition, and this is not a problem beyond the skill of most competent musicians.

Similarly, a chorus on the screen need not appear as a group of people singing together, much less as the conventional stage chorus. The effect of choral singing can be produced by screen composition made up of a number of single individuals. One can go even further in the application of this method. Granted the power of creating musical effects in its own way, the screen can weld together, in a fluid and rhythmic pattern, a great variety of independent sounds and images. Waves and rain, wind and thunder, birds and animals with their different "voices," rushing trains and tooting automobile horns, screeching sirens, church bells, and rattling machine shops—all these and innumerable others can be brought together to form an orchestra of images and sounds that has its existence only upon the surface of the screen. If the idea seems far-fetched, it can hardly be denied that there is opportunity here at least for some very striking and novel jazz-music effects.

In the treatment of dancing, split-screen composition provides an escape both from the artificialities of the musical-comedy stage and from the fantastic unrealities of camera tricks, with their cavorting grand pianos or dancers fleeting from floor to floor in defiance of all laws of physics. Split-screen composition does not impose artificialities upon the dancers. In fact, it can produce rhythmic patterns without having the characters themselves go through the postures and movements of dance. All the split screen requires is that the surface of the screen be regarded as a dance floor upon which a group of independent images, constantly changing in size and position, engages in a pattern of rhythmic movement. To take a simple example, a parade of fashion models, which in most movies is a dull and humorless affair, can be turned into a spectacle of live and scintillating beauty if made to appear as if it is filing past in three or four parallel bands—like so many horizontal or vertical panels, with the figures moving in a variety of directions.

There is also another important advantage in the device of the split screen. By alternating images occupying different positions on the screen, a degree of rhythmic emphasis can be achieved that is entirely beyond the power of ordinary filmic treatment, which unfolds images in single file. However, this is hardly the place to go into technical details. Suffice it to say that in visualizing all the possibilities and effects of screen composition, one has to picture the screen as a huge keyboard instrument in which every square foot of surface represents a different note—one that can be sounded at will. (*New York Times*, June 9, 1935)

1. *The End of St. Petersburg* 1927 Vsevolod Pudovkin

2. *The Cabinet of Dr. Caligari* 1920 Robert Wiene

3. *The Last Laugh* 1924 F. W. Murnau

4. *Ten Days That Shook the World* (a.k.a. *October*) 1927 Sergei Eisenstein

5. *All Quiet on the Western Front* 1930 Lewis Milestone

6. *The Circus* 1928 Charles Chaplin

7. *The Last Command* 1928 Josef von Sternberg

8. *The Crowd* 1928 King Vidor

9. *The Wedding March* 1928 Erich von Stroheim

10. *Nana* 1926 Jean Renoir

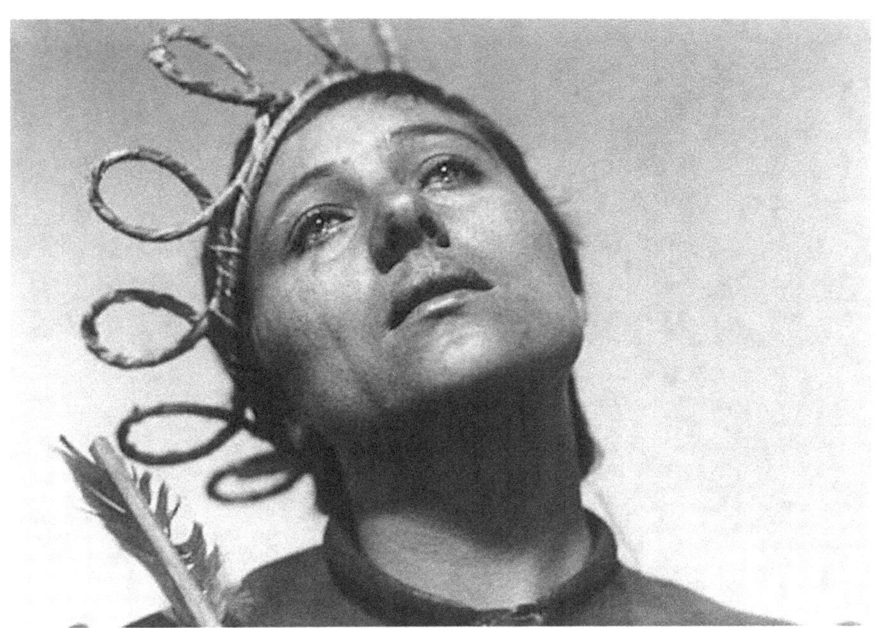

11. *The Passion of Joan of Arc* 1928 Carl-Theodor Dreyer

12. *Blackmail* 1929 Alfred Hitchcock

13. *Arsenal* 1929 Alexander Dovzhenko

14. *Pandora's Box* 1929 G. W. Pabst

15. *Anna Christie* 1930 Clarence Brown

16. *Old and New* (a.k.a. *The General Line*) 1929 Sergei Eisenstein

17. *Storm over Asia* 1928 Vsevolod Pudovkin

18. *The Big House* 1930 George Hill

19. *The Dawn Patrol* 1930 Howard Hawks

20. *Abraham Lincoln* 1930 D. W. Griffith

21. *Animal Crackers* 1930 Victor Heerman

22. *Earth* 1930 Alexander Dovzhenko

23. *Billy the Kid* 1930 King Vidor

24. *Morocco* 1930 Josef von Sternberg

25. *Sous les toits de Paris* (*Under the Roofs of Paris*) 1930 René Clair

26. *The Blue Angel* 1930 Josef von Sternberg

27. *City Lights* 1931 Charles Chaplin

28. *Trader Horn* 1930 W. S. Van Dyke

29. *Tabu* 1931 F. W. Murnau

30. *The Front Page* 1931 Lewis Milestone

31. *The Beggar's Opera* (a.k.a. *The Threepenny Opera*) 1931 G. W. Pabst

32. *The Maltese Falcon* 1931 Roy Del Ruth

33. *An American Tragedy* 1931 Josef von Sternberg

34. *Street Scene* 1931 King Vidor

35. *Horse Feathers* 1932 Norman Z. McLeod

36. *Back Street* 1932 John M. Stahl

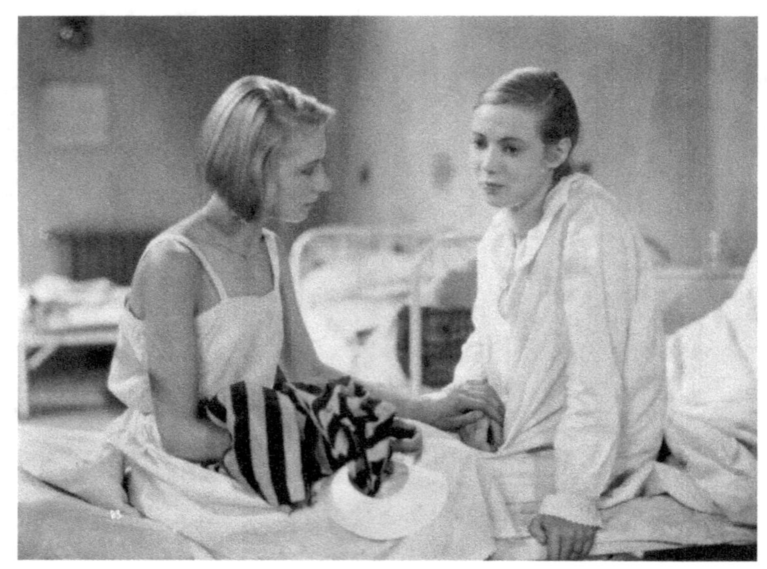

37. *Mädchen in Uniform* (*Girls in Uniform*) 1931 Leontine Sagan

38. *Kameradschaft* (*Comradeship*) 1931 G. W. Pabst

39. *I Am a Fugitive from a Chain Gang* 1932 Mervyn LeRoy

40. *Trouble in Paradise* 1932 Ernst Lubitsch

Reviews

1. Realism au Naturel: *Chang: A Drama of the Wilderness* (1927), dir. Merian C. Cooper & Ernest B. Schoedsack.

It is well to be reminded that there are places on this planet where man is still a plaything of nature and his life a never-ending struggle against her blind forces. Such a place is the faraway and inaccessible Siamese jungle that Messrs. Cooper and Schoedsack exhibit in their interesting film called *Chang* [1927].

There danger lurks behind every bush. Man's life and labor are continuously exposed to the attacks of giant snakes, bears, leopards, tigers, and wild elephants. The last are the most to be feared, and one of the most effective scenes in *Chang* is the one showing a herd of elephants literally razing to the ground—like so many card boxes—a whole native village. Here then is human life, which ever and again caps a redoubtable effort with the bitterness of defeat. No better material could be desired for a drama. And yet *Chang* is not drama—not even melodrama, which it is said to be in the official program.

In saying this, I do not want to detract from the credit that is due the authors of the film for the infinite pains and exceptional risks they took in securing their material. As films go today, theirs is an achievement. But the claim put forward on their behalf is hardly justified. It is just as a dramatic narrative that *Chang* fails. We are shown a native couple engaged in the daily pursuits of primitive farming. We see their peaceful life occasionally disturbed by encounters with leopards and tigers—encounters in which man proves always victorious. Then comes their greatest calamity, the destruction of their home by an enraged mother-elephant; and a similar fate befalls a neighboring village. Miraculously, no man is killed; the villagers organize a pursuit of the elephants; they succeed in driving practically the whole herd into a trap—and thus our pioneer couple is seen again building a new homestead with a tamed elephant for their obedient servant.

The story, even as it stands, should have provided sufficient opportunities for drama against the background of a relentless and awe-inspiring jungle. But in *Chang* the jungle is shown not so much in the pictures as in the subtitles (preposterously inept to boot), and man's struggle for existence is hardly ever conveyed—much less made to appear as a heroic fight against an implacable foe. The authors are not entirely to blame for this. The natives photographed were not actors, nor could they be expected to sacrifice their lives for the sake of a certain effect.

Again, the conditions under which the picture was made were not of a kind that would enable a director to build his effects according to plan. But all this only goes to show that mere realism is not enough. A film, to be truly dramatic, must organize its material as a dynamic sequence in which all scenes are emotionally related to one another. There is no such unity in *Chang*. (*The Nation*, May 18, 1927)

2. Douglas Fairbanks: *The Gaucho* (1927), dir. F. Richard Jones.

After *The Thief of Bagdad* [1924, dir. Raoul Walsh] and *The Black Pirate* [1926, dir. Albert Parker] comes *The Gaucho* [1927, dir. Richard F. Jones]—a film decidedly inferior to its two predecessors. It is easy to dismiss Douglas Fairbanks as an artist. His reliance on acrobatic stunts, his monotonous repetition of the same character, and his undisguised playing for effect brand him as an actor lacking in imagination and weak in interpretative powers.

If acting were all that mattered in movies, one would be content to accept this criticism as the final verdict on Douglas Fairbanks. But acting is not all—not even half—of the cinema. And when the acting does appear bad by reason of its failing to appear convincing, this failure may actually be due to causes far different from the deficiencies of the acting itself. I am not referring here to the extraordinary manipulations of the film record that take place in the cutting room, though, obviously, these can make or damn the acting. In Fairbanks's case the trouble lies elsewhere. It is to be found in the general direction of his pictures, and this is particularly evident in *The Gaucho*.

At the outset the fact must be admitted that Fairbanks's pictures are inevitably "vehicles" for Fairbanks's acting. There is no question that he is the principal passenger there, and that the vehicles are out for the special object of driving him to his appointed destination. But what is his destination? In *The Thief of Bagdad* and *The Black Pirate* one was almost persuaded to think that the fairyland of Oriental romance and the fancy of bedizened buccaneering were the objects of Fairbanks's histrionic efforts. With all his heroics, he seemed to belong to the backgrounds and the worlds of these two motion pictures. He was plausible. He was human.

In *The Gaucho*, Fairbanks and the background in which he moves are two different entities. The background tells the story in the conventional but straightforward way made familiar in most American movies. But now Fairbanks comes on the scene indulging in various acrobatic stunts, and one is immediately struck by a peculiarity that did not seem to be so conspicuous in his earlier pictures. Each time Fairbanks performs, he strikes an attitude (with the movement of his hand and a completely self-satisfied grin) that suggests not so such a dashing cavalier of a bandit as a clever acrobat waiting for a round of applause or a curtain call after performing an act on a vaudeville stage.

No censure is implied in this description. Fairbanks is essentially a vaudeville actor of the acrobatic type. He has earned success on the screen by a frank exploitation of his personality. On occasions he tried, and not without a measure of success, to adapt his manner of acting to the character of his background. In *The Gaucho* he made no such attempt, and the result is that the film is disrupted in action and painfully discordant in style. And yet this result was not inevitable. Even granting Fairbanks's disposition toward the effects of vaudeville acting, the direction of the picture could have been pulled round to satisfy this condition. In other words, the vaudeville style of acting should have extended from Fairbanks to the rest of the movie.

Moreover, let it be clearly understood: vaudeville does not mean either the grotesque or the caricatured. All it means is a frank display of the actor's skill direct to the audience. Fairbanks chooses to give his own acting a certain musical-comedy touch, which somewhat cheapens its effect. This, of course, could be easily avoided while still keeping within the artificial convention decided upon. But if the musical-comedy style for Fairbanks himself is deemed indispensable, then musical comedy let it be—from the beginning to the end of the picture. (*The Nation*, January 25, 1928)

3. Tramp and Clown: *The Circus* (1928), dir. Charlie Chaplin.

Looking at our great and incomparable Charlie Chaplin, I feel as if I should pat myself on the back. Did I not argue as long as fifteen years ago that the ordinary "legitimate" actors should be barred from the motion picture? It was of these actors that I said in 1913 [in "The Cinema as Art," published 1916]: "Are they aware that the cinematographic play is the most abstract form of the pantomime? Do they realize that if there is any stage on which the laws of movement should reign supreme, it is the cinematographic stage? If they did they would not have monopolized the cinematographic play, but would have left it to the dancers, clowns, and acrobats, who do know something about the laws of movement."

A few years later came Charlie, the perfect clown and acrobat, and by way of confirming my dictum, at once leapt to such heights of artistic distinction that ever since there have been only two kinds of motion-picture actors: Charlie Chaplin and the rest. The classification is based not only on the singularity of Chaplin's genius, but equally so on the singularity of his methods as an actor. This fact, however, is often ignored. Chaplin's mannerisms, the peculiar traits of the screen character he has created, have been imitated and plagiarized times without number. On the other hand, his consistent pantomimic acting (I cannot recall a single picture in which Chaplin moves his lips as if actually speaking), his emphasis on expressive movement (his gait, for instance), and his puppet-like, essentially non-realistic treatment of his role—these are the characteristics of Chaplin's acting that may have found many imitators, but certainly none who show anything like Chaplin's appreciation of their meaning and importance.

Those who induced Charlie Chaplin to try the movies did not suspect him of being more than a "funny man," though he came from the vaudeville stage—the stage that still preserves some of the great traditions of "pure" acting. In vaudeville he learned how to create an image and convey emotion by a movement of the body, a twist of the head, or a doll-like fixedness of expression; from vaudeville also he has carried the sense of dramatic composition: the use of emphasis in a portrait-like portrayal, the appreciation of rhythmic pattern, the knowledge of the exact location for the dramatic accent. Had he stopped with this and remained merely a master of technique, he would have achieved something rare in the motion picture. But he went farther. He created a character—a creature entirely fantastic, utterly impossible in real life, yet so human, so lovable in its childish naïveté and pathetic helplessness, so uproariously humorous in its grotesque ingenuities that it has acquired significance equal to that of any of the historic types of the stage.

And now *The Circus* [1928]. The poor tramp; fame and fortune; hunger for food; hunger for friendliness and love. He has unwittingly got into trouble with the police, attempts to escape, and loses them and himself in a mirror-maze. He disguises himself as one of the front-side specimens of a Noah's Ark, but is discovered and chased into a circus. In saving himself from the police, he has incidentally become a member of the troupe and has caught an egg for breakfast by chasing a hen, when a fair lady in distress, a circus equestrian, puts him in his proper stride as the gallant knight-errant that he truly is. A knight-errant, a lovelorn Pierrot, an impish harlequin, our hero then proceeds to reveal himself in a series of episodes among which are two feats of inspiration: a scene in a lion's cage and a scene in which he walks a tightrope with the help of a disguised cable.

Descent from the tightrope—the climax of the story—and the downward slide of fortune are simultaneous and he is "gradually fired"—a gross exaggeration. Poor and helpless, he will not allow the fair lady of his heart to join her fortunes with his but restores her instead to his more prosperous rival, and quietly withdrawing from the selfish people who no longer need him, resumes his lonely wanderings through the world. The sad ending of the photoplay is significant. The tragic mask is increasingly apparent in the comic make-up of the waif whom the world has so tenderly taken to its heart. The irresponsible harlequin is receding. The tendency may or may not enrich Chaplin's art.

In *The Circus*, nonetheless, Chaplin is again at his very best. His inexhaustible comic imagination has provided the picture with a more than ample supply of side-splitting "stunts" of characteristic Chaplinesque quality, the most striking of these being the aforementioned scenes at the Noah's Ark and the lion's cage. The "big scene" of the picture, in which Charlie performs some amazing feats in tightrope walking, is funny too, but suffers somewhat from the attempt to join the wistful buffoonery of Charlie's little trick to the cruder and different fun of his helplessness in disengaging himself from the attacking monkeys. (This latter portion thus strikes a somewhat alien, discordant note. Its scarcely premeditated effect may be ascribed to the change in dramatic style of the scene, which, from a situation artificial and farcical, passes into realism and borders on tragedy.) And through all these mirth-provoking scenes there flits the unforgettable image that has so endeared itself to the world—the image of a childishly simple and quixotically noble Pierrot who occasionally borrows the impishness of Harlequin.

In *The Circus*, as one might guess, Chaplin's is a solo performance. The rest of the actors are not more than competent, and the direction of the picture as a whole lacks distinction. This last quality is disappointing. *The Circus* is neat and competent but here as previously, its author has failed fully to rise to the opportunity placed before him by the extraordinarily fantastic world of the character he has created. Chaplin showed his mettle as director in *The Woman of Paris* [1923], and though there is no place for realism of this kind in his own grotesqueries, there is place in them for something that he is preeminently fitted to accomplish. Perhaps one day Chaplin will turn his mind to this richly promising field of experimental effort, where the great screen genius of our time may be able to find for the photoplay as a whole the fully expressive visual form he has found for himself.

Chaplin's style of acting and all his dramatic upbringing proclaim him for what he actually is: a superb vaudeville comedian. We have motion pictures that are equivalent to comedy and drama. But we still have no motion-picture vaudeville, i.e., entertainment that shuns illusionist effects and makes its appeal direct to the audience, simply and solely as entertainment. There is waiting for Chaplin, then, a full-sized job worthy of his genius. (*The Nation*, February 29, 1928, & *The Dial*, May 1928)

4. Character and Drama: *The Last Command* (1928), dir. Josef von Sternberg; *The Crowd* (1928), dir. King Vidor.

Allowing for the determined enthusiasm of the publicity agents, one feels that Hollywood is quite sincerely convinced of the outstanding artistic merit of *The Last Command* [1928, dir. Josef von Sternberg] and *The Crowd* [1928, dir. King Vidor]—two of the recent crop of "specials." This, of course, is as it should be in Hollywood. For my part, I fail to see much if anything in these two pictures that can properly be described as standing out. On the other hand, I see a great deal that stands decidedly below the level of achievement revealed by both Emil Jannings and King Vidor in their earlier work.

One feels particularly sorry for Jannings. This very serious, inquiring, and gifted actor is succumbing to the slick efficiency of the rubber stamp and the perverse incompetence of the studio hand that seem to pervade the Hollywood scene. In *The Last Laugh* [1924, dir. F. W. Murnau] and *Variety* [1925, dir. E. A. Dupont]—thanks largely to the exceptional quality of the directing—Jannings' acting was the focusing center of a dynamic pattern. It sustained the ebb and flow of the emotional forces involved; it provided the highlights for moments of tense, overcharged drama and the low lights for moments of relaxation and comic relief. Characterization, more prominent in *The Last Laugh* than in *Variety*, was designed for such a purpose in *The Last Command*, and therefore intended to form part and parcel of the dynamic pattern. In *The Way of All Flesh* [1927, dir. Victor Fleming], by contrast, characterization came much more to the fore, and thus inevitably threw the whole dramatic scheme out of balance. This was particularly emphasized by the excellence of Emil Jannings' acting in the descriptive introduction of the story, in contrast to the conventional treatment of his character in the subsequent narrative development.

The Last Command is a step still further away from a consistent emotional pattern unfolded in visual images. Though obviously selected for the sake of its final scene—the pathetic "last command" of an old Russian general, acting as a Hollywood extra—the story does nothing to rouse the spectator to the appreciation of this climax beyond picturing crudely, at times rather stupidly, the events on the fighting front that brought about the overthrow of the generals and the triumph of the Revolution. On the other hand, the portrait of the general, though it occupies half the film, comes nowhere near the subtlety and richness of Jannings' characterization in *The Way of All Flesh*. The total effect is of a picture that lacks distinction; it runs smoothly from scene to scene with the sleekness of an article written according to a well-known formula.

In *The Crowd*, King Vidor, the director, had an opportunity to treat an interesting subject in an interesting way. He made a feeble attempt to avail himself of this opportunity but abandoned it very soon. I am not surprised at his failure, since he seems to owe it to the same quality that ensured his success in *The Big Parade* [1925, dir. King Vidor]. It will be recalled that the latter picture achieved its great distinction not through any original conception of filmic drama, but rather through its masterly treatment of very conventional material. It was daring in realistic detail while remaining romantic and sentimental in its general mood. In a word, *The Big Parade* was brilliant in its superficiality—which latter quality did not seem so objectionable because the scale of the picture demanded a big brush.

King Vidor was faced with a vastly different problem in *The Crowd*. The story of a young office clerk—one of the millions who make the wheels go round in such big cities as New York—called for a finer brush and a more delicate treatment than were necessary in *The Big Parade*. Here was a psychological drama set against a sociological background. For a daring interpretation in visual images diametrically organized, there could have been no better opportunity. After a few faltering steps, however, Vidor decided that the job was not for him. He rejected both psychology and sociology, and instead turned to "character" as his principal weapon. He chose his types with the same sureness of touch as in *The Big Parade*—types torn from real, everyday life—but he afforded them the same treatment: farcical exaggeration and fake emotion. As for the background, Vidor showed some very striking views of skyscrapers and one particularly striking picture of a large office; but he never attempted to relate these images to the life story of his hero, or to weave them into the emotional pattern of the picture.

One technical innovation in *The Crowd* deserves notice—the use of double exposure, with a reduced image instead of the ordinary flashback, in which the thoughts of a character are shown as pictures inside his head. But even in this device there is subordination of cinematic effect to the requirements of a crudely conceived realism. Alas, Hollywood. (*New York Times*, April 18, 1928)

5. The Russian Contribution: *Czar Ivan the Terrible* (1926), dir. Yuri Tarich; *The End of St. Petersburg* (1927), dir. Vsevolod Pudovkin.

Judging by what has been written in America of such Russian films as *Battleship Potemkin* [1925, dir. Sergei Eisenstein], *Czar Ivan the Terrible* [a.k.a. *The Wings of a Serf*; 1926, dir. Yuri Tarich], and *The End of St. Petersburg* [1927, dir. Vsevolod Pudovkin], the proper way of expressing oneself on the subject of Russian movies is by beating the big drum and shouting at the top of one's voice. Screaming, for those who like it, is also permissible. Perhaps all this is as it should be. Perhaps it is natural that a discussion of the cinema, as of everything else connected with Soviet Russia, should be tinged with a certain amount of sensationalism. The enhanced interest in and appreciation of Soviet art—if such is the effect of this sensationalism—is all to the good. But what is one to do if, like the present critic, one has no talent for beating the drum? Apparently one will have to be content with a dispassionate discussion of the merits of Soviet films irrespective of other considerations.

At the outset let this important point be properly understood. Whatever other qualities or defects Soviet movies may have, the very fact of their Soviet origin is in a sense an artistic quality. This "Soviet origin" has rightly come to be regarded as the emblem of fearless grappling with reality, of tearing down the shams that have been set up by the class-prejudices of the bourgeois world. There is such a thing in art as the pathos of stark truth, and today Soviet films seem to be the chief providers of this rare and hence so invigorating article. Nor is this all. The "Soviet origin" is entitled to credit for another artistic quality of importance: it is responsible for an independence of outlook that refuses to bow before established conventions and is always ready to test new forms, new methods, and new ideas.

How much of the appeal of Soviet films is due to the characteristic difference of their matter and manner, and how much to their intrinsic artistic qualities, is not a question that can easily be answered. It would seem that the shouting and screaming about them should be ascribed in the main to the appreciation of their "difference," while the intrinsic appeal of these works, where it is present, should be regarded as a contributory factor in helping to enhance the very qualities that make Soviet pictures so startlingly "different."

For my part, I accept with gratitude the stark truth in the matter of Soviet films and the ardor for social justice in the light of which this truth is bared. It is possible that the day will arrive when the nakedness of life, by reason of its very familiarity, will cease to impress in the cinema, as it has ceased to do in modern literature—not to mention the nakedness of the human body in primitive communities. But for the present the Soviet starkness impresses, and I am thankful. There are scenes in *Czar Ivan the Terrible* and *The End of St. Petersburg*, as there were earlier in *Battleship Potemkin*, that almost stagger one by their undisguised ghastliness and brutality. Yet one welcomes even the ghastliness and brutality when one remembers such a *charlotte russe* from Hollywood as John Barrymore's *Tempest* [1928, dir. Sam Taylor]. (Incidentally, in Hollywood the French Revolution of commercial fiction still passes for the Russian Revolution of 1917. The scenes of tribunals and crowds, and the stock phrases about "aristocrats," seem to come straight out of *The Two Orphans* [1915, dir. Herbert Brenon; remade as *Orphans of the Storm* (1921, dir. D. W. Griffith)] and other such popular romances.)

My gratitude to the Russians for the manner in which they present their material is somewhat less fervent, as it is tempered and conditioned by considerations of intrinsic artistic quality. In *Battleship Potemkin*, the story of the mutiny as told on the screen catches something of the pulse of drama. Its emotion is conveyed through the direct physical appeal to our senses of various forms of movement. *Potemkin*'s tempo, as revealed in its suspenses, climaxes, and pauses, threads the story with a throbbing dramatic unity that is felt as if it were corporally alive. It is thus that *Potemkin* achieves cinematic dramatization, albeit in a manner that is still faltering and crude. But the achievement itself is a triumph of art, and this is *Potemkin*'s justification for being regarded as a landmark in the evolution of motion pictures.

Nothing approaching this achievement can be claimed for either *Czar Ivan the Terrible* or *The End of St. Petersburg*. The former film, conventional in its story, is also largely conventional in its form except in one scene—the scene of the czar's orgy, which shows a certain originality in the rhythmic treatment of its dance sequence. Yuri Tarich, who directed the picture, deserves all credit. But the chief honors in the film go to Leonid Leonidov for his extraordinary impersonation of

Ivan the Terrible. Nothing so subtle and yet so dynamically expressive has ever before been seen on the screen. Leonidov does not merely register an expression; he gives it suspense and movement, which make it a part of the whole drama. The screwed-up eye and the concealed smile with which he watches the humiliation of a *boyard* offender are unforgettable, and represent the high-water mark of movie acting. The characterization on the part of the other actors is also excellent, but the film as a whole, striking in many ways as it is, lacks unity, and to that extent it fails in fashioning out of its interesting material a truly cinematic drama.

The End of St. Petersburg, though less conventional in its story and general treatment than *Czar Ivan the Terrible*, is nevertheless even less impressive as a drama. This is rather surprising, as the material is there and the director, Vsevolod Pudovkin, gives innumerable instances of his ability to see things in an original, revealing light. All the same, the film seems to be singularly lacking in substance. The story, which begins with a promise of picturing the downfall of the old aristocratic world, soon resolves itself into a wholly tendentious and somewhat abstract recounting of the familiar factors that brought about the Russian Revolution: the callousness of the masters, the brutality of the world war, the starvation of the people, and, finally, their victorious rising. The life of the masters is only hinted at, with one or two deftly satirical touches; and the life of the masses is also only barely outlined in purely schematic and needlessly monochromatic scenes.

The feature that distinguishes *The End of St. Petersburg* and places it considerably above the average product is the passionate fervor of its photography. It is a cameraman's picture, with the cameraman's constant search for the most characteristic angle and sometimes the most symbolic object. But a motion picture is more than merely a sequence of still views, however quickly they follow one another and however expressive is their arrested imagery. Indeed, in *The End of St. Petersburg*, there is perhaps more of this symbolic, if not literary, imagery than the picture can hold.

The End of St. Petersburg is worthy of all the enthusiasm that has been showered on it, if only for its striking "difference" from the Hollywood article, which it shows in its earnest, even fearless tackling of human life and in its mordant penetration into the visual substance of the Russian world. As a photographic record of the reconstructed events of the Revolution, it is superb. As a dynamic narrative—a cinematic drama—it is loosely connected, jerky, and, well, often flat. (*The Nation*, July 25, 1928)

6. The Language of Images: *Ten Days That Shook the World,* a.k.a. *October* (1927), dir. Sergei Eisenstein; *The Wedding March* (1928), dir. Erich von Stroheim.

At this stage of the season's progress, Sergei Eisenstein's *Ten Days That Shook the World* [a.k.a. *October,* 1927] must be adjudged, among the movie offerings, as indisputably the most significant. It is unnecessary to dwell on the fact that it is not a great picture. The critics who found it confusing and sometimes even boring were perfectly right. It does confuse people who are not familiar with the events of the October Revolution, who know nothing about the struggle between the different revolutionary factions, and to whom the topography of St. Petersburg is a hidden secret. Nor is it possible to deny that the film often sacrifices tempo by marking time in sequences that contain no action or are excessively repetitious. This much goes by general agreement into the debit side of the picture's account. Eisenstein himself admits the confusion and the lack of sustained dramatic development, pleading, in justification, the pressure of time and aims or effects other than dramatic ones.

His plea shall be readily granted. One absolves Eisenstein of blame for failing to produce drama, for with the magnificent material in his hands—material pictorially and theatrically as striking as that in his *Battleship Potemkin* [1925]—he could easily have achieved success had he only chosen to repeat himself, or to follow more conventional lines. Deliberately, however, he steered his course toward a different goal—the goal not of a gradually prepared dramatic climax and its resolution, but of a recital of events with the recitalist's personal "angle" conspicuously in evidence.

In the final analysis, there are two schools of thought about the movie art of today. One school regards the motion picture as a procession of visual images related to one another through their meaning. The other school maintains that the only significant relationship is that based on the movement of the images, or their dynamic interplay. Hollywood, with the exception of F. W. Murnau and to some extent of King Vidor and Paul Fejos, has always adhered to the first theory. To the second school belongs the whole modern group of Russian movie directors—Lev Kuleshov, Dziga Vertov, Vsevolod Pudovkin, and Eisenstein. Only the Russians are developing their theory much farther than it ever occurred to the Americans to do. Not content with ignoring the Hollywood formula for dramatic construction, they are attempting to build the language of *cinematic* images. Their believe that visual images, like words, can be joined through movement into sentences, with the difference that the cementing medium is provided by the associations arising out of the meaning of the moving images—the logic of facts, so to speak—and not by deductions deriving from etymological forms, as in the words of sentences.

In *Ten Days That Shook the World* Eisenstein makes great hay out of this linguistic concept. The problem that engaged his special attention was that of the cinematic equivalent of metaphors and other figures of speech, as well as qualifying clauses, which in verbal language serve to express the speaker's personal attitude toward the subject of his narration. In the present case, Eisenstein confined his personal reaction to satirical comment on the enemies of the Revolution: he points a mocking finger at the self-regarding Alexander Kerensky by introducing the statue of a woman holding a wreath, as if about to crown the hero, or by placing him side by side with a statue of Napoleon; he pokes fun at Kerensky's ministers by showing their dreamy musings to the accompaniment of heavenly melodies, played on harps by ethereal ladies; he stresses the moral of a telephone conversation between Kerensky and a Cossack stableman by showing the buttocks of munching horses, as a sign of the latter's so-called neutrality.

It is impossible to deny considerable interest in Eisenstein's experiment. It is suggestive. It may add to the resources of the cinema. It may bring about a new, essentially descriptive genre of screen art. But such an experiment is fundamentally anti-dynamic and anti-dramatic, and as such lies off the main road of artistic progress in this medium. Far more important than these exercises in linguistic ideography are some of Eisenstein's startling visual effects, produced by purely dynamic means. Such is the effect of machine-gun fire with its rapid staccato beat, which is conveyed almost with the reality of sound. Eisenstein achieves this by alternating very rapidly two or three different sequences of guns and gunners, one sequence light and the other dark, while also changing the position of objects, which results in the visual effect of intermittent spurts of shooting.

It remains to be added that in spite of its rococo discursiveness and its lack of organized dramatic development, *Ten Days That Shook the World* is replete with magnificent scenes of mass movement, with amazingly observed characters (a gallery of types that can never be forgotten), and with extremely striking, even beautiful camera shots.

Of the other pictures lately shown on Broadway the most satisfying was *Shadows of Fear* [a.k.a. *Thérèse Raquin*, 1928]—a straightforward realistic drama directed by Jacques Feyder with a subtlety reminiscent of Chaplin's *Woman of Paris* [1923]. Murnau's *Four Devils* [1928], though less firmly knit than his *Sunrise* [1927], and though sharing with the latter a certain lack of warmth in the composition of its characters, shows the hand of a master in its flowing style, which shapes and modulates its equally fluid emotional content. Fejos's *Lonesome* [1928] has the same dynamic quality as *Four Devils* and shows many extremely interesting, suggestive effects, such as the combination of a number of independent images within the same frame. It is marred, however, by an unnecessary talking sequence.

Erich von Stroheim's *Wedding March* [1928], redolent with old-fashioned sentimentality from the days of *The Blue Danube* [1926, dir. Frederic Zelnik], is interesting only for its insistence on realistic detail—an insistence so screeching and sometimes so incongruous that it loses even the little virtue that one might be willing to concede it. W. S. Van Dyke and Robert Flaherty's *White Shadows* [1928], depicting the life of South Sea islanders, is a very effective picture—in fact, too effective, with a sleekness and prettifying that are characteristic of Hollywood. King Vidor's *Show People* [1928] itself is a fairly amusing comedy, though most of its laughs, one is sorry to say, come from the subtitles. (*The Nation*, December 26, 1928)

7. There *Are* Silent Pictures: *Nana* (1926), dir. Jean Renoir; *The Passion of Joan of Arc* (1928), dir. Carl-Theodor Dreyer.

The sense of physical discomfort—the jarring of rasping sounds on one's ear—is still one of the things we have to put up with in witnessing the slow progress of the talking picture. In this respect the silent picture can proudly point to its freedom of anything that hurts the eyes—a freedom of not more than ten years' standing, but today absolute and taken for granted. And yet, in spite of this great advantage over the talking picture, it is enough to see a few silent specimens of Hollywood's most ambitious efforts to understand the failure of the silent picture to stem the advancing tide of its noisy rival.

There are on Broadway at present three silent "specials" of Hollywood manufacture: *The Four Feathers* [1929, dir. Merian C. Cooper], *Evangeline* [1929, dir. Edwin Carewe], and *The Single Standard* [1929, dir. John S. Robertson]. Conventional and stereotyped as they are, they have the quality of their defect—the characteristic Hollywood workmanship that reveals itself in smoothness of action, splendid photography, and the skillful casting of character parts. The defect itself, however, is too fundamental to be neutralized or even disguised by its superficial attractions. The standardization of form and the resulting moronization of content rob the Hollywood picture of that flexibility of treatment which is essential to effective dramatic statement.

Now, just at the moment when the situation would seem to call for some striking, directly impressive effect, the Hollywood director, chained to his conventions, calls in the orchestra and the sound machine and thinks he has done his duty. The three pictures mentioned above, though they are silent, are no exception to this rule. Not only do they expound stories that are puerile (the heroics of *The Four Feathers* are simply inept), but they also fail to produce even the crude thrill of a dramatic climax. *Evangeline*, although a little more advanced in its technique, is dramatically the least convincing of the three. *The Four Feathers* has a few minor thrills supplied by scenes of wild animal life in Africa; but they are rather artificially connected with the main theme of the story and contribute very little to its dramatic development. As for *The Single Standard*, it is largely Miss Greta Garbo—take it or leave it. For my part, I am inclined to leave it.

Nonetheless, Hollywood does not hold a monopoly on cinematic ineffectiveness, as we are reminded by the frequent foreign importations that find refuge in the so-called little cinema theaters. There is *Nana* [1926], for instance, which, we are informed, was directed in France "by Jean Renoir, son of the distinguished French impressionist painter, with the cooperation of members of Émile Zola's family." Shades of Renoir *père* and Émile Zola! Are they to be held responsible for this talentless concoction undistinguished by a single cinematic quality and marred by terrible overacting by [Catherine Hessling] in the part of Nana, who is made not merely vulgar, as well she should be, but singularly unattractive to boot?

As a specimen of the cinematic sterility of British directors, there was recently *The Constant Nymph* [1928, dir. Adrian Brunel]—acclaimed as a masterpiece in England but more accurately described as the Hollywood average of ten years ago—insensitive, flat, and amateurish. It was a relief after this to see *Piccadilly* [1929], another picture made in England though directed by A. E. Dupont, the famous German director of *Variety* [1925]. Here were genuine workmanship and an unmistakable sense of cinematic values. Dupont's tempo is sometimes too slow, he lingers too fondly over details of small dramatic significance, but he does produce a flow of images that merge imperceptibly into one another—a dynamic quality previously best illustrated in Sergei Eisenstein's *Battleship Potemkin* [1925]—and he does convey a sense of cinematic unity and balance. Unfortunately, the cheap "mystery" ending of the story utterly spoils the dramatic movement of the film, coming almost as an anti-climax. Still, the acting in *Piccadilly* is also above the average English standard, particularly that of King Hou Chang, who plays Jim, and of Anna May Wong, performing the part of the Chinese dancer.

Of other current silent pictures, *The Fight for the Matterhorn* [1928, dir. Mario Bonnard & Nunzio Malasomma] deserves notice for striking photography and interesting natural scenery. Its drama does not come to much, but at any rate it is unobjectionable. The most interesting silent picture that has reached Broadway for some time, however, is *Penal Servitude* [a.k.a. *In Old Siberia*; 1928, dir. Yuli Raizman]. It is a strange film with many obvious faults. The contrast between the brutal tyrannies of prison officials toward their prisoners and the petty diversions of these prison officials against the background of provincial society—an excellent idea in itself—somehow is never translated into a dramatic unity; the two thematic strands remain separate. The characters themselves are exaggeratedly grotesque types and their make-up is frequently crude. But in spite of these deficiencies, *Penal Servitude* is a fresh and stimulating picture. It has remarkable atmospheric effects secured with a moving camera (apparently these effects are considerably cut in the present version), and it shows originality in its dramatic treatment. As the first work of a young director, Yuli Raizman, this picture is distinctly promising.

It is rather curious that the defects and qualities of this film should be completely reversed in another remarkable Russian picture not previously noticed here. *Women of Ryazan* [a.k.a. *The Village of Sin*, 1927] is the work of a young woman director, Olga Preobrazhenskaya.

Compared with Raizman's movie, hers shows a rather conventional choice of characters, but unlike the other one, it succeeds in welding its material into a dramatic unity by means of a treatment that has the quality of a sober and somewhat detached factuality, resembling the natural flow of modern *vers libre*. *Women of Ryazan* is also distinguished by the remarkable pictorial beauty of some of its scenes, notably a windswept wheat field.

This occasion is as good as any for referring to a film that, though shown a few months ago, is still eagerly discussed among movie enthusiasts. There is no denying the fact that *The Passion of Joan of Arc* [1928], directed by Carl-Theodor Dreyer and produced in France, is a movie of outstanding originality. Dreyer's emphasis on the facial expressions of his characters, who are shown mostly in monumentally sculpturesque close-ups, represents a technique that is decidedly fresh and unconventional, as is his use of the camera, which is made to follow the characters as if it were the eyes of a seated spectator watching the trial. Thus the whole drama is unfolded before us as if we were actually present in the court. The result of this peculiar use of the camera can hardly be described as cinematically, as well as dramatically, successful. The restricted camera movement retards the action and gives the picture a decided static quality. The method of conveying dramatic development by means of changes in facial expression lends further emphasis to this static quality.

Thus, instead of finding an adequate cinematic form in which to show the mental tortures of Joan and the reactions of her prosecutors, Dreyer has reduced the drama of the situation to rather obvious factual mimicry illustrating the subtitled dialogue, which is thus made to bear the whole burden of dramatic movement. Clearly, the picture should have been made as a talkie. Dreyer deserves all credit for his extraordinary photography, however, and must be complimented on the daring with which he has flouted the Hollywood formulas. Few directors seem to have the courage and originality to do so. (*The Nation*, August 21, 1929)

8. A Year of Talkies . . . Advancing: *Applause* (1929), dir. Rouben Mamoulian; *Blackmail* (1929), dir. Alfred Hitchcock.

It is only a year since *The Jazz Singer* [1927, dir. Alan Crosland] broke upon us, but the revolution occasioned by this sudden appearance of a talking photoplay has been as thorough as could possibly be imagined. The one regrettable result of the sound revolution has been the virtual disappearance of the silent picture from the bigger houses on Broadway. Thus the week beginning June 9th witnessed, among Broadway first runs, fourteen talking pictures and only three silent ones. One need not share the sophomoric enthusiasm that has recently developed for the silent picture, or pay much attention to the confused and often ignorant theories with which this enthusiasm is usually buttressed, to feel distressed at the sight of such wholesale slaughter.

It looks, then, as if the silent picture as an entertainment for the masses is definitely facing extinction. A year or so until the picture houses are "wired" for sound in this country, a little longer perhaps in other parts of the world, and the only silent pictures left will be those especially intended for the small ranks of admirers of cinematic art. But, deploring this fact as we may, let us also remember that among the films made during the past twenty-five years one would be hard put to count an equal number of cinematic masterpieces (apart from Charlie Chaplin's work, most, though by no means all, of which is certain to survive, thanks to Chaplin's own genius as a performer).

In a sense, therefore, one may welcome the present commercial eclipse of the silent picture as a means of its emancipation from Hollywood, with the possibility of its renaissance on an entirely new aesthetic foundation. The technical improvements forecast by the talkies, such as enlarged projection and effects of color and depth, are also sure to redound to the benefit of the silent picture, whose means will thus be enriched for the conquest of forms of expression that are no less fascinating than the flat monochrome of the film of today.

Now we may ask what progress has been made during the year of talkies. Judging by the opinions voiced in the press, the progress must have been enormous. On closer examination, however, one finds that it is usually the fickle critic's conversion to the talking picture that is announced as improvement of the pictures themselves. So far it is in the most important direction that one finds the least advancement. An absolutely faultless reproduction of human speech is obviously the first consideration in a talking picture. And yet today, as a year ago, we are still treated to hollow, squawking, and lisping voices, even to imperfect synchronization. To quote a few instances, in *Coquette* [1929, dir. Sam Taylor], Mary Pickford's voice was too painful to listen to (women's voices, it would seem, generally suffer more than men's), and in *Broadway* [1929, dir. Paul Fejos], one saw the flapping lips of the characters while the sound seemed to come from an entirely different direction.

It is not for a layman to discuss frequencies, acoustics, and other technical matters, but it is clear that far from sufficient care is being taken to insure perfect sound reproduction in the movie theaters, which is the only part of the process of direct and paramount interest to the audience. The very fact that in some pictures shown on Broadway the reproduction sounded well-nigh perfect (as in *The Rainbow Man* [1929, dir. Fred C. Newmeyer], for instance, which this writer heard from a seat very close to the screen), while in other pictures it was almost unbearable, is proof positive that producers are too much in a hurry to display their product. In these mechanical matters, even at the present stage of their progress, there should be no such thing as taking potluck when one goes to a talking movie.

And how have the talkies fared as dramatic entertainment? When they first appeared, those who were able to cast off old prejudices instantly saw that the thing worked—that it got its dramatic effects over as easily as the stage, and more easily than the silent picture—and this in spite of its obvious crudity. Today we still say that the thing works, though the crudity is only a little less obvious than it used to be. Unquestionably, there has been a noticeable advance in the general treatment of screenplays. Scenes run more smoothly into one another, acting is less stiff, and effects are increasingly more cinematic.

The action in *Bulldog Drummond* [1929, dir. F. Richard Jones], for example, is as swift and continuous as in any old Hollywood mystery drama. In *Madame X* [1929, dir. Lionel Barrymore], Ruth Chatterton is the acme of naturalness. In *The Trial of Mary Dugan* [1929, dir. Bayard Veiller], the pointing of the district attorney's finger at the accused, with the lawyer's voice offscreen, and similar instances in other pictures—thus separating the voice from the image of its owner—provide examples of distinctively cinematic technique. Another instance of such technique is *Broadway*'s attempt to introduce a fade-out of sound.

And yet, stage models still govern their screen versions in the major parts. And for reasons that it is difficult to discern, the total effect of the talking picture is generally thin, lacking in substance. Strange as it may appear, a silent picture seems to be freighted with sensory appeal. A picture like *The Last Laugh* [1924, dir. F. W. Murnau] is a veritable eye-full. In the talkies, much as you may be moved by the drama, you feel it is a drama that takes place in a world of ghosts. Perhaps the introduction of stereoscopic projection, coupled with color, will solve this problem.

That said, there are two reasons why Rouben Mamoulian's *Applause* [1928] is one of the most significant talking pictures that has yet been produced in the United States. Its first claim to distinction is that rare thing: the artist's touch, a quality that proclaims a cultured and sensitive mind attuned to the medium of its expression. Its second claim rests on its convincing demonstration of the ability of the talking picture to create drama that is not modeled after the stage.

Mamoulian is a newcomer to the movies. But the man who directed *Porgy* [1927] on Broadway did not come empty-handed to his new task. He brought with him an extremely fine sense of pictorial and dramatic values. His story was conventional—one of those sentimentalized romances of backstage life that film producers are now feeding the public—and his actors were hardly above the average as far as Broadway standards go. Yet in spite of the rather poor material he had to work with, Mamoulian has created, if not quite a masterpiece, at least a genuine work of art that occasionally thrills one with its distinctive beauty and sardonic humor.

Perhaps Mamoulian's most striking achievement is the sustained sense of unity, of atmosphere, with which he infuses *Applause* as a whole. The sordidness of its realistic detail is not to be gainsaid, yet how mordant and spicy it is, how different in its imaginative treatment from the countless scenes of chorus girls onstage as found in even the best Hollywood films! Particularly striking, also, is the opening sequence showing a desolate street with bits of paper blown by the wind, then a solitary dog running this way and that, followed by groups of excited children, and, finally, as a climax, the street parade of the burlesque troupe, with the volume of sound rising from moment to moment until it swells to a cacophonous blare of the actors' trumpets.

Since Dudley Murphy's *St. Louis Blues* [1929], a very remarkable little picture in its own way, this is unquestionably the most satisfying instance of the cinematic treatment of sound. Another instance, even more important in its implications because of the far-reaching developments it foreshadows, is to be found in Mamoulian's use of the split screen—that is, two independent scenes shown side by side, at the same time. Taken as a whole, however, *Applause* is not free from some significant defects. The dramatic import of its dialogue is not put forward so well as that of the visual images, and there is a consequent loss of emotional effect. Nor is Mamoulian's almost continuous use of the moving camera wholly convincing. It slows up action where an imaginative cutting, like that in Eisenstein's *Battleship Potemkin* [1925], would have given speed and concentration of interest. Besides, with its bouncing horizon and its emphasis upon the outline of the image, the moving camera gives a view of the world as it might be seen by an elephant from an enclosed car, rather than by a human being walking out in the open.

The British picture *Blackmail* [1929, dir. Alfred Hitchcock], for its part, is a creditable piece of work. It tells its story smoothly and effectively, with due regard for dramatic climaxes. But while intelligent and on occasion even ingenious, it lacks the imaginative quality that stamps a work of art. The best that can be said for *Blackmail* is that, as a talkie, it does as well as an average silent picture would.

As for musical comedy, the best one that has come out of Hollywood, no doubt, is *Sunny Side Up* [1929, dir. David Butler]. As mere comedy it is excruciatingly funny, as musical entertainment it is— well, let us say, harmless. As an example of smart and dashing Hollywood workmanship at its finest, however, *Sunny Side Up* is unique. (*The Nation,* June 26, 1929, & October 30, 1929)

9. Talkies and Dummies: *Disraeli* (1929), dir. Alfred E. Green; *Young Nowheres* (1929), dir. Frank Lloyd.

Not having seen George Arliss in *Disraeli* [1929, dir. Alfred E. Green] when it was produced as a stage play [1911, Louis N. Parker], I am deprived of the necessary basis of comparison in judging his performance in the screen version of the same work. Arliss, of course, is a very polished actor and, moreover, one of considerable resource—a rare quality among modern actors. The talkie in question conveys all this quite unmistakably. Thanks to the spoken dialogue— and one feels that without it the picture would not nearly be so effective—Arliss's subtleties of characterization are brought home to the spectator with all the poignancy of effect that one may wish for. In fact, they are brought home more successfully than could be done from the stage.

But this new invention of the talking picture is a curious medium. It has given the screen a degree of realism that in its silent form it never had. It is not that spoken dialogue as such is necessarily realistic. A purely cinematic and at the same time non-realistic use of human speech is not only feasible but inevitable with the advance of screen art. Where, however, as in *Disraeli,* the characters are portrayed as we would see them in normal life, the element of speech becomes a powerful actor in creating the illusion of reality.

And here a curious phenomenon arises. Instinctively, we become aware of something checking the complete illusion of life. The characters, natural as they are, appear to lack the essential warmth, material solidity, and individual isolation of real people. Clearly, the thing that is missing here is the sensation of natural colors and stereoscopic space. Until the moving picture solves this problem—and some recent experiments have brought this moment almost within its reach—realistic plays on the screen will always and unavoidably fall short of their counterparts on the stage. As far as the present version of *Disraeli* is concerned, it may be pronounced a fairly good entertainment provided one likes the playwright Louis Parker's Sardouesque stagecraft.

Young Nowheres [1929, dir. Frank Lloyd] itself is one of the more successful talkies. It is well recorded and well photographed, and is distinguished by the very able acting of Richard Barthelmess. But its story, though a relief after all the garish pictures of stage life, is too sugar-coated for our jaded palates. Surely even elevator boys, not to speak of girl typists, are not so "green" and helpless as this movie would ask us to believe. Since the advent of such talkies, the silent pictures have withdrawn to the "little cinema theaters." The result is that, unfortunately, there are today very few silent films worth showing.

The Soul of France [1928, dir. André Dugès & Alexandre Ryder], shown at the Film Guild Cinema, for its part is a thoroughly banal and sentimental glorification of patriotic frenzy during the World War. The Russian movie *Scandal* [1929, dir. Ivan Perestiani], also at the Film Guild, although more human and not infrequently, though sometimes unintentionally, amusing, is conventional in its technique and is spoiled by loquacious titling. Perhaps the worst picture seen in a long time, however, is *Rasputin* [1928, dir. Nikolai Larin & Boris Nevolin]. It would be difficult to find its equal for cinematic incompetence, amateurish acting, and stupidity of narrative.

Alas, even films heralded in New York as great achievements of cinematic art turn out to be, in the majority of cases, extremely disappointing. A case in point is Alberto Cavalcanti's *Sea Fever* [1928]. In its attempt to create a mood by mere views of scenery, long pauses, and slow acting, it succeeds only in making one thoroughly bored. One feels that the director was searching for some elusive, poetic quality but that he utterly failed to capture it—in striking contrast to John Mansfield's 1902 poem "Sea Fever," which is quoted throughout the picture. (*The Nation*, November 13, 1929)

10. A Miracle: *Arsenal* (1928), dir. Alexander Dovzhenko.

They are still coming from Russia those breathtaking revelations of genius that instantly make cinematic history. You may doubt this statement if you see *Arsenal* [1928, dir. Alexander Dovzhenko] only once. I was doubtful myself when I saw it for the first time. But I have no doubts now after my second visit to the theater. *Arsenal* is one of the most beautiful motion pictures that have ever been shown. In Russia today they judge works of art by their social significance; the artist, like any craftsman, must execute a "social order." Alexander Dovzhenko, the director of *Arsenal*, has fulfilled this requirement, I understand, to the complete satisfaction of his customer. But he has done more. He has produced a piece of palpitating reality that transcends its immediate political message, and that reaches into the ideal realm where rights are rights and wrongs are wrongs simply because the artist willed them to be so.

I am not sure, for instance, that communism as a religious cult is any less grotesque and funny than is the cult of nationalism. What does it matter? When I see *Arsenal*, communism is right with me and nationalism all wrong, and I laugh at the Ukrainian patriots glorying in their embroidered shirts and cascades of patriotic oratory, or hate their cool executioners who shoot Bolsheviks like rats, while my heart goes out to the poor dying soldier who, in his death-bed letter to his parents, inquires if he may kill officers and bourgeois if he meets them on the street. There it is. The artist has made you accept his characters in the light in which he wants them to be seen, and you surrender yourself to the spell of his art because he has succeeded in creating an independent, ideal world, entirely self-sustained and coherently compact, which has its own life and its own emotional logic.

It is strange that one should be so conscious of this inner unity, given that the first impression one gets from *Arsenal* is that of utter incoherence. There is hardly any story in the film. Groups of soldiers fight other groups of soldiers, incidental characters spring up from nowhere and disappear into nowhere, and you hardly know who is who or what it is all about. But once you have become familiar with the faces and grasped the general line of action, every character and every scene fall into their proper place as part of an emotional pattern. It is the great achievement of Dovzhenko that he has built this pattern and bound his picture together by means of a purely cinematic treatment of rhythm. Nothing so rich in contrasts, so subtle in nuances, has yet been done on the screen. The fury of the revolutionary struggle, its tragedies and its hilarities, are all brought out by variations in rhythm that range from complete stillness, with characters posing like statues, to breathless speed that carries everything before it like so much litter in a gale.

The episode of a runaway train, for example—outwardly unconnected with the story—acquires symbolic significance as a rhythmic accent in a symphony of struggle that is the real story of *Arsenal.* There are two or three scenes, however, in which the symbolism appears to be somewhat forced, as the characters, standing still in unnatural positions, do symbolical duty in a picture of life that is essentially realistic. But if this is a blemish, it is a minor one. The movie as a whole is an amazing production, no less rich in its technical resourcefulness than in its dramatic sense of human character. Moreover, it is splendidly acted.

In *The Last Performance* [1929] Paul Fejos, for his part, has probably directed his best film. At least it shows a marked originality in treatment—unaccompanied, however, by anything equally original in the appreciation of dramatic values. (*The Nation*, November 27, 1929)

11. The Eye and the Heart: *The New Babylon* (1929), dir. Grigori Kozintsev & Leonid Trauberg; *Condemned* (1929), dir. Wesley Ruggles.

In considering works of literature and drama we have come to recognize that the mere sequence of events described does not constitute their whole "story." The manner in which the events are described and unfolded is as much a part of the story as are the events themselves. The same consideration obviously applies to the motion picture. Like novels and plays the motion picture tells the story with a multitude of means that all contribute to the total effect. The only difference is that its means are peculiarly its own, and especially so in the case of the silent picture. It will be remembered that the American silent picture, now defunct, relied for its effect mainly on the action of the characters. The Germans and the Russians between them, while giving a peculiar national twist to their plots, have also brought into play a number of other means of expression. Notably, they have emphasized the pictorial appeal to the eye and dynamic or rhythmic continuity. It is still a debatable question whether the pictorial or the dynamic emphasis is the more potent, and whether the former when applied in the motion picture should not be completely dissociated from the forms that it developed in the art of painting, and made to seek a purely cinematic form in the dynamic foundation of the motion picture itself.

In my opinion, the art of the cinema has no business to imitate the art of painting either in the matter of composition, of lighting effects, of surface texture, or of the treatment of human character. Least of all can it afford to do it when it attempts to tell a story of dramatic significance. But I should not say that films that lay particular stress on their pictorial appeal are not interesting. Some of them will titillate your pictorial palate, if you happen to have one, with such choice relishes that you will forget everything else. *The New Babylon* [1929], the latest Russian arrival, almost comes within this class. Anyone who remembers his Manet, his Renoir, or his Degas will find their characters suddenly come to life with all the atmosphere that their masters gave them, and almost with their masters' brush strokes. They do not strike attitudes as painters' models but move about with perfect poise and naturalness; sometimes they even indulge in a veritable orgy of movement. Yet they always retain a certain quality of reality about them, as if they were ghosts masquerading in human clothes. If it were not a story of the Paris Commune that these characters unfold before us we might possibly accept them for real beings, but the Maeterlinckian touch of otherworldliness in the midst of the struggle for a new life in a real world seems to defeat the very message of the story.

Those who like stories of adventure, with all the romance that pertains to their heroes, will enjoy Ronald Colman in his latest debonair effort called *Condemned* [1929]. One does not apply the criteria of psychological truth to pictures of this kind. All one asks of them is that they should be plausible. And *Condemned* is plausible besides being amusing, racy, and, in the end, quite thrilling. It is also rich in detail in depicting the life of the penal colony on Devil's Island, though with the accent on Colman's deviltry the devil of the island somewhat recedes into the background.

It is just because *The Trespasser* [1929, Edmund Goulding] tries to deal with serious matters of life (a strong-willed woman elopes and gives birth out of wedlock without telling her ex-husband) that one must pronounce it a less satisfying picture than *Condemned*. Gloria Swanson acquits herself creditably in this her first appearance in a talking picture, but the story is utterly unreal for our day. (*The Nation*, December 11, 1929)

12. Mostly "For the Family": *The Taming of the Shrew* (1929), dir. Sam Taylor; *Pandora's Box* (1929), dir. G. W. Pabst.

Broadway may go on eagerly pursuing "sophistication," a near relative of "corruption by something spurious or foreign," but Hollywood sticks to simple human nature, which in the matter of dramatic entertainment demands no more than the plainest fare and rather enjoys what the doctors call "roughage."

Thus to Douglas Fairbanks and Mary Pickford go the well-deserved plaudits of their admirers, who, in *The Taming of the Shrew* [1929, dir. Sam Taylor], get as much genuine fun as could be extracted from Shakespeare by the rough though good-natured process of squeezing him into the Hollywood mold of slapstick comedy. I am not particularly aggrieved about the Bard's discomfiture, for, after all, *The Taming of the Shrew* was only the Hollywood fare of its day. But it is to be regretted that in carrying out his interesting experiment, Fairbanks made no attempt to use some of the excellent material in the play for a more original and more cinematic treatment of the dialogue. As it stands, Fairbanks's adaptation is merely a silent picture of the conventional pattern, with the subtitles spoken by the actors instead of being read by the audience. Even so, there is very little dialogue, while long stretches of the film are given over to silent comic "business." That would hardly disturb the peace of the great magician of words, albeit his phrasing is less felicitous in this comedy than in many of his other plays.

Shakespeare, however, wrote for his coarse contemporaries, who had a voracious appetite for finely spun words, whereas Fairbanks has to please our more civilized children of the Henry Ford age, who have left most of the bother of growing up and aging to their machines, while, like all children, they revel in the spectacle of people tumbling into the mud or rolling down steps, of chairs' and cushions' being thrown about, or of any other horseplay. More is the pity, as Fairbanks is an ideal Petruchio (I regret I cannot say the same of Pickford as Katherina) and can speak his lines, when he has the chance, with a gusto and a sensuous delight in the sound of words that could not be bettered. With the camera used searchingly and dramatically, the duel of wits in the first scene between Petruchio and Katherina could therefore have been made a sparkling and glamorous thing. Instead, most of the lines in this scene have been cut out, and the whip has been enthroned where wit was supposed to reign.

The public that likes boisterous fun in its feminine part is even more thrilled, on its masculine side, by sentimental crooning about "a kiss in the morning and a kiss at night." Rudy Vallee is an unassuming young man with a pleasant voice, and in *The Vagabond Lover* [1929, dir. Marshall Neilan] he gives his admirers what they long for—a succession of songs to the accompaniment of a jazz band, which makes their hearts melt and fills their beings with a glow of romance. Those who write to Vallee can also get his signed photograph; of this privilege, announced over the radio, the Vallee worshipers have lately been availing themselves to the tune of about 5,000 photos a day.

If the two films just reviewed were made expressly "for the family," the American censors saw to it that the German film *Pandora's Box* [1929, dir. G. W. Pabst] conformed to the same standard of morality. In the process the original, which was obviously intended for adults only, lost a great deal in footage and, what is more, its only *raison d'être*, since besides its rather pleasing photography this ponderous and indifferently acted picture has little to commend it to any moviegoer. (*The Nation*, December 25, 1929)

13. As You Were: *The Virginian* (1929), dir. Victor Fleming; *The Mighty* (1929), dir. John Cromwell.

A curious change has come over Hollywood within the space of a single year. Last winter when the film producers decided to take a plunge into the production of talking pictures, Hollywood was all in a state of turmoil as it peered anxiously into the future and made frantic efforts to adjust itself to the new conditions. Today, to judge by its recent movies, it must be again enjoying the comfortable feeling of restored stability, in fact, of being back where it was before all this rumpus began. There is indeed something almost uncanny in the ease with which the new medium has been turned to the old uses and the whole industry placed back on its accustomed rails. After all the talk about the revolution that the talking picture was going to create in the art of the cinema, one is startled to find that the

Hollywood talkie of today is barely distinguishable from its familiar silent predecessor.

To be sure, subtitles have given place to spoken dialogue, but in refutation of the early fears that dialogue is bound to slow up action, one finds the talkie just as fast-moving as the silent picture ever was. Side by side with this undeniably positive achievement, Hollywood has succeeded in retaining practically all the other features that characterized its typical product. In spite of the Russians and the Germans, it still glories in the straight photography that refuses to look for anything but the obvious. Its treatment of character and dramatic situation is still as impersonal as it is in a newsreel. And in its choice of subject matter, with a few rare exceptions, it clings stubbornly to the kind of story that is best appreciated by juvenile intelligence.

But even on the existing popular level of Hollywood pictures, there are degrees of quality and some established standards of competence. It is by bearing in mind these standards that one can comment at all on the recent crop of movies to appear on Broadway. Choosing the most notable among the latter, it is possible to say that *The Virginian* [1929, dir. Victor Fleming] is quite up to the standard of a good Hollywood western, with perhaps a little more respect for the realities of the life described than is usual in this highly conventional but entertaining genre; that *The Mighty* [1929, dir. John Cromwell] is as thrilling a drama of the underworld as can possibly be—that is, for a story of a gunman reformed by the love of a respectable young lady and enforcing the law against his old associates; and that *The Laughing Lady* [1929, dir. Victor Schertzinger], which attempts a portrait of society life, is rather more deliberate and heavy in the mechanics of its plot than can be accepted even by movie-trained credulity.

For real originality in the use of sound on the screen, one has to turn to the remarkable animated cartoons designed by Walt Disney. One of them, *Springtime* [1929], belonging to the *Silly Symphony* series [1929-39], is shown on the same program with *The Virginian*. Like its predecessor in the same series, *The Skeleton Dance* [1929, dir. Walt

Disney], *Springtime* makes an extremely clever use of characteristic rhythm and melody to enhance its grotesque humor and fancy. (*The Nation*, January 22, 1930)

14. Screen Musical Comedy I: *The Love Parade* (1929), dir. Ernst Lubitsch.

A great deal can be said for as well as against the exact reproduction of a stage performance in a motion picture. But to stress this issue today would be to overlook the fact that the technical powers of the motion picture are still wholly inadequate for creating the illusion of a performance *that is enacted within the walls of a theater*. Nothing less than such an illusion can justify the use of stage technique on the screen, and the penalty for ignoring such a truth is a painful incongruity that often borders on the inept.

Screen adaptations of musical comedies are particularly open to criticism on this score. For the current season, the Hollywood workshops have been turning them out by the dozen, with the majority patterned faithfully after their stage model. In the few cases where music and dancing were incidental and woven more or less intelligently into the story, the pictures were at least bearable, and occasionally, as in *Sunny Side Up* [1929, dir. David Butler], even quite entertaining. It is, however, the attempt to adapt to the screen the conventional genre of stage musical comedy that deserves greater consideration, in spite of the poverty of artistic thought that it represents.

It scarcely needs pointing out that the conventions of musical comedy derive whatever meaning they have from their being a frank entertainment on a stage that is physically connected with the audience. The characters' suddenly breaking into song or forming themselves into dancing columns never consists of anything more than mere actors whose only concern is to entertain those who are watching their performance. For its part, the audience expects from them nothing more. It disregards the absurdities of the plot or the antics of the characters, because it never associates them with real life.

The screen imitators of musical comedy seem to be ignorant of this essential relationship between the actor and the spectator. They place their characters in perfectly natural surroundings, introduce them as perfectly normal people, and then make them behave as if they were escaped lunatics. Far be it from me to suggest that highly conventionalized acting is impossible on the screen. On the contrary, it is one of the things that the motion picture needs most, but the convention used must spring from the peculiar properties of the cinema and not from those of the stage.

Today the screen, in the strict sense of the term, is merely a neutral surface for carrying images, and only helps to emphasize the gap that divides the picture from the audience. But it is the only possible link between the two, and to make this link perform its service as liaison, the visual images must be hitched to the screen. In other words, the screen must become a physical reality in the eyes of the audience, a part of the theater building that provides the graphic frame of reference for the very being of characters in space, as well as for the form in which they are presented to view. By this means a motion picture will not merely be demonstrated or exhibited, but will actually be performed before the spectator, and a basis will be supplied for conventionalized acting of every kind, including that of musical comedy.

The absence of such a cinematic approach in *The Love Parade* [1929, dir. Ernst Lubitsch] is particularly regrettable, for, apart from its treatment of singing, this picture is a very remarkable achievement in cinematic comedy. The surprising thing about *The Love Parade* is that its most telling comic effects are produced not by Maurice Chevalier's acting, which in this movie is only moderately good, but by the deft juxtaposition and contrast of scenes provided by the director, Ernst Lubitsch. In the field of light comedy, Hollywood has no greater master than Lubitsch.

One wishes there were the same avoidance of the heavy or obvious in *Sally* [1929, dir. John Francis Dillon]. This film shops the charming personality of Marilyn Miller to some advantage, but it is a routine piece of work in all other respects. (*The Nation*, February 5, 1930)

15. A Soviet Fantasy: *A Fragment of an Empire* (1929), dir. Fridrikh Ermler; *Demon of the Steppes* (1926), dir. Cheslav Sabinsky & Lev Sheffer.

Political sympathies enter to such a large extent into the public appreciation of Russian films that it is something of a problem to consider *A Fragment of an Empire* [1929] on its merits exclusively as a motion picture. Here is unquestionably an unusual piece of work if measured by the standards of Hollywood. It deals with the interesting if not quite original theme of a man who suddenly finds himself in a new world, unaware of the changes that took place while he was suffering from the effects of amnesia. It also employs some very striking images to describe the man's experiences and reactions. Moreover—which is rare—the acting in it is reserved and sensitive. With all this excellent material *A Fragment of an Empire* might have been a great movie. It actually falls short of this by a very considerable margin.

Perhaps the most disappointing thing about it is its treatment of the new ways of life in Soviet Russia as they reveal themselves to the primitive mind of a peasant worker who remembers only the Russia of the czars. The war scenes that make up the first half of the picture, though not quite relevant to the theme and somewhat overburdened with symbolism, are magnificently conceived. One expects an equal wealth of imagery and an equal sense of dramatic contrast in the scenes that describe the impact of the new life on a mind that has been bound by tradition and ruled by the idea of the sacred rights of master over his men, of husband over his wife, of father over his children. Here was an opportunity to show the remarkable changes wrought by the revolution in the status and mentality of the worker.

But just at this point inspiration seems to have deserted the authors of the picture. Their hero, on recovering memory and returning to Petrograd, is thrown into a state of utter bewilderment by such trivial changes as a monument to Lenin—of whom he had probably never heard—a block of new buildings, the short skirts worn by women, and the fact that the old owner of the factory in which he used to work no longer owns it. On the other hand, the picture makes hardly any attempt to show the reactions of the man to his new social standing and new opportunities for enjoying life. In fact, in one respect, namely, the relationship between husband and wife, *A Fragment of an Empire* seems to suggest that there has been no change at all, our hero recovering his wife from a man whom she has been obeying with as much docility as she had probably obeyed her previous spouse.

Of the two other silent films recently shown, suffice it to say that *Demon of the Steppes* [1926] is a rather mediocre Russian item, and *The Last Night* [1928, A. W. Sandberg] a somewhat better German one. Richard Barthelmess, who distinguished himself in the part of a Chinaman in D. W. Griffith's *Broken Blossoms* [1919], plays another Chinaman in *Son of the Gods* [1930, Frank Lloyd], an effort to show the injustice of racial discrimination that culminates in a complete surrender to existing prejudices. The Oriental color of the picture is about as authentic as Hollywood can make it, and the same must be said of the credibility of the story. The only feature of the picture deserving praise is the very able acting of Constance Bennett.

The appearance of a singer from the Metropolitan Opera in a full-length motion picture may be a portent of the times, indicating the trend toward a screen opera, but Lawrence Tibbett's vocalizing in *The Rogue Song* [1930, Lionel Barrymore] fails to make this musical travesty a notable achievement in any other respect. Except for a few ballet scenes, the movie is quite crude. One wonders what its makers were thinking . . . or at which audience they were aiming. (*The Nation*, February 19, 1930)

16. Inflated "Grandeur": *Happy Days* (1929), dir. Benjamin Stoloff; *Puttin' on the Ritz* (1930), dir. Edward Sloman.

I do not know if any psychologist has tried to analyze the peculiar complexes that dominate the minds of the film-manufacturing colony in Hollywood, but I am certain that the people there suffer from some strange mental disease. Taken individually they seem to have the normal quota of intelligence, technical competence, and even imagination. In any collective effort, however, they almost invariably sink to sheer puerility. Witness the present Hollywood craze for plots dealing with stage life. Picture after picture has shown us the miraculous rise of an unknown vaudeville actor to stardom on Broadway.

Why, you will ask, this persistent riding to death of a patently trivial subject? Because the public demands it? No, I am sure the reason is simply that Hollywood finds in stage life the easiest formula for making a song-and-dance show realistically plausible. It has obviously never occurred to the film producers that actors today are much more anxious to attain stardom in Hollywood than on Broadway. Nor has it occurred to them that a film-within-a-film provides as many opportunities for singing and dancing as does a play-within-a-play or, to be more precise, a play-within-a-film. But then, to make singing and dancing expressly cinematic, something that belongs intrinsically to the screen instead of being a slavish copy of the stage, requires a little thinking and a little imagination, whereas aping the stage requires none.

It is this strange preference for the trite and hackneyed that makes *Happy Days* [1929] such a painful disappointment. For *Happy Days* is not an ordinary picture. It is an experiment designed to herald forth a new achievement in cinematic technique—the enlarged projection. You would think that with the increased screen space at their command, the producers would have tried to present their entertainers (since the picture is largely a revue) in all the variety of simultaneous contrasts and juxtapositions made possible by the enlarged projection. You would expect to see the screen surface used for weaving decorative and rhythmic patterns built up of different groups of actors and dancers on the principle of parallel action. But what do you find? A not particularly bright comic introduction of stage life leading up to a glorified but uncommonly dull minstrel show, both of which derive no greater benefit from the larger screen than the ability to show an increased number of people at the same time or a full-sized figure on a scale approximating the normal. Neither of these advantages is of much importance except for reproducing the effect of the stage.

By contrast with *Happy Days, Puttin' on the Ritz* [1930] may almost pass for a Hollywood masterpiece. To be sure, it has its defects—the inevitable story of a vaudeville team and all the stage business that goes with it—but it breaks away from the routine in a number of scenes, notably, in Harry Richman's spirited dance against the perfervid movements of the chorus. For this alone, Edward Sloman, the director, deserves high praise.

Praise is also due to George Arliss for his brilliant acting in *The Green Goddess* [1930, Alfred E. Green], a slight but entertaining skit by William Archer that does not obtrude its stage descent on the screen, although it does not achieve any cinematic distinction, either. As a comedy, *Not So Dumb* [1930] is itself sufficiently amusing, with Marion Davies proving herself a very able comedienne. King Vidor's direction of the picture, however, is only competent, and from him, of all Hollywood directors, we are entitled to expect something far more inspiring. (*The Nation*, March 5, 1930)

17. Color: *The Vagabond King* (1930), dir. Ludwig Berger; *Men Without Women* (1930), dir. John Ford.

It has been frequently maintained that the screen has no need of color—in fact, that the use of color in the motion picture is a step backward from the goal of artistic perfection. On the other hand, in the whole range of problems that have occupied the minds of film producers during the past twenty years, none has aroused greater interest or has been pursued with greater deliberation than the problem of color. Today the technical goal has been practically reached. Color has been captured for the screen. It is true that the hues reproduced are not always faithful to nature and, what is even more important, are not always pleasant to the eye. But even with these shortcomings, Technicolor, the process that has been the most successful in the field, may be said to have solved the problem within a measurable distance of the ideal. There remains the question: Do we need color in the movies? Does it add anything to their powers of artistic expression? The answer may be profitably sought in some of the recent color pictures, of which *The Vagabond King* (1930) and *Song of the West* (1930, Ray Enright) are the latest to arrive on Broadway.

The evidence in this matter supplied by *Song of the West* can be easily disposed of, since it merely demonstrates the fact that bad color does not improve an otherwise bad picture. Indeed, it is very doubtful if any color, no matter how good, could have saved this insipid and poorly acted operetta, which manages to squeeze a modern revue chorus into a story of the days of "the covered wagon." As it is, smudgy color, glaring lights, and feeble composition, relieved only by one or two rather delicate close-ups, contribute neither to the illusion of real life nor to the enhancement of the dramatic or the decorative effect.

To pass from *Song of the West* to *The Vagabond King* is to realize the enormous possibilities that are latent in the use of color. Even if we concede considerable merit to the story, dialogue, and acting in *The Vagabond King* (in spite of the incongruity of the conventions that the film borrows from the stage), it is its color that makes this picture so different from others and so vibrant with dramatic sentiment and pictorial loveliness. The romantic fantasy of François Villon's seven-day adventure as the king of France called for an emotional atmosphere that would combine purity and lust, serenity and frenzy. In the picture this atmosphere is suggested mostly by the play of color. Not only is the quality of color in many single scenes most appealing to the eye, but it also succeeds in charging some of the scenes with a greatly enhanced dramatic significance.

The naïve enthusiasts who have been denouncing color in favor of black and white as the only "art" form of the movies must be either color-blind or simply ignorant of the artistic quality that distinguishes one visual sensation from another. There can be no question that color is one of the most important means of cinematic expression. The irony of the situation is that it is derided by those who profess to be concerned with the art of the cinema, while it is brought into practical use and developed by those to whom "art," like hypocrisy, is only a tribute that vice pays to virtue.

So much of the Hollywood output is banal and trivial that any picture showing serious interest in human life is assured of attracting general attention. *Men Without Women* (1930), a picture shown at Manhattan's Roxy and the Film Guild, reveals this commendable concern with real life and does so in a series of tensely dramatic and largely convincing scenes. This is a picture decidedly worth seeing. (*The Nation*, March 19, 1930)

18. Small Mercies: *China Express* (1929), dir. Ilya Trauberg; *Anna Christie* (1930), dir. Clarence Brown.

In Soviet Russia the cinematic artist, like any other artist, is supposed to be concerned only with the cause of communism. Very often he will deny that he is an artist at all, claiming, as Sergei Eisenstein does, that he is merely an engineer, a technician. It is therefore something of a paradox that, outside Russia, Soviet films have been acclaimed as masterpieces of cinematic art, superior to anything produced in other countries, whereas these pictures' preoccupation with communism has been regarded as their least important feature. But paradox or not, Soviet directors continue to surprise foreign audiences by the vigor and resourcefulness of their imagination.

China Express [a.k.a. *The Blue Express*; 1929, dir. Ilya Trauberg] fully maintains this reputation for high imaginative quality. Treated as a dramatic poem, it unfolds its story with a tremendous power of imagery and motion, ending in a breathtaking climax featuring a rushing train that no power on earth seems to be able to stop. This apotheosis of a rebellion as the symbol of the Chinese Revolution [of 1911], together with the sustained dramatic movement of the picture and the rich variety of its characteristic human material, speaks highly for the art of its director, Ilya Trauberg. They prove not quite sufficient, however, to make the movie wholly convincing. The obstacle is chiefly in the scenario, which treats its social theme in a way that is too conventional to impart to the picture the quality of a fresh and independent approach to life, which was so notable a feature of some of earlier Russian films.

China Express is not merely the story of some passengers on a train. It is an attempt to show a cross-section of China, with all the conflicting interests of its different classes. Here we have the downtrodden coolies, the babbling liberal merchants, the ruthless representative of the ruling European capitalists, and the native military who are the capitalists' obedient tools. The story is set in motion by means of the attempted rape of a Chinese child by a white overseer, which leads to a rising of the coolies and their seizure of the train by victory over the indigenous troops and their European masters. Now this may be good communism, but the schematic relationship of characters according to formula, and their automatic falling into groups of heroes and villains, can scarcely be described as a fresh and independent view of life.

Soviet films, let it be said, represent the highest development of the silent cinema. The advance made by the Hollywood talkies has been chiefly technical; artistically, the talkies are still in the nursery. The high praise bestowed on some recent American movies leaves this opinion unshaken. One finds very little that oversteps Hollywood conventions in the much-lauded *Sarah and Son* [1930, dir. Dorothy Arzner], for example, although one may admit that Ruth Chatterton acts her part with complete sincerity and splendid restraint, and that the general treatment of the picture is skillful. Nor can *Anna Christie* [1930, dir. Clarence Brown], with Greta Garbo in the principal role, be accepted as a notable achievement in cinematic art. Again, it may be admitted that Garbo acquits herself quite creditably, particularly in scenes such as the opening one. On the other hand, even her performance is rather uneven, failing pitifully in the big scene at the end; while the film as a whole, largely through poor direction, fails to maintain dramatic unity and suspense. (*The Nation*, April 2, 1930)

19. Delightful Lunacy: *The Man from Blankley's* (1930), dir. Alfred E. Green; *Mammy* (1930), dir. Michael Curtiz.

Today the author's part in the talking picture is undoubtedly much more important than it used to be in the days of the silent picture, but his exact contribution still remains a great deal of a mystery. As an example one may quote *The Man from Blankley's* [1930], the honors of whose authorship are distributed by the program among the "author," the "screen adaptor," and the "dialogist." In this case, therefore, unless one has read the original 1903 play by F. Anstey [Thomas Anstey Guthrie], one really does not know whether the credit for the delightful dialogue of the picture should go to him or to the "dialogist"; nor does one know whether upon him or the "screen adaptor" should be fastened the blame for the thinness of the plot and the triviality of some of the scenes. Despite this uncertainty, however, let it be stated with all haste that *The Man from Blankley's* is a picture decidedly different from the general run of Hollywood productions. It has "quality"—the quality of subtle and imaginative literary intelligence—shining through its lines, though it lacks similar distinction in its dramatic and cinematic aspects.

It gives one a quite pleasant shock to discover a world as poignantly grotesque and whimsical as that in *Alice in Wonderland* [1865, Lewis Carroll] or in Anton Chekhov's *The Wedding* [1889] in what ostensibly is unpretentious farcical comedy poking gentle fun at a collection of Victorian freaks. Indeed, the Dickensian flavor of the picture, to which reference is made in the program, extends no farther than the make-up and costumes of its characters, whereas there is a distinct echo of Carroll and Chekhov in the delicious disquisition on the peculiarities of scarabs, and in such bits of conversation as the remark by one of the guests that "hair does not grow under the legs of a rhinoceros." The striking resemblance of *The Man from Blankley's* to *The Wedding* can hardly escape notice, particularly in the parallel of a lord and a general who to themselves act the parts of hired guests at party. But in both scripts the plot is only a peg on which the authors hang the wistful lunacy of their characters, and one's only regret is that compared with Chekhov's play, *The Man from Blankley's* is just a little too tame. John Barrymore does play the tipsy lord excellently, and of the rest of the cast the midgety Tiny Jones in the small part of Miss Bule mingles her eccentricity with almost enough pathos to create a memorable image. But apart from its dialogue and acting the picture can boast of no cinematic virtues. It imitates the stage quite expertly, but gets no farther than that. It is to be hoped that even Hollywood will one day realize that cinematic treatment of dialogue is not confined to close-ups of the speaking characters.

Though Hollywood has not yet learned how to give music from the screen instead of reproducing it as it is given from the stage, *Song o' My Heart* [1930, Frank Borzage], starring John McCormack, deserves praise for the technical quality of its reproduction of sound and the apposite simplicity as well as persuasive tranquility of its acting and setting.

Speaking of music, one does not look for any kind of "sophistication" in Al Jolson's pictures, but it seems as if the brand of sentimental appeal so skillfully exploited by this artist were beginning to wear rather thin. *Mammy* [1930, Michael Curtiz] is, of course, another instance of backstage life, this time of the minstrel variety, and with its simulacrum of a plot it provides Jolson with sufficient opportunities for singing Irving Berlin's reminiscences of the world's music direct from the stage platform. Jolson is a gifted enough artist to try get away from a formula beginning to pall: I shall wait. (*The Nation*, April 16, 1930)

20. End of the Road: *Journey's End* (1930), dir. James Whale.

Is *Journey's End* [1930, dir. James Whale] the movie masterpiece that it is claimed to be, or is its popularity merely a passing vogue? Whatever the answer, it is clear that the story owes its present success not so much to the fidelity with which it reproduces life at the front line (its picture of that life sins rather on the side of idealization) as to the moral appeal of the unobtrusive and matter-of-fact gallantry that culminates its action. But having already asked "What price glory?" it is quite possible that some day some of us may also ask, "What price gallantry?" We may become critical not only about the business of killing, but also about the business of being killed. For it is true that we admire gallantry in others because we recognize the ordeal that being in their place would be to us; because, too, as a rule we are directly or indirectly benefited by these feats of heroism, and therefore cannot possibly regard them as deserving anything but our greatest admiration.

Hence, as long as society is conceded the right to call upon the individual to perform the supreme sacrifice, so long shall we have this far-from-disinterested cult of heroism, and so long will the "gentlemanly" Anglo-Saxons glory at the spectacle of gallantry that is unobtrusive and self-effacing. To brand the specific code of honor that permeates *Journey's End* as bourgeois (which it undoubtedly is) will no more solve the problem than to invoke the same code, with appropriate adjustments, in behalf of proletarian class rule or the Nietzschean superman. After all, it does not really make much difference whether one is invited to destroy oneself for the greater glory or a nation, of a class, of the human race as a whole, or of the improved human species of a million years hence.

With these reservations concerning the fundamental values embodied in *Journey's End*, one must admit that the actual spectacle of guiltless men walking docilely their "last mile" is in itself stirring enough to hold one in its grip from first scene to last. In this respect the film version of *Journey's End* is even more tense than the original stage play of the same title [1928, R. C. Sherriff], for it is less diluted by the orderly's amusing remarks on food and, unlike the play, provides a few scenes of actual fighting. It also gains in comparison by the greater detail and relief that the cinematic treatment bestows on its characters.

On the other hand, tersely as the story is told on the screen, it lacks the more subtle play of contrasts that marks the progress of action on the stage; and the movie additionally fails to create the atmosphere of uncanny ordinariness and uneventfulness that hides the inferno of war horrors—something which the stage somehow succeeds in suggesting. Nevertheless, of its kind the film is a remarkable achievement, notable for the success with which it has preserved the dramatic qualities that went into the making of the original play. It would be an exaggeration to say that *Journey's End* is a cinematic masterpiece, for it never attempts to assert its independence of the stage and to express itself entirely in terms of the cinema; but the picture is skillful and intelligent as far as it goes, and this is no small merit for anything that comes out of Hollywood.

Under a Texas Moon [1930, dir. Michael Curtiz] is as different from *Journey's End* as a light extravaganza can be from the grim realities of life. Unlike the latter picture, too, it shows a divided mind in both its narrative and its direction, with the disastrous result that inevitably follows such indecision. The trouble with the movie is that its producers could not make up their minds whether it was to be a piece of exaggerated romanticism or a satire on such romanticism. Had the satire been left out, the movie would have gained immensely, and Frank Fay would have been able to make the character he plays with such penetration and charm a piece of truly unique and subtle portraiture. (*The Nation*, April 30, 1930)

21. Eisenstein and Pudovkin: *Old and New*, a.k.a. *The General Line* (1929), dir. Sergei Eisenstein; *Storm over Asia* (1928), dir. Vsevolod Pudovkin.

If I tried to list the scenes that impressed me most in *Old and New* [a.k.a. *The General Line*, 1929], Sergei Eisenstein's remarkable sermon on the advantages of collective farming, I should be inclined to select these: the pathetic figures of a man and a woman as they pull a barrow for want of a horse; the enormous mass of smooth and glistening flesh displayed by the *kulak* couple; the "juicy" portraits of priests praying for rain, interspersed for sardonic contrast with close-ups of bleating sheep; the wheat fields swept by wind; the gorgeous stud bulls with their quivering bulk. All these may be described as portrait studies, here and there reminiscent of such Russian painters as Ilya Repin, Boris Kustodiev, and Vasily Perov, but conceived dynamically, not as still pictures, and brimful of characteristic detail.

Perhaps it will even be no exaggeration to say that *Old and New* resolves itself largely into a serious of marvelously executed cinematic portraits of men, beasts, and machines, portraits observed with a revealing penetration and the precision of a master—but strung together on a thread of narrative that carries with it no particular appeal either to the mind or to the heart. The movie was of course made primarily for the Russian peasant, as part of the campaign to carry the "general line" of Communist policy into the villages. It is therefore not to be expected that the demonstration, however ingeniously conceived, of a cream separator or a tractor would be found equally impressive by an American audience. But with all due allowance for this difference, it is still doubtful whether *Old and New* is capable of converting *anybody* to its message; and the fault, I think, does not lie with the message. Regarded merely as an argument for collective farming, the film quite obviously takes too many things for granted. On the other hand, as the story of a successful struggle for the life of such a collective farm, it is too tame and schematic in its dramatic development to make one thrill in sympathetic response.

This is not to say that *Old and New* does not contain a number of highly effective and original scenes, as previous noted. The episode of the "wedding" between a stud bull and a common cow, serving as the village bride, itself is extremely amusing, not to say exciting; so, too, is the race between the tractor and the village carts, with the delightful interlude during which the driver of the tractor, to mend his engine, helps himself to the proffered skirt of a female enthusiast. But it does seem to me that Eisenstein's preoccupation with conveying ideas by means of a specially developed cinematic language is inevitably leading him into a blind alley, for it excludes the purely sensual and emotional appeal of the structural foundation of the cinema—its rhythmic and dramatic progression. His *Battleship Potemkin* [1925] undoubtedly gained its success because of the stress laid on the film's rhythmic and dramatic structure, elementary as this still was in its case. But *Ten Days That Shook the World* [a.k.a. *October*, 1927] was a step away from turning into analysis instead of synthesis, from becoming a series of loosely related descriptive episodes rather than demonstrating a unified dynamic-cum-thematic pattern. And *Old and New* is an even further, still more disintegrating step in the same direction. (*The Nation*, May 14, 1930)

Speaking of disintegrating steps, it is difficult to say what particular qualities in Vsevolod Pudovkin's *Storm over Asia* [1928] aroused so much enthusiasm in France and Germany, unless it be the film's rather cheap thrust at British imperialism (disguised, in the American version of the film, as White Russian imperialism). Apart from this, the only thing that seems to be of interest in the picture is its record of the exotic types and manners of Mongolia. (*The Nation*, May 14, 1930, & October 1, 1930)

22. American Natives and Nature: *The Silent Enemy* (1930), dir. H. P. Carver; *King of Jazz* (1930), dir. John Murray Anderson.

After innumerable travel pictures in which the less familiar parts of the world are presented in the manner of a snapshot album, with the tourist or the big-game hunter conspicuously in the fore, one turns with pleasure to a picture like *The Silent Enemy*, from which one does learn something about the life of a primitive tribe, with the joys and sorrows—particularly sorrows—that are attendant on it. Of course, the genre derives from Robert Flaherty's *Moana* [1926]—still unsurpassed for subtle observation and photographic beauty—and his also very interesting *Nanook of the North* [1922]. The next important contribution, a few years later, was made by Merian Cooper and Ernest Schoedsack with their *Grass: A Nation's Battle for Life* [1925] and *Chang: A Drama of the Wilderness* [1927].

It is from *Grass* that *The Silent Enemy*, like the recently shown British picture *The Wild Horse Stampede* [1926, Clifford Smith], derives more directly, all three pictures illustrating the same idea and differing from one another no more than is required by the differing peculiarities of the tribes they describe and the territories in which the episodes take place. In *Grass* we were given a vivid picture of a Persian tribe crossing a formidable mountain ridge in search of new pasture lands; *The Wild Horse Stampede* described a search for new hunting grounds by a Sudanese tribe; and now *The Silent Enemy*, with still greater vividness, tells us of the search for fresh hunting grounds by the Ojibway Indians in the Great Lakes district of Canada.

After suffering the great hardships of a long trek through snow-covered wilds, the Indian tribe arrives in time to intercept the migrating herds of caribou. We are shown the overwhelming spectacle of the stampede of the animals—a photographic feat that seems to surpass everything of the kind this writer has seen on the screen, even if one assumes that much of the action was "staged." H. P. Carver, who directed the picture, and his assistants deserve every credit for the skill shown in the shooting of this scene, as well as of many other marvelously observed incidents in the life of wild animals. Great praise is also due the natives for their "acting," which is extraordinarily expressive while remaining perfectly unforced and natural. On the debit side, however, one must note the conventional treatment of the plot, with heroism, villainy, and "love interest" injected in approved fairy-tale fashion.

In the field of the talking picture, and of the screen revue in particular, *King of Jazz*, directed by John Murray Anderson [1930], marks another step of progress. Following *Paramount on Parade* [1930, Dorothy Arzner et al.], which rose above the customary ineptitudes of Hollywood in the matter of sketches, *King of Jazz* rises above other revues in discarding the stage setting and making a fuller use of the methods of the silent picture, with a stress on the spectacular that is somewhat reminiscent of *Intolerance* [1916, D. W. Griffith]. We must now wait for the next step—a revue making cinematic use of speech and music as well as of visual images. (*The Nation*, May 28, 1930)

23. Stark War: *All Quiet on the Western Front* (1930), dir. Lewis Milestone; *Westfront 1918* (1930), dir. G. W. Pabst.

According to one of Bernard Shaw's pet theories, in the matter of ideas the stage is usually ten years behind literature. It would be difficult to say how far behind the cinema is, for as a rule it cares precious little about ideas. But there is one exception. Let the idea attract public interest, let the work of fiction in which it has found expression be a bestseller, and no expense will keep the film companies from producing the book as a movie as quickly as they can get the rights. During the past year the Great War was the most popular subject in literature, and for once, to refute Bernard Shaw, also on the stage; and so the novel of *All Quiet on the Western Front* [1929, Erich Maria Remarque], as well as the play *Journey's End* [1928, R. C. Sherriff], has already found its way onto the screen. Need it be added that both cost tremendous sums to produce (two million, it is said, in the case of *All Quiet*), and that both have been unprecedented box-office successes?

There can be little doubt that Remarque's *All Quiet on the Western Front* is not a great literary masterpiece. At least this was the conclusion that I arrived at after I had found that nearly every page of the book required a special focusing of imagination in order to bring out in clear relief the episodes and facts that stud the author's guileless and inarticulate prose. Nevertheless, there is no denying the interest and importance of the story as a human document. No book had spoken so courageously and, granting the necessary effort of mental readjustment, so vividly of the sheer horror of war—of man's relapse into bestiality, with its frenzy of fear and rage, of his physical suffering and moral prostration.

It is as just as a document that *All Quiet on the Western Front* [1930, dir. Lewis Milestone] emerges in a film of the same name—a terrifying record that reveals the carnage of war with staggering force. Battle scenes have been represented in many a picture, but *All Quiet* surpasses them all in the stark horror and madness of the business of fighting. Although the movie is not devoid of gentler moods, and is sprinkled generously with captivating humor, the predominant impression is that of life in the raw, of existence stripped of all adornments and bared to the bone. For this reason, the total effect produced is not so much the tragedy of war as its callous cruelty. One is shaken, and then staggered, even almost ready to sob, but one is not really thrilled. Probably because of the elemental quality of its material, *All Quiet* is not so good a drama as the film of *Journey's End* [1930, dir. James Whale]; but its appeal is more immediate and, technically, it is a superior piece of cinematic craftsmanship for which achievement Lewis Milestone, who directed the work, deserves unstinted praise.

It is the same fidelity to fact, the same documentary value of a record, that to me, in my ignorance of German, seems to be the most important feature of the German war film *Westfront 1918* [1930, dir. G. W. Pabst]. Scenes of actual fighting have perhaps been somewhat overdone on the screen, but in this picture they still succeed in making one shudder at the horror of the whole ghastly business. One realizes, however, that the effect is achieved not so much by a few supremely revealing images, like those unforgettable scenes in *The End of St. Petersburg* [1927, dir. Vsevolod Pudovkin] or *Fragment of an Empire* [1929, dir. Fridrikh Ermler], as by the cruder method of piling up the purely physical terrors of ceaseless bombardment and brutal fighting. The story itself appears to be convincing enough, though, in spite of director G. W. Pabst's preoccupation with psychoanalysis, it does not strike one as a very subtle or profound study of human behavior. (*The Nation*, June 11, 1930, & March 18, 1931)

24. A Lesson from Moscow: *Cain and Artem* (1929), dir. Pavel Petrov-Bytov.

It is to be assumed that only the best of the Soviet pictures are exported abroad. But whatever those kept for home consumption may be, no country has yet equaled the Soviet record on the movie screens of America as set during the past season in the following, extraordinary series of films: *Arsenal* [1928, dir. Alexander Dovzhenko], *New Babylon*

[1929, dir. Grigori Kozintsev & Leonid Trauberg], *A Fragment of an Empire* [1929, dir. Fridrikh Ermler], *China Express* [a.k.a. *The Blue Express*; 1929, dir. Ilya Trauberg], *Old and New* [a.k.a. *The General Line*; 1929, dir. Sergei Eisenstein], and *Turksib* [1929, dir. Viktor A. Turin], to which now we have to add *Cain and Artem* [1929, dir. Pavel Petrov-Bytov]. Without claiming for all these works the exalted name of masterpiece, it must be admitted that their general level of excellence is something altogether unprecedented in the history of the cinema. Whether one approves, or does not approve, of the main line of development in the Soviet cinema, Moscow's leadership today is as indisputable as it is highly welcome.

The latest Soviet arrival, *Cain and Artem*, would have made a sensation if it had appeared three years ago when the silent film was still holding sway. In these days of the talking picture, it would do Hollywood an unholy amount of good to learn this picture's methods of telling a plain, straightforward story both intelligently and imaginatively. Unlike so many Soviet films, *Cain and Artem* has no political ax to grind, or perhaps it has just enough to observe the Soviet proprieties without appreciably spoiling the story. The movie is as broad in its appeal, as tersely dramatic, and as full of color as Hollywood could wish. But over and above this, it has something that so far only Moscow has been able to supply—a freedom from the stereotyped and a genuine pathos.

The plot of the *Cain and Artem*, which is based on Maxim Gorky's 1898 short story, is concerned with the romance of the wife of an elderly fishmonger with a handsome longshoreman, Artem, the sullen and bullying hero of a marketplace in a small Volga town. With the help of a few hired toughs, the jealous husband nearly succeeds in doing away with Artem; but taken care of by a little Jew, Cain, a mender of boots, Artem recovers, while the fishmonger's wife, believing Artem dead, drowns herself in despair.

Around this simple plot, the director, Pavel Petrov-Bytov, has painted a portrait, rich in vibrant colors, of the stifling, stagnant life of the little toiling and trading folk in old Russia. The marketplace is the focus of that life, and as one striking detail after another is presented, the spectacle of a few sensitive souls suffering in the midst of dismal poverty, filth, brutality, and superstition takes on the quality of something that is tangibly real. Then the plot begins to develop, and the dramatic situation, growing in intensity, passes through a series of rising climaxes. Here again the director's masterly treatment brings out the utmost in each situation, and now and then strikes a note of marked originality, as in the use of distorted images, or in the cross-cutting to the woman as she walks down the steps to the river bank and the view of the water ahead.

Next to the richness of characteristic detail and its telling use for dramatic effect, the most notable feature of the movie is Emil Gal's acting in the part of Cain. This is a rare example of acting in which it is impossible to detect a single false note—so convincing and so moving is it in revealing the beauty of character that otherwise irradiates the unkempt and sorry image of the little Jew. Among the blemishes that mar the picture, the most significant is the too theatrical conception of the part of Artem, which finds its expression even in his make-up as a kind of tattered toreador. (*The Nation*, June 25, 1930)

25. Enter Japan: *Slums of Tokyo* (1928), dir. Teinosuke Kinugasa.

We hear very little about Japanese films. Many hundreds are said to be produced annually in Japan, but so far New York has seen only two: *A Daughter of Two Fathers* [a.k.a. *The Situation of the Human World*; 1928, Gosho Heinosuke], shown last summer, and *Slums of Tokyo* [a.k.a. *Crossroads*; 1928, dir. Teinosule Kinugasa], the current picture at the Fifty-Fifth Street Playhouse. It is difficult to say on such slender evidence how far one may regard these two works as representative of the Japanese cinema. One may note only that they are distinctly different from the typical American and European movies. The quality that sets the Japanese films apart is mainly their peculiar earnestness. No sophistication of any kind is visible in them. Traditional moral values are never questioned. The struggle with the adversities or life is couched in terms of extreme simplicity; the point of view has the naïveté characteristic of primitive communities. To the Western mind this makes the same sort of appeal that the natural simplicity of children does. It is refreshing in its ingenuousness.

But such an appeal also has its weak points. Having outgrown the patriarchal stage of family life, we find it difficult to be moved by the spectacle of paternal love as it rises in triumph over all obstacles, or to be thrilled by the self-sacrificing loyalty of a sister to her erring brother. There is a sentimental attitude here that cannot but seem forced to our Western eyes. This largely accounts for the failure of the two pictures mentioned to be fully convincing. One feels this particularly about *Slums of Tokyo*, which expounds upon the sister-brother theme, although here the failure is partly attributable to a theatrical treatment of the material that was less evident in *A Daughter of Two Fathers*. The latter clearly belonged to the naturalistic school of filmmaking and consequently shared all the limitations of that school. By contrast, *Slums of Tokyo* exhibits a cinematic technique of considerable imaginative power, but it is technique that has the serious defect of echoing the conventions of the Japanese national stage.

The principal character in this movie, Rikiya, whose infatuation with a geisha results in his losing his sight at the hands of a rival, is played by an actor whose make-up and bodily gestures are clearly reminiscent of those very conventions. Much as we may admire masks on the stage, where the setting is wholly conventional, on the screen, amidst the surroundings of natural life, the barest suggestion of such artifice strikes a harshly discordant note. Moreover, the high emotional tension apparent behind the emphasized movements and facial expressions of this actor suggests a deaf mute struggling to break into speech—an effect that makes one feel as if this *silent* picture were incomplete without spoken dialogue. The cumulative effect is that the *Slums of Tokyo*, though produced with evident care and photographic skill, and though abounding in extremely interesting glimpses of Japanese life, rather drags in telling its story and falls short at its most dramatic moments. (*The Nation*, July 23, 1930)

26. Where Broadway Scores: *Holiday* (1930), dir. Edward H. Griffith; *The Big House* (1930), dir. George Hill.

Those inscrutable ways of Providence! Haven't we all been bewailing the pernicious influence of Broadway on the youthful and inexperienced talkie? Haven't we been deploring the latter's readiness to ape the ways and habits of the stage, while suppressing the promptings of its own cinematic nature? Today we have to admit that Broadway's influence has not been all for the bad. With the milk of Broadway dialogue, Hollywood has been obliged to imbibe some of its intelligence as well. No doubt, from the perspective of even a few years, Broadway successes are apt to lose a great deal of their glamor. But in one respect they are undeniably superior to Hollywood creations: they represent adult standards of intelligence if not always of artistic appreciation. Injection of intelligence into pictures by means of dialogue may not be an unmixed blessing from the point of view of future developments, but the future will take care of itself. For the present it is a relief to encounter movies that are not made expressly for the juvenile mind.

In this class belongs *Holiday* [1930, dir. Edward H. Griffith], based on Philip Barry's 1928 play of the same name. Of cinematic values expressive of its own medium *Holiday* has none. It has hardly a scene to suggest the searching power of the camera. The development of its plot is borne entirely by its dialogue, and no attempt is made to indulge in cinematic embroidery on the principal theme of the film, the rebellion of romantic youth against Babbittry—even when the story provides such an excellent opportunity as the ballroom scene. In short, the direction of the movie follows faithfully the stage model.

Still, *Holiday* is undoubtedly one of the best talkies yet produced. It is distinguished both by the quality of the play and by the acting. Its story and dialogue, if not profound or important, are fresh and entertaining. Its acting is light and expressive. Ann Harding in the part of Linda Seton deserves the highest honors, for not only is her acting polished, but, what is more, it is convincing—no mean achievement in a part as vague and contradictory as that of Linda. Harding is also the fortunate possessor of a rare gift among screen actresses, a voice of a very beautiful timbre, with a tragic note in its well-modulated range of expressions that rings true.

Even if we have to come down a step, intellectually, in adjusting ourselves to the true Hollywood standards, we cannot help giving credit to, and even grudgingly admiring, the display of realistic thrills that is provided by *The Big House* [1930, dir. George Hill]. This is a mighty good melodrama rising to a climax in the breathtaking spectacle of a pitched battle between mutinous convicts and the authorities. Apart from this scene, the chief interest of the film lies in its portrait of prison life, a subject sufficiently unfamiliar to the majority of moviegoers to seem startling. It is, of course, only for the experts to say whether the details of the portrait are entirely authentic. Surely they have enough truth in them, however, to serve as a needed revelation of so ghastly an aspect of our civilization. Probably the effect of *The Big House* would be even stronger if the narrative showed a little more originality and eschewed stock characters. But Hollywood will be Hollywood—and still is. (*The Nation*, August 6, 1930)

27. Ingredients: *The Dawn Patrol* (1930), dir. Howard Hawks; *Manslaughter* (1930), dir. George Abbott.

Exciting physical action, suspense, and surprise in the plot, as well as characters that look "different"—these ingredients of a good Hollywood movie are most effective when they are served together in a well-balanced mixture. Thus the three films under review, *The Dawn Patrol* [1930, dir. Howard Hawks], *Manslaughter* [1930, dir. George Abbott], and *Grumpy* [1930, dir. George Cukor & Cyril Gardner], would probably be vastly more entertaining if the qualities they severally represent were joined in a single picture. As they are, these works provide excellent illustration of the inadequacy of one-sided growth.

The Dawn Patrol, for instance, is based mainly on the physical thrill of aerial warfare. Although following in the trail of several other, similar pictures, it succeeds in contriving a number of scenes of aerial bombardment and fighting that are undeniably exciting. But it must have been clear to the producers that this was not enough, for a considerable part of the movie is used in building up a situation that is supposed to invest the fighting episodes with dramatic significance. We are introduced to the life of a group of pilot-officers on a section of the British front where the daily flying operations are inevitably accompanied by the loss of a few men. Resentment against this seemingly deliberate slaughter flares up now and again, and bitter words are exchanged between those issuing the orders and those obliged to carry them out. But the war goes on, and so does the daily sacrifice of the fliers.

One notices the similarity of the theme to that of *Journey's End* [1930, dir. James Whale], as well as a few resemblances in the minor episodes of the two films. The similarity in itself need not be counted as a sin in *The Dawn Patrol*—although the Cockney orderly is becoming something of a bore. A far more important defect is that the picture never succeeds in shaping its plot—the little that it has—into anything psychologically convincing. The conflicts among the officers seem to be so deliberate as to be forced; nor is the lack of motivation compensated for by any arresting character portraiture. On the contrary, most of the characters are utterly colorless, as is also the acting, with the notable exception of the minor part of Lieutenant Phipps, which is played by Edmund Breon with great subtlety.

In *Manslaughter*, for its part, there is little physical action; nor is any attempt made in it to suggest a more profound reading of character than is to be found in the archness of a society girl or the zeal for rectitude of an honest lawyer. On the other hand, although its "dramatic struggle of beauty and wealth against the law" is no more exciting than it reads, it is handled by George Abbott, who directed the movie, with such suave deftness that one almost accepts the story at face value. At all events, the picture has a visual swing about it that makes watching it a pleasure for the eye. The attempt to superimpose sounds and to externalize the auditory sensations of the heroine deserves notice, although, as in *Blackmail* [1929, dir. Alfred Hitchcock], it fails of effect owing to the abrupt change of style.

Characterization as practically the sole ingredient of the film, to the exclusion of physical movement and any serious plot, is exemplified by *Grumpy*, in which Cyril Maude re-creates for the screen his famous portrait of a freakish old gentleman turned Sherlock Holmes. In spite of its pronounced theatrical quality, this is a delightful and highly entertaining performance. But apart from Maude, the movie is rather poor. The developments of its very slight plot are treated with a heavy hand, and the supporting cast is mediocre. But Maude himself is really good fun. (*The Nation*, August 20, 1930)

28. Devil or Angel: *Hell's Angels* (1929), dir. Howard Hughes; *Moby Dick* (1930), dir. Lloyd Bacon.

So much has been made of the fact that it cost nearly four million dollars to produce *Hell's Angels* [1929], Howard Hughes's epic of war in the air, that I am prompted to state with all haste that the picture is not nearly so bad as the fact referred to might lead one to expect. On the other hand, I am also compelled to admit that it is not so good as it might have been, perhaps at a quarter of its actual cost, had its producer [Hughes, who also directed] known better where to look for his value. One has the feeling that the film succeeds mainly in spite of his conscious efforts. For the really exciting scenes in *Hell's Angels* are of two kinds: instances of superb photography, like the view of the Zeppelin as it speeds its way through the clouds, or the breathtaking scene of a falling airplane, followed by the camera throughout its progress without a single cut; and, secondly, instances of purely spectacular action, like the burning of the Zeppelin or the destruction of the munitions depot.

In all these scenes the effect produced is truly magnificent. But if the beauty of the photography seems to have been merely incidental to the use of the material, the spectacular thrills mentioned, I suspect, were themselves not quite authentic. And it was realistic authenticity—so we are repeatedly told in the program—that was the declared aim of the producer, and which accounted for most of the expenditure of the four million. The battle scenes in the air between the British and German squadrons are a costly attempt at realism, it must be said. But interesting as these are in parts, particularly in the long-shot views of the free-for-all dogfight, they are not very impressive as a whole. The far too numerous close-ups of men and machines with which this sequence is studded are, in spite of their seeming authenticity, as obviously theatrical as any studio close-ups would be. Nor is there visible in this sequence much dramatic and rhythmic organization by way of montage. One misses the heightened and almost tangible sense of movement that one found in *The Big Parade* [1925, dir. King Vidor] or *Battleship Potemkin* [1925, dir. Sergei Eisenstein].

So far no mention has been made of the story of the picture. Perhaps it is just as well, for, poor on all accounts, it becomes intolerable because of the persistence with which it thrusts its lurid banalities into the procession of aerial splendors. A really interesting story for a movie like *Hell's Angels* should have stuck to the clouds rather than to the earth. Indeed, it is a pity that the dramatic possibilities of clouds are made so little use of in this picture. There is a hint at such a dramatic effect in the Zeppelin sequence when the airship suddenly disappears in a cloud. For the rest, we get our clouds merely as a pictorial background. And yet what wonderful *dramatis personae* they would have made had the hide-and-seek motif of the plot been more consistently developed. Judging the film by what it has, however, rather than by what it has not, *Hell's Angels*, on the whole, is a very creditable production, with some moments of surpassing beauty.

The new sound version of *Moby Dick* [1930, dir. Lloyd Bacon] impresses one as a very tame and conventional treatment of a subject that, in the hands of a cinematic genius, might have equaled the stupendous quality of Herman Melville's 1851 masterpiece. In this case, suffice it to say that the overwhelming grandeur of the image of the whale finds no better expression than a few shots of actual whale hunting, supplemented by shots of a wooden model. As for Captain Arab, John Barrymore's Satanism does not seem very convincing. What else can I say? (*The Nation*, September 3, 1930)

29. Griffith's New Epic: *Abraham Lincoln* (1930), dir. D. W. Griffith.

In this still undeveloped and primitive art of the movies, which is ruled by standards several degrees below those that are acknowledged in other arts, fame and achievement mean precisely as much as you are willing to grant them. There can be no doubt, for instance, that the bombastic platitudes and mawkish sentimentality of such films as *The Birth of a Nation* [1915], *Intolerance* [1916], *Orphans of the Storm* [1921], and *Way Down East* [1920] are the very qualities that endeared their author, D. W. Griffith, to the masses of the American public. Yet it would be unfair to judge Griffith only by his reputation as a popular movie director. His main claim to be included in the first rank of the artists of the cinema is based on something much more solid than the frothy sentiment of his grand epics. In Griffith the art of the motion picture had its first real craftsman—one who knew how to tell a story by means of the camera and the editing. A pioneer in the use of such devices as parallel action, the close-up, and the fade-out, he at the same time showed himself to be the complete master of his material, and to have a sense of dramatic action and expressive detail that placed him head and shoulders above his early contemporaries.

Now, in *Abraham Lincoln* [1930], Griffith is attempting to recapture some of his old glory. By the standards of his early work, he almost succeeds in doing so. *Abraham Lincoln* has an epic grandeur comparable to that of *The Birth of a Nation*. But the art of the motion picture has not remained still during the past ten years, at least outside America; and its more recent advances, one feels, take a great deal of luster out of Griffith's present achievement.

It is to be counted to Griffith's credit that the story of *Abraham Lincoln* is completely free of the false pathos that made the refrain of "the cradle, endlessly rocking" in *Intolerance* so painfully vulgar. The forthright simplicity of the new film has much genuine charm, and one could hardly wish for anything better in the matter of the delineation of character and general atmosphere. Lincoln himself, as played by Walter Huston, and most of the other characters are completely convincing. The moving scene of the bleak, bare tree stumps in the opening and concluding shots demonstrates Griffith's sense of pictorial atmosphere. Indeed, the photography is excellent throughout *Abraham Lincoln*, and one notes with pleasure the battle scenes as examples of perfectly "clean and neat" warfare, which is so different from the inevitable mud and corpses in shell holes of the other recent war movies.

It is only when the picture is viewed as a whole that one realizes its essential defect, its lack of dramatic quality. Probably, because of its discursiveness, which sprang inevitably from the desire to cover as much ground as possible, the real drama that was in Lincoln's life story somehow fails to emerge. Though well maintained, the interest in the story never culminates in one of those sweeping climaxes that made the early Griffith films so effective.

Though *Abraham Lincoln* may signify Griffith's return to popular favor and box-office success, then, it discloses no evidence of a step forward in the direction of the cinematic uses of sound. As a talkie, *Abraham Lincoln* is a good old silent Griffith film. And much as we are pleased to renew acquaintance with an old master, we should have liked it more if we saw as much originality in his tackling of the new problems of the cinema as he had shown in the past in tackling the problems of his day. (*The Nation*, September 17, 1930)

30. Screen Musical Comedy II: *Monte Carlo* (1930), dir. Ernst Lubitsch; *Animal Crackers* (1930), dir. Victor Heerman.

Musical comedy is not a subject to be approached lightly by a critic. He may be excused for writing about it in the facetious tone characteristic of the genre itself, but may he be serious about it? At the risk of appearing a lowbrow to some, and a bore to others, I propose to be nothing but serious in discussing *Monte Carlo* [1930, dir. Ernst Lubitsch] and *Animal Crackers* [1930, dir. Victor Heerman]. After all, entertaining as these two pictures are, the question as to why they are not more entertaining does not seem to be particularly funny, though their comedy, of course, is—comedy that, by the very nature of things, belongs to all things Hollywood.

Strictly speaking, the problem is not the same in both movies. *Animal Crackers* is essentially a farce in which a quartet of delightful loonies is let loose regardless of consequences. Since the loonies are those excellent entertainers the Marx Brothers, the only quarrel I can pick with the picture is the tameness of its direction apart from its dialogue and gags. A little detail, the painted moustache of Groucho's make-up, may serve to illustrate this point. That a character supposed to be merely a freak should be thus stamped as a stage comedian is an incongruity to be explained only by the inability of the actor and director to shake off their memories of the theater.

Incidental in *Animal Crackers*, this problem of the stage and its conventions becomes the dominant factor in *Monte Carlo*. Here we are presented with the deft and at times very witty efforts of that grand master of Hollywood, Ernst Lubitsch, to acclimatize the theatrical musical comedy to the screen. Let it be it remembered that the musical comedy in question is not that of *The Jazz Singer* [1927, dir. Alan Crosland] or *The Dance of Life* [1929, dir. John Cromwell & A. Edward Sutherland], where singing and dancing flowed naturally from the fact that the characters were singers and dancers. No, in *Monte Carlo* as in his earlier *Love Parade* [1929], Lubitsch is out to capture the very spirit of the artificial, conventional musical comedy, with its music and dancing as means of dramatic expression independent of the realistic requirements of the plot.

It must be admitted that these realistic requirements have stymied Lubitsch here, as they have stymied others elsewhere. In fact, every time he introduces singing (in solos, duets, and even choruses), he feels obliged to disguise the procedure by some device, at which he is often extremely ingenious. It must even be regretfully stated that *most* of Lubitsch's ingenuity in *Monte Carlo* is directed at disguising the staginess of the musical-comedy convention, whereas in *The Love Parade* he allowed himself a few brilliantly successful flings at something much more creative and original—namely, combining independent sounds and images by the process of cutting. Seeing that the final solution of the problem of musical acting on the screen can be found only in the direction of such an assembling of sounds and images, I am baffled by the short-sightedness of the Hollywood producers, who have not yet commissioned a single director to explore to the full this tremendous field of cinematic possibilities.

The artistic justification of musical comedy on the theater stage lies in its frank emphasis of its own staginess. But no actor on the screen can make the audience accept him as an actor. He is, and will always remain, a character. On the screen the power of direct contact with the audience can be wielded only by one person, the man who pulls the strings behind the scenes: the director. In order to achieve this aim, however, he must stress the arrangement, the graphic pattern, of his images on the screen in their interrelation with sounds. There is much more to be done in this area than merely to diversify visual images that are strung together by continuous dialogue, song, or orchestral accompaniment, as in most of *Monte Carlo*; or to combine independent, characteristic sounds into a dramatic unison, whether simultaneous as in the train scenes of *Monte Carlo* or consecutive as in the episode of the barking dogs in *The Love Parade*. I particularly look forward to the use of split-screen technique, which more than any other technique promises to help develop a purely cinematic convention of musical comedy—as well as straight drama. (*The Nation*, October 1, 1930)

31. The Grafted Narrative: *The White Hell of Pitz Palu* (1929), dir. Arnold Fanck & G. W. Pabst; *With Byrd at the South Pole* (1930, doc.), dir. Julian Johnson.

So thanks to Admiral Richard Byrd and his companions we can now actually look at the South Pole. And what a desolate place it is! No enchanted castle that hides a sleeping beauty, no dragons, no monsters of any kind—only a wilderness of snow, bleak and dreary. I doubt that the place is interesting enough to attract the tourist even were trips there as cheap as they are to Paris. But that is the trouble with so many of these mysteries of the world. Stripped of their secrets, they are so utterly unexciting.

This is not to say that Byrd's adventure lacked in excitement. There were perils enough and to spare, and the Antarctic blizzards were as much on their guard to thwart the intrepid explorers as any dragons could have been. It was only by a long and careful study of the habits of these blizzards that Byrd succeeded in slipping through and reaching his goal. Even then he had to fall back as fast as he could to escape their fury. A glorious adventure! As tensely dramatic as any exploit on the part of ancient heroes.

To have preserved its thrill by means of an authentic record on film would have been a service to humanity. *With Byrd at the South Pole* [1930, doc.; dir. Julian Johnston] does not quite convey this thrill, although it tries to make up for the missing drama in its record of the Antarctic through a machine-gun rattle of spoken comment. But if the climax of the movie is somewhat flat, there is a great deal that is exciting as well as amusing in the rest of it. One recalls the magnificent views of the barrier ice-shelf, the amazing scene that shows whales popping out of the water within a few feet of the members of the expedition, the all-but-human penguins as they take stock of the invaders, the amusing glimpses into the family life of seals, the wonderful dogs. The film also records innumerable fine scenes of the little band of adventurers as they construct their homes, fight the blizzards, explore, study, and indulge in the amenities of social life in

Antarctica—all the time displaying the superb determination that eventually brought them to their goal. As a travel picture, *With Byrd at the South Pole* is one of the best.

And now for a different kind of travel picture . . . Although a great deal of the danger so frequently encountered by characters in screen thrillers is nothing but screen illusion, there is no denying the purely physical appeal of such a record of Alpine adventure as *The White Hell of Pitz Palu* [1929, dir. Arnold Fanck & G. W. Pabst]. Here nature itself is alive with drama as it bares its gaping abysses, rises in towering walls of ice, or breaks into the fury of blizzards and avalanches. Added to this, there is a visual loneliness that casts a sweet enchantment even over the perils of Alpine mountaineering, or at least so it appears to one ensconced in a comfortable seat as he watches the Alpine glories so amazingly recorded in this German film. But, of course, the wonders of the Alps do not make up the entire picture. It has a fictional story, too—a rather juvenile affair of no particular consequence, but good enough to do duty as the framework for the thrills of climbing a most formidable peak, and as the vehicle for some fairly able acting.

There is one feature of this American version of the film that deserves special consideration. Like the earlier documentary of Byrd's expedition to the South Pole, *The White Hell of Pitz Palu* is accompanied here and there by spoken narrative. Charles McNamee, of radio fame, is the narrator in the present case, but his efforts, like those of Floyd Gibbons in *With Byrd at the South Pole*, never succeed in heightening the drama of the story. In fact, they rather detract from it. One has to admit, of course, that the flights of both these narrators into lyrical and dramatic rhetoric are tinged, and rather heavily, with tabloid bathos. But it would be unfair to blame them alone for their failure. The idea of a spoken narrative running parallel with the movie is not only legitimate in itself, but is also extremely promising as a novel cinematic form. It must be applied intelligently, however, and this implies a relationship between words and images that makes them inseparable from one another.

It is said that in Japan, silent films have always been explained to the audience in a highly dramatized commentary supplied by a special, permanently employed actor. To a large extent this is an easy substitute for foreign titles. But a silent movie, made as a silent movie, should hardly require such extraneous help. It is only when images are used to *illustrate* a spoken narrative that the combination of the two becomes natural, and it is only when pictures and words bear a close correspondence to one another that their joint use becomes effective. To be fully successful, however, this presupposes a new "hieroglyphic" technique of which Hollywood today has not the ghost of a notion. (*The Nation,* July 9, 1930, & October 15, 1930)

32. The Mother of Us All: *Earth* (1930), dir. Alexander Dovzhenko.

There are many features in *Earth* [1930], a Soviet film directed by Alexander Dovzhenko, that will make it extremely popular in certain art-minded sections of the public. In the pictorial loveliness of its scenes, for instance, it has few equals. One can hardly fail to be impressed by the rich mellowness of its wheat fields and skies, the noble gorgeousness of its pedigreed cattle, the quiet lusciousness of its fruit, the loving delineation of its interesting Ukrainian types. The lyrical mood that pervades the picture will also put it in a class apart, imparting a poetic quality that seems to lift the story above ordinary life.

At times *Earth* even goes so far as to discard the natural movements of its characters and to substitute for them stylized posing or highly exaggerated action. Indeed, though the narrative is ostensibly political in its message—the story of a bitter conflict between a *kulak*, or rich peasant, and an "activist," a supporter of the Communist land policy— it is wrapped in a pantheistic sentiment that spreads a veil of eternity over all incidents of human life, reducing the dramatic conflict to a mere episode in the endless cycle of birth, love, and death.

Such poetic earnestness as this, such artistic and intellectual superiority over the commercial trivialities of Hollywood, are bound, I repeat, to earn the film the enthusiastic applause of the art-house audience. For my part, however, I must confess to a rather painful disappointment. The early reports from Moscow, where the picture was hailed as the supreme achievement of Soviet cinematic art, and the memories of Dovzhenko's glorious masterpiece, *Arsenal* [1928], held out the prospect of a new miracle. Alas, the miracle never came to pass. The man of genius chose to exploit his weaknesses rather than his strength. Thus we have had to see the riotous exuberance of *Arsenal* give place to the disciplined uniformity of *Earth*, the overwhelming dynamism and symphonic rhythm of the former recede before the static pictorial loneliness of the latter; while symbolic eccentricities that were casual in *Arsenal* have now become a dominant feature, unconvincing and forced where they find expression in mannered acting and rather platitudinous in their imagery.

To top matters off, the poetic sentiment that has, in *Earth*, displaced the fervent passion of *Arsenal*'s thoroughly communistic treatment of its story does not strike me as being particularly profound or significant. There is no denying, of course, the extraordinary power of Dovzhenko's imagination, but it seems rather late in the day to draw from the symbolist bag such ancient devices as the masklike face and the stylized movement, both of which, moreover, demand a stylized setting.

Judged by Hollywood standards, *Earth* is a great picture. Judged by the standards of *The Last Laugh* [1924, dir. F. W. Murnau], *Battleship Potemkin* [1925, dir. Sergei Eisenstein], and Dovzhenko's own *Arsenal*, it is a cinematic aberration and a step backward. (*The Nation*, October 29, 1930)

33. The Romantic Western: *Billy the Kid* (1930), dir. King Vidor; *The Big Trail* (1930), dir. Raoul Walsh.

The Wild West is again very prominently with us on the screen. Time was when the western film was the most popular as well as the most characteristic product of cinematic art. To the majority of its admirers it provided, to use the cant phrase, "an easy escape from actuality."

Yet there were also many who did not eschew actuality but who enjoyed a western for the sheer force of its physical movement, for its sweeping dynamics, just as they enjoyed a good circus show. The present revival of the western film raises the problem of whether, in its new form of the talkie, it has preserved the old elements of its appeal, and whether the western can still find favor with lowbrows and highbrows alike.

It is very probable that there are as many people today as there used to be who are genuinely stirred by the "romance" of the Wild West. To these, the screen-made romance of the *talking* West is likely to be a little less stirring, for with the use of dialogue a picture becomes either more intellectual or more stupid. In the old western, acting was of slight importance, whereas action was the very lifeblood of the movie. Today the use of dialogue makes acting much more important than before, and this means either that the characterization and psychology are more true to life, with the resultant loss of romance, or that the picture confines itself to the traditional stock types and situations and therefore uses dialogue that is downright silly. On the other hand, the action, the sheer dynamic, of the western plot has suffered greatly from the dilution with words and the consequent slowing down of tempo. On the face of this, it would seem that our more intellectual admirers of the western, who cannot stomach the genre in cold print in magazine stories but who used to enjoy its purely sensuous appeal on the silent screen, will find its new form rather a strain on their intellectual forbearance.

These reflections are illustrated in different degrees by the three western films under review. *Billy the Kid* [1930, dir. King Vidor] tells a credible story distinguished by well-marked characterization and natural dialogue. It is these qualities, however, which, while enhancing its realism, also deflate its romance and retard its movement. *The Big Trail* [1930, dir. Raoul Walsh] is more conventional in characterization and dialogue, but lays greater stress on mass scenes and panoramic effects, in which it is undeniably highly impressive. It must be pointed out, though, that sound has added nothing to the appeal of the picture, perhaps has even taken something away through its stilted dialogue, whereas in its purely visual effects the movie is reminiscent of many previous historical epics of the West.

An interesting feature of both *The Big Trail* and *Billy the Kid* is the employment of the wide screen, but one cannot help regretting that neither King Vidor nor Raoul Walsh saw any uses for this valuable device other than those that enhance realism. Finally, we have *The Girl of the Golden West* [1930, dir. John Francis Dillon], a screen version of David Belasco's 1905 play, which attempts to get away from the stereotyped psychology of the western romance and in doing so achieves neither romance nor psychology.

Of the foreign talkies so far shown in New York, one has attracted considerable attention. The British movie called *Murder!* [1930], the work of Alfred Hitchcock, who earlier directed the talkie *Blackmail* [1929], is excellently acted and shows a commendable desire to make the utmost use of the cinematic possibilities of sound. Unfortunately, the sense of dramatic and filmic style is not a strong point with Hitchcock, and his would-be original idea of getting inside the minds of the characters results only in a few weird effects without much thematic significance. (*The Nation*, November 12, 1930)

34. The Wages of Talent: *Kismet* (1930), dir. John Francis Dillon; *Playboy of Paris* (1930), dir. Ludwig Berger.

It is an old complaint that Hollywood kills talent, kills it because huge, soulless organizations can neither tolerate talent nor understand it. The fact has been made familiar to us by the fate of several foreign and American actors and directors who went to Hollywood with the reputation of distinguished artists. It would be an exaggeration to say that all of them have been crushed by the machine, but happy exceptions undeniably have been very few. Perhaps Sergei Eisenstein, the cancellation of whose contract with the Paramount Company has recently been announced, should thank the gods for escaping with his skin; the intelligent public, however, cannot but feel disappointed at the blasting of its hopes for higher standards of art from Hollywood as the result of Eisenstein's vitalizing influence.

If in the case of Eisenstein one suspects considerations other than artistic to have been the cause of his retirement, two other instances of the neglect of talent that are revealed in two recent films must be ascribed wholly to artistic ignorance and crass commercialism. At the Hollywood Theater, *Kismet* [1930], with Otis Skinner in the principal role, illustrates the blight of ignorance. One recalls a highly symbolic little episode that occurred in the same Hollywood Theater a few months earlier. A short film was shown as one of the opening items on the program. It commemorated the silver anniversary of the cinematic activities of Warner Brothers, and a galaxy of the company's stars was gathered for the occasion around a horseshoe table and introduced to the audience. What with the stellar smiles and occasional songs and the general splendor of the surroundings, the scene undoubtedly was very impressive, if rather dull. The fly in the ointment was the intolerably bright little girl, appropriately called "Miss Vitaphone," who did the introducing. But the unintended symbolism of the scene was revealed elsewhere. The *unannounced* old gentleman who opened the proceedings by introducing the impossible child was none other than Otis Skinner himself.

Somehow one cannot help feeling that in his present film, *Kismet*, Skinner has been served by his producers with as little respect for his talent as he was in that affair of the celebration. One would have thought that the presence of an actor of Skinner's attainments would have inspired the producers and directors with the desire to second his imaginative effort. They might have remembered, for instance, that the second-rate pastiche of a stage play also known as *Kismet* had swing and vigor that sprang from its color, from its exaggerated action, from its grotesque characterization. Because of that it showed speed even on the slow-moving stage. But the only trace of color to be found in the film adaptation is that preserved in the contrasts and resourceful virtuosity of Skinner's acting. With its slow and even tempo, with its lack of color and contrast, the film represents no more than a humdrum display of Hollywood's Oriental lore, and fails miserably to bring into relief Skinner's beautiful diction and masterful technique.

The Playboy of Paris, featuring Maurice Chevalier, is another instance of indifference to talent. That the picture is amusing in its crude way and is a great box-office success should not blind us to the fact that we are actually witnessing the burial of a very gifted artist, one with an effervescent and impish personality, under the weight of the obvious banalities of juvenile comedy. Chevalier is being Americanized, Hollywood-style, and if this goes on a little longer there will be no Maurice Chevalier left. Phfft! (*The Nation*, November 26, 1930)

35. The Travel Picture: *Wild Men of the Kalihari* (1930; doc), dir. C. Ernest Cadle; *Morocco* (1930), dir. Josef von Sternberg.

The experiment of a special theater for filmed news launched over a year ago by the Newsreel Theater must be pronounced a complete success, at least if the attendances at the theater can be taken as a criterion. The fact is very gratifying for those who believe in a differentiated cinema, a cinema that sets itself the aim of satisfying the more or less special interests and tastes of the various sections of the public. Under this heading comes the interest in educational subjects, and if the example of the Newsreel Theater finds imitators, as it should, there is no doubt that a theater devoted exclusively to educational films will be generously supported by the public.

At present the Cameo Theater bids fair to develop into such a specialized house. So far it has given particular prominence to travel pictures, of which *The Wild Men of Kalihari* [1930], following almost on the heels of *Africa Speaks!* [1930, Walter Futter], has been the latest exhibit. Other theaters, too, are of course showing travel pictures, and it is a significant fact that the same week that saw *The Wild Men of Kalihari* at the Cameo also saw *Hunting Tigers in India* [1930] at the Roxy and *Mediterranean Cruise* [1930] at the Fifth Avenue Playhouse. On the other hand, it must be admitted that, interesting as some travel films undoubtedly are, they are apt to pall when one has seen a few of them.

The trouble lies in the pictures themselves. Even when they do not repeat one another (natives and wild animals of "the dark continent" have been done almost to death), there are inherent limitations in the conventional type of travel film that make it largely ineffective. For one thing, it is not enough for a film to show a series of views and scenes that are interesting in real life. This is done in *Mediterranean Cruise*, a movie that suffers somewhat from poor photography. Scenery and people, however beautiful or unfamiliar they may be, can never impress the eye from the screen if they are nothing more than camera records devoid of any unifying concept or emotion. A travel film does not need a story in the sense of a plot, but it needs one in the sense of a connected exposition of a scientific idea, of an emotional narrative, or of a pictorial vision.

A similar criticism applies to *The Wild Men of Kalihari*, which claims to set on record the exploration of a scientific expedition, but manages only to romp inconsequentially about the African continent, to wind up in a rather flat account of the Kalihari Bushmen. How much more interesting the picture could have been had it tried to connect the Bushmen with the story of the recent finds of prehistoric human remains in South Africa!

There is, of course, a way of enhancing interest in a travel film by selecting dramatic episodes, as *Hunting Tigers in India* does with a fair measure of success by showing an Indian hunting pursuit with a force of 150 elephants closing in on three tigers. Or one can enhance dramatic situations by faking them, as was done in *Africa Speaks!* But by far the better way of improving the travel film is that of using the camera in order to illustrate an intellectual concept or to relate an emotional experience. A scientist in particular is overdue on the screen, on which anthropology, ethnography, and zoology, as disciplines, would be much more effective than the rambling observations of amateur travelers. In fact, the entire field of popular science should be brought to the screen for the edification of the man in the street. And it should be done by scientific institutions in cooperation with film producers rather than by the method that seems to be invading this particular field.

The advertiser, you see, is awakening to the possibilities of the screen. Within the same week there have been *Mediterranean Cruise*, manufactured by a great German shipping company and advertising its boat service, and a short film at the Rivoli, a revival of an earlier newsreel, which is presented "by the courtesy" of a well-known cigarette manufacturing company. The scientific short lends itself easily to such uses of publicity, as has been demonstrated in several pictures shown in the smaller theaters. The question is how far this development will go. It is only to be hoped that the practice will be discouraged, and that the insidious influence of the advertisers will be prevented from bringing the movies to a still lower level than they have already reached.

Morocco [1930], by the way, may be recommended as fair entertainment. *Just Imagine* [1930, David Butler] is decidedly not. (*The Nation*, December 10, 1930)

36. Selling Sophistication: *Fast and Loose* (1930), dir. Fred C. Newmeyer; *Laughter* (1930), dir. Harry d'Abbadie d'Arrast.

It is all very well for literary critics to discuss absolute standards and relative standards, standards (loud cheers) and standards (boos and catcalls). The movie critic has very little use for such fine distinctions. The only standard acknowledged in the movies is the Main Street standard, and whatever may be said of Main Street, I doubt if even Gilbert Chesterton will claim for it a highly developed sense of artistic discrimination. This is one of the reasons why it may be profitable sometimes to consider films not so much for what they are when judged by themselves as for the light they throw on the views and sentiments of the audience they have been made to please.

This week I have been moved to adopt this course by two pictures that seem to be particularly characteristic of the state of mind of the big public. They are *Fast and Loose* [1930], shown at the Paramount, and *Laughter* [1930], which preceded it there a week or two earlier. Of both of them it must be said that in their lightness of touch and their pains (sufficiently disguised) to get away from the obvious, they represent Hollywood at its best. That this best does not amount to very much if measured by the creative standard need not be stressed in this instance. The important fact about the two pictures is the evidence they contain of the workings of the Main Street mind. The evidence is of course indirect, for it comes only from the makers of the films; but these shrewd judges of their public know what they are doing, and when we see them selling "sophistication" to Main Street we can be sure that this is the sort of sophistication that Main Street wants and appreciates.

So, behold sophistication, grade "Society." We are introduced to a banker's family in a Long Island home. Bankers being the height of the social ambition of Main Street—the American equivalent, so to speak, of their lordships across the Ocean—the one in *Fast and Loose* is treated with all the deference that is due his rank. But unlike the bankers themselves, Main Street is rather scornful of British aristocracy, and accordingly it gets the silly ass of an English lord to satisfy its democratic resentment. So far it is all pretty orthodox. But with the young members of the family enters sophistication, or the want of it. The spoiled and irresponsible son and daughter kick against the boredom of conventional existence, the son deciding to marry a chorus girl, and the daughter choosing for her mate a young mechanic whom she meets at night bathing in a lonely spot. The affair of the daughter, a girl of Rossettian beauty as portrayed by Miriam Hopkins, is the high spot of the fast and loose behavior of the young sophisticates. One is startled at the discovery of the familiar twists and tricks of Shaw's *You Never Can Tell* [1899] and *Man and Superman* [1903] suddenly bobbing up in a film that uses them not only to shock its audience, but also to teach the lesson of the moral superiority of Main Street over Park Avenue.

In *Laughter* we are treated to another variety of sophistication that is being sold to Main Street—sophistication, grade "Artistic Bohemia." Here a young chorus girl married to a banker rebels against her loveless bondage to cars, frocks, and jewels, and goes back to her artist-musician to listen to him humming his latest masterpiece in the Café de la Paix, Paris. It is extraordinary how tenacious of life is this conception of an artist. It is true, his long hair has gone, but in the divine simplicity of his heart he still breaks into other people's houses, treats himself to anything he finds there, and even plays the piano with a leg of chicken in his hand. Main Street is sure to be hugely pleased, to a point, with this superb indifference to Emily Post's precepts of propriety.

As a descriptive picture of native life in Siberia *Igdenbu* [1930, dir. Amo Bek-Nazaryan], for its part, is highly recommended. Its story is rather weak, and in its treatment it does not come up to the level of *Moana* [1926, Robert Flaherty] or *Nanook of the North* [1922, Robert Flaherty], but it occasionally approaches them, and there is much in it that is truly beautiful. *Razlom* [a.k.a. *The Break-Up*; 1930, Lev Zamkovoy] deals with a revolutionary theme in a highly conventional manner— not a highly revolutionary one. (*The Nation*, December 24, 1930)

37. One Notable Achievement: *Sous les toits de Paris* (1930), dir. René Clair; *The Blue Angel* (1930), dir. Josef von Sternberg.

René Clair, the author and director of *Sous les toits de Paris* [*Under the Roofs of Paris*, 1930], enjoys the combined benefits of great talent and good fortune. He has produced a picture that in many ways is a little masterpiece, and he has been lucky enough to be the first artist in a field that has been dominated by Hollywood robots. Indeed, so great is one's relief and delight at seeing a fresh mind, unencumbered with hollow conventions and equipped with fine taste, subtle wit, and imaginative insight, apply itself to fashioning a work of art—so great is one's relief that the shortcomings of the film inevitably recede into the background. There I shall leave them for the moment, to stress the more important fact—the fascination and charm of Clair's offspring.

The quality of the movie is revealed almost from its opening scenes. The characters have hardly been introduced when the story halts on a scene in which a group of Parisian tenement dwellers, led by a young peddler of songs, engages in solemn singing in the fashion of the Salvation Army. The length of the song, the dullness of the music, and the solemnity of the voices would have been enough to condemn this scene for any Hollywood talkie. But here comes the miracle of art. By introducing a slight action, so slight that it is almost entirely confined to an exchange of glances between the peddler and a prowling pickpocket, the artist sets off the vital force. Instantly the characters become intensely alive, the singing acquires the quality of suspense, and the whole scene begins to sparkle with humor and to throb with the pulse of human life.

By vivifying touches such as this, René Clair transforms one scene after another into a palpitating reality. We observe their effect in the episode of the two friends' interrupting their altercation to turn on the fashionably dressed passers-by who stop to gaze at them; in the scene of another fight where a gramophone keeps wailing after the tune has played itself out, and where the face of a silent café *habitué* reveals a gamut of expressions that follows the action with a tale of its own; and in several other episodes throughout *Sous les toits de Paris*, too numerous to be listed here. All this testifies to the freshness of approach and the sense of vital, significant detail with which Clair treats the material of human life in this film. His imaginative vision of this life is the source of the authentic Parisian atmosphere that distinguishes his motion picture, that makes it so stimulating in its sober earnestness.

But greatly as I admire this creative interpretation of the material of life and the flawless acting in which it is embodied, I am not prepared to regard *Sous les toits de Paris* as an important advance in the solution of the problem of cinematic form in the talkies. Clair undoubtedly achieves a fair measure of success in blending scenes containing dialogue with scenes lacking dialogue. He succeeds, however, only by the extensive use of music, of which, as it happens, he has an abundant supply in his story and setting. But even he is occasionally obliged to resort to music as mere accompaniment, as in the old silent movies; and this method, if applied to less musical stories, would be dodging the issue of cinematic dialogue.

Compared with *Sous les toits de Paris*, *The Blue Angel* [1930, dir. Josef von Sternberg] and *The Royal Family* [1930, dir. George Cukor & Cyril Gardner] are negligible. But they are entertaining enough as Hollywood films go. *The Blue Angel*, a German picture made by a Hollywood director, is a conventional melodrama; *The Royal Family*, a comedy bordering on farce. The former is a little more sensitive and cinematic, the latter more stagy. Both remain safely within conventional viewpoints and methods of treatment. (*The Nation*, January 7, 1931)

38. The Underworld: *The Criminal Code* (1931), dir. Howard Hawks; *Paid* (1930), dir. Sam Wood.

Gangsters and racketeers play so prominent a part in American life today that it would be little short of a miracle if their exploits were ignored by the movies. Nor are they. In fact, the number of films dealing with the underworld and its criminal activities is altogether too great. The actual proportion of these films in the total Hollywood output cannot be stated for lack of data. But it can hardly be very small, and if casual observation is to be trusted, there is reason to believe that the number is growing steadily. It is sufficient to mention that the week under review saw two new pictures in New York belonging to this class, while several more were being shown in neighboring places.

Of course, there can be no objection to underworld films on the ground that they make crime too attractive. It is the business of the movies, as it is of the theater, to reflect life, and American life is American life. The trouble with these pictures is that they reflect the life of the underworld in a light that is altogether false. They crown the holdup man and the safe-cracker with the romantic halo of bravery and adventure—a halo that helps to disguise their fundamental moronism. Nor do these pictures ever make the slightest attempt to relate the criminal class to its societal source, the economics and ethos of rapacious capitalism.

Yet the glorification of the gangster, pursued mostly for the sake of cheap sensationalism, does not stop at this. To judge by some recent movies of prison life, of which two, *The Criminal Code* [1931, dir. Howard Hawks] and *Paid* [1930, dir. Sam Wood], have just arrived on Broadway, the criminal is not only admired as a hero, but also pitied as a victim, a victim not of this acquisitive society of ours but of its soulless law that demands an eye for an eye. It is true that the two films mentioned, which are both adaptations of well-known stage dramas (*The Criminal Code* is the title of a 1929 play of the same name, by Martin Flavin; *Paid* is the screen name of the play *Within the Law* [1912, Bayard Veiller]), choose for their victims of the law two innocent characters; but this innocence is purely accidental, and the chief interest of the pictures, as well as their main emotional appeal, lies in their denunciation of punitive law and its instrument, the prison. Granting the brutal vindictiveness of the penal system, one cannot help feeling that this sentimentalizing over poor gunmen, side by side with the meek acceptance of the conditions that breed the gunmen and create the prisons in the first place, fosters a hypocritical attitude toward the existing social evils.

Barring this false view of crime and punishment, it must be admitted that both *The Criminal Code* and *Paid* achieve considerable success in the presentation of their respective narratives. The portrait of prison life in the former is not so rich in detail as it was in *The Big House* [1930, dir. George Hill], but it is sufficiently harrowing to keep one spellbound. The drama is also capably acted, particularly by Walter Huston, though even he is not completely free of a certain stage effect in speech and bearing. For its part, *Paid* does not deal so much with prison life as with its effect on a proud and resourceful young woman who went to jail without guilt, and who left it with the determination to avenge herself for her suffering. There is a great naturalness in the acting of this film, with the chief honors both for stirring acting and striking beauty going to Joan Crawford.

Ronald Colman is also a person with a "crime record" on the screen, but in *The Devil to Pay* [1930, dir. George Fitzmaurice] he is only a delightful, happy-go-lucky adventurer in life with a chivalrous regard for the ladies' feelings and quite an unusual disregard of money. This motion particular picture, then, is a sparkling and wholly entertaining trifle. (*The Nation*, January 21, 1931)

39. Shaw's First Movie: *How He Lied to Her Husband* (1931), dir. Cecil Lewis.

The inevitable has happened. For years George Bernard Shaw turned a deaf ear to all proposals to put his plays on the screen. He has at last relented, and one of his early works, the one-act *How He Lied to Her Husband* [1904], has been made into a short talkie [1931, dir. Cecil Lewis] by an English company. There was doubtless great wisdom in Shaw's refusal to submit to the ministrations of the Hollywood experts. For one thing, he spared us the disappointment of seeing his showman's display of a nimble and effervescent mind brought down to the level of infantile understanding. He also spared us the painful experience of sitting through some of the worst films that could possibly be made. For as silent pictures, shorn of their conversational brilliance, Shaw's plays, with the possible exception of *The Devil's Disciple* [1897; filmed 1959, dir. Harold Hecht], would have been particularly lacking in the qualities that make the flesh and blood of a good motion picture. In talkies he is on safer ground, though one still has grave doubts whether any of his bigger dramas can be successfully adapted to the screen.

How He Lied to Her Husband, regarded as an augury of what is to come, is disappointing. The film was produced under Shaw's personal supervision; and it is rather a pity, for Shaw's ideas of direction, which cramp his plays even on the stage, are little short of disastrous when applied to the movies. He evidently does not sense the difference between the cinema and the stage. Though Cecil Lewis, who directed the picture, has given it a pleasant fluidity of alternating shots, Lewis has adhered to the dramatic original in practically everything else. So much so, indeed, that he has confined the entire action to a single room, showing even that setting exclusively from one end, as if, like a stage set, it had only three walls.

But what seems to matter even more, where quality is concerned, is the essential theatricality of the whole piece. The theatrical intimacy of contact with the audience that enables the actor to make his points on the stage is still unobtainable in the talkies, however. A deficiency affecting all the sound genres, it makes itself felt with special force in the conventional dramatic genre, and *How He Lied to Her Husband*, with its invented situation of a husband's welcoming and even demanding admiration for his wife from a lover who feigns indifference to her, has decidedly all the earmarks of a dramatic stunt. On the screen this simply does not work.

Yet even this failure does not quite explain the paucity of effect produced by the film. The truth is that besides its situation—a not very happy conceit at best—the play has little to offer. What is most surprising of all, it has none of the Shavian brilliance of dialogue and none of the sudden twists of characterization that have made Bernard Shaw's reputation as a dramatist. One is still kept in a state of amused bewilderment while watching the antics of his four-act comedy *You Never Can Tell* [1899], but *How He Lied to Her Husband* is not even mildly amusing. The one relieving feature of the picture is the acting of Vera Lennox [as Aurora Bompas]. The finesse of her craftsmanship is admirable—if nothing else in the picture is. (*The Nation*, February 4, 1931)

40. Glories of the Epic: *Cimarron* (1931), dir. Wesley Ruggles; *The Fighting Caravans* (1931), dir. Otto Brower & David Burton.

By and large, it is a good thing for the movies that now and again a Hollywood company turns to a historical subject and produces an epic. The triteness of so many film comedies and dramas, though inherent in their stories, would have figured less prominently if their main characters had been shown against a historical background of active humanity. At least, the advantage of the epic method has been demonstrated in a number of films in which the employment of large masses of people shifted the interest from the central figures to the mass action that surged around them.

It is true that when Hollywood turns to the masses it never does so for their own sake; it never treats them as a compact organism welded together by common interests and sentiments. Pictures like *Battleship Potemkin* [1925, dir. Sergei Eisenstein], *Grass* [1925, doc.; Merian C. Cooper & Ernest B. Schoedsack], or even *The Silent Enemy* [1930, doc.; dir. H. P. Carver] are not made in Hollywood. The Hollywood practice is to keep the masses on the fringes of the plot, using them only for spectacular effects or merely as a background for the principal characters. Even so, the employment of large numbers of people actively participating in the progress of the narrative is a cinematic virtue. It creates opportunities for sweeping movement, adds swing and intensity to the action, and at the same time avoids the pitfalls of the cheap psychology that usually distinguishes Hollywood's central characters.

Cimarron [1931, dir. Wesley Ruggles], the latest epic on to arrive in New York, is a case in point. Like its numerous predecessors in this genre, this film takes for its subject the thrills and turmoils of the pioneering era. It departs, however, from the type of story made almost traditional by *The Covered Wagon* [1923, dir. James Cruze] in that instead of a single episode such as a trek across the country, with all the hardships and adventures involved, *Cimarron* depicts the rise of a modern community out of the wilderness of an Indian territory. The scenes describing the life in the new settlement form the best part of the picture and are both exciting and informative. Here we get not only the familiar trimmings of the romance of the Wild West with its gunplay and lawlessness, but also an insight into the life of a bustling, go-getting community that is highly typical of the American scene and has the quality of national uniqueness.

The episode of a church service in a gambling hall, the setting up of a newspaper to defend and promote civic righteousness, the trial of a prostitute whose presence in the settlement rouses the ire of respectable wives—these scenes provide a vivid illustration of the characteristic methods of grappling with the problems of communal life that belong exclusively to the United States. But just as the portrait of the growing community with its various types and swift action is rich in human interest and captivating in panoramic imagery, the story of the principal character around which the movie is built seems, by comparison, lacking in substance and at times even crudely conventional. The heroic exploits of Yancey Cravat, the public-spirited lawyer with the steady hand of a crack shot and the crusader's urge for "empire-building," belong more properly to the traditional romance of the western film and seem out of place in this sober, realistic setting. But for these misdirected heroics and the disappointingly flat ending, *Cimarron* might have been a truly remarkable picture. As it is, it is only interesting.

Of *The Fighting Caravans* [1931, dir. Otto Brower & David Burton], one cannot say even that. The mysteries of the Hollywood mind are beyond human probing. But there is something baffling in the misuse of opportunities exemplified in this motion picture. With all the money spent on it, one might have expected at least a touch of originality in the story and treatment. *The Fighting Caravans* does no more, however, than rehash an old theme, almost repeating the recent epic *The Big Trail* [1930, dir. Raoul Walsh], in comparison with which it is much less competent and infinitely more inept. (*The Nation*, February 18, 1931)

41. Chaplin Falters: *City Lights* (1931), dir. Charlie Chaplin; *Trader Horn* (1931), dir. W. S. Van Dyke.

Charlie Chaplin's latest picture, *City Lights* [1931], has been greeted with the general acclaim of the press, an acclaim so fervent that it surpasses even the unmeasured enthusiasm over his past performances. The three cheers of publicity (largely gratuitous, no doubt) that preceded the showing of the movie have possibly had something to do with this. Likewise, so has the impressive fact that a silent film is coming out of dialogue-ridden Hollywood. But the magic of Chaplin's name must have been the strongest factor. Only this can account for the acclamation of *City Lights* as the crowning achievement of Chaplin's art.

The truth is, *City Lights* is the feeblest of his longer pictures. *The Kid* [1921], *The Gold Rush* [1925], and *The Circus* [1928]—I am one of the unfortunate few who missed seeing *The Pilgrim* [1923]—gave us the mature Chaplin, less spontaneous, perhaps, than in his still earlier *A Dog's Life* [1918] or *Shoulder Arms* [1918], but just as subtle in his whimsicalities and a little more wistful. In *City Lights* there are few whimsicalities, while what was intended to be wistfulness has clearly degenerated into something decidedly maudlin.

One has feared for some time that this was going to happen. There were alarming signs of it in *The Circus*, although they were heavily outweighed by the amazing ingenuity of the episodes that revealed the fantastic naturalness of the little tramp. In *City Lights* the only scenes that have this fantastic quality are those depicting the desperate venture of our hero into the business of prizefighting. There we get our old Chaplin, the personification of a helpless and guileless soul who resorts to grotesquely fantastic, though essentially natural, devices to get him out of a tight corner.

In Chaplin's art what he does has always been as important as how he does it. His little tricks and unexpected twists of action may be described as "gags," but there is a world of difference between them and, for instance, the ones that are used by Harold Lloyd. Lloyd's gags are merely external situations in no way connected with his screen personality, which, by the way, is little more than a void. Chaplin's gags, by contrast, spring from the very nature of the character he has created and are the principal means of revealing that character.

It is precisely because of Chaplin's ingenious reactions to the situations in which he finds himself that we have come to love the absurd little fellow; we would gladly imitate him if we could only divest ourselves of our respectable habits. To be sure, we laugh at his droll ways, but we also pity him for always being at odds with the world, a round peg in a square hole. Thus there is pathos enough in the character himself, such that it doesn't require any stressing by means of a sentimental plot. Chaplin's growing seriousness, his desire to be more than a mere comedian, has deceived him into holding sentiment more precious than fun. He has paid dearly for this error of judgment by producing, in *City Lights*, a picture of which less than a quarter does credit to his genius.

If I ask for more fantasy in Chaplin's films, I should be content, not to say pleased, with much less of it in a movie like *Trader Horn* [1931, dir. W. S. Van Dyke]. Somehow the fantasy there fails to blend with the realistic background. The blame for this must be laid largely at the feet of that entertaining spinner of yarns, the character of Aloysius Horn, though the director, too, is guilty of some quite uncalled-for crudities. Apart from this, the picture is a magnificent record of wild life in Central Africa, abounding in thrilling episodes and scenic splendors. The natives who play a prominent part in the story prove to be excellent actors, and they are approached in this among the white members of the cast only by Harry Carey in his fine characterization of Trader Horn. (*The Nation*, March 4, 1931)

42. Nature and Artifice: *Rango* (1931), dir. Ernest B. Schoedsack; *The Easiest Way* (1931), dir. Jack Conway.

The time is probably not far off when television tours will be conducted through the most inaccessible parts of the world, and we shall be watching the life of the jungle, the desert, and the deep sea as today with the help of newspapers we watch the happenings in the capitals of Europe. It is possible that we shall become so familiar with that life that we shall not even bother to watch it. Be that as it may, and in spite of the numerous films that have already familiarized us with the habits and doings of the wild denizens of Asia and Africa, there are few sights today so capable of sending a thrill up our spine as the spectacle of a lion or a tiger attacking its prey or engaging in mortal combat with some other powerful fighter. For that matter, jungle comedy is hardly less fascinating than jungle drama, particularly when it is provided by those star comedians of the animal world, the apes and monkeys.

Ernest Schoedsack's *Rango* [1931], the latest contribution to the subject of jungle life, maintains a happy balance of comedy and drama, and succeeds so well, with such directness and intimacy, in capturing the fun, the terror, and the pervading watchful atmosphere of the jungle that it must unhesitatingly be classed with the very best of its kind. It is true that it has not the sweep and action that distinguished its more ambitious predecessor *Chang* (made by the same Schoedsack in cooperation with Merian Cooper), but it is superior to the earlier picture in conveying the sense of lurking danger that makes the jungle itself into a living thing. The film shows up equally well in comparison with *Trader Horn* [1931, W. S. Van Dyke]. Though lacking the variety of the latter, it reveals a greater unity of mood and theme, and moreover gains immeasurably in its power of appeal by confining itself strictly to the facts of nature, instead of encumbering itself, as *Trader Horn* does, with an inept love story.

Once again the primary material of the film—the facts of life— proves to be the only relieving feature in an otherwise banal and juvenile picture, *The Easiest Way* [1931]. The struggle of a poor but of course beautiful girl in trying to escape from the position of "kept woman" and marry the man she loves is just regular Hollywood piffle; but the opening scenes, showing the family life in a tenement house, deserve praise for incisiveness and color.

No considerations of fidelity to life can enter into the discussion of the screen opera *Pagliacci* [1931, Joe W. Coffman]. Here, by the very nature of the genre, everything is frank artifice, and from start to finish the characters and the action remain entirely conventional. The main question in a production of this kind is the quality of the music and singing. In the present instance all that need be said is that the reproduction of voices is only moderately successful. As a first experiment the film is important. But a really satisfying screen opera is still in the limbo of the future . . . as are many other things in the field of artistic endeavor. (*The Nation*, March 18, 1931)

43. With Benefit of Music: H_2O (1929, doc. short), dir. Ralph Steiner; *Mechanical Principles* (1931, doc. short), dir. Ralph Steiner.

Since its earliest days the moving picture has always appeared before the public arm in arm with music. There has never been a satisfactory explanation of this alliance, although, on the face of it, it has often seemed not a little incongruous. Why should a silent film need music at all? Clearly, a film that finds its complete expression in visual images can gain nothing through the addition of musical accompaniment. More likely it will even suffer from such intrusion of a foreign medium, for music will be either repeating what is already present in the film, or adding something of its own to what in itself is a complete and perfectly balanced composition. To see a silent film "cold," that is, unaccompanied by music, has been the recognized test of its success or failure in standing on its own feet. Needless to say, the vast majority of silent films never passed this test. Denied the support of music, they appeared emaciated, bloodless, lacking in emotional appeal and dramatic accent. It was to cover these sins of artistic incompetence that music was dragged in as a ready dispenser of emotional stimuli.

But if music supplied poor films with what they lacked—and apart from realistic sound effects, the thing they lacked most was intrinsic dramatic rhythm—it seemed natural to conclude that better music would add further to the appeal of the film. To be sure, the musical exercises of the movie orchestras, not to mention the young ladies who earned their livelihood by strumming the movie pianos, could stand a great deal of improvement. A more intelligent selection, arrangement, and synchronization of the musical material would have been a decided step forward. Paradoxically enough, it has been the much-maligned talking picture that has accomplished this improvement, even if it has been far from perfect in its reproduction of sound. But this still left much to be desired in the eyes, or rather ears, of the devotees of music. The younger composers of the more advanced school have been attracted by the problem, and at the recent Copland-Sessions concert at the Broadhurst Theater the public was given the opportunity to appraise some of their efforts in this direction.

It is not for me to pass an opinion on the music that accompanied the showing of the five films on that occasion. The fact that was more important than the quality of the music was its utter irrelevancy to the films shown. It was almost incredible. Here were three composers obviously appreciative of their own medium—one of them, Darius Milhaud, already enjoying world-wide fame—deciding to lend their talents to the creation of a composite form of art, the musical film. And how did they go about it? First, they chose films that were the least suitable for musical treatment (and in the case of Milhaud, unworthy of any attention at all); and, secondly, having chosen the films, they proceeded to ignore the very foundation of the moving picture as a medium, its inner dynamics, its rhythm. In the face of this obvious blindness to the inner structure of the film, one can only wonder why they ever bothered to try their hand at something so far from their special interests and comprehension as the art of the film.

The pity of it all is that three of the films shown, the works of Ralph Steiner, deserved better consideration. Steiner has not yet developed into a cinematic artist. He is still essentially a photographer of still subjects. He has an excellent eye for graphic form and pattern, but has not yet learned the importance of dynamic organization of the raw material of the camera. In H_2O, his first picture, the variety of patterns was so amazingly effective that it made up for the lack of dynamic unity in the picture as a whole. His two other little pictures, *Surf and Seaweed* and *Mechanical Principles*, were less interesting in their material and even more spineless in their cinematic structure. Alas, the accompanying music only emphasized their shortcomings. (*The Nation*, April 1, 1931)

44. Too Much Halo: *The Front Page* (1931), dir. Lewis Milestone; *Tabu* (1931), dir. F. W. Murnau.

We are all interested in newspapers and what newspapermen write about their calling. The business of supplying us with our daily scandal, if we are to believe these chroniclers turned novelists and playwrights, is in itself full of scandal. Moreover, it has its thrills, which, as they are portrayed in books and plays, can stand comparison with the most exciting experiences from the world of crime. We are reminded of all this by that extraordinarily vivid 1928 drama of newspaper life titled *The Front Page,* by Ben Hecht and Charles MacArthur, which has now emerged as a film [1931, dir. Lewis Milestone].

Granting *The Front Page* its trenchant dialogue and the sculpturesque sureness of its characterization, the only question it stirs in my mind is whether this work gives a true depiction of the newspaper world. It is the glamor, the romantic halo, surrounding the characters of *The Front Page* that arouses one's suspicions about the authenticity of the men portrayed. Aren't they a trifle too hard-boiled to be wholly credible? And if the authors are right in their characterization, aren't they guilty of a certain lack of honesty in treating this hard-boiled cynicism as standing for some superior knowledge and understanding of life, instead of being merely what it is, a protective mechanism of interior intelligence against the *demands* of life? Perhaps if we had been allowed a glimpse under the callous masks worn by these reporters, we might have found their owners more human. On the other hand, so clearly do they stand out as individuals under the vitalizing treatment of Hecht and MacArthur that one is inclined to forego further probing and to accept them for what they appear to be—racketeers of publicity, whose habitual sitting in judgment on other people gives them the prestige of superior intellect.

The movie, one of the most satisfying during the current season, again shows us Lewis Milestone, who directed *All Quiet on the Western Front* [1930], as one of the most sensitive and intelligent directors in

Hollywood. His treatment is distinguished not by any striking contrasts of light and shade, by any emphasis of action, but by an atmospheric unity in which all characters and all action flow in a constant stream as parts of a single whole. One is brought to realize this dramatic unity when the flow is suddenly arrested by a lyrical interlude between the condemned man, Earl Williams, and his streetwalker friend, a scene that both emotionally and dramatically belongs to a different world. Neither this episode, however, nor the conventional episodes (they are fortunately few) of the upcoming marriage of the star reporter, Hildy Johnson, nor the romantic embellishment of the newspaperman and his profession—none of these scenes are sufficient to destroy the air of verisimilitude that pervades the picture.

That air is sustained largely by the effortless, expert acting to be found in *The Front Page*. By far the highest honors in this regard go to Adolphe Menjou, who gives as polished a performance of a gruff and unscrupulous editor as he used to give of a man about town. In the role of the reporter Johnson, Pat O'Brien himself is rather colorless, but his confrères in the court pressroom are as bright and glittering a group of character actors as has ever appeared on the screen [Edward Everett Horton, Walter Catlett, Matt Moore, Frank McHugh, and Phil Tead].

Tabu: A Story of the South Seas [1931] adds little to the artistic reputation of F. W. Murnau, who died in a car accident a few days before the opening of his film in New York. Murnau's greatest achievement was *The Last Laugh* [1924], produced in cooperation with Karl Freund and Emil Jannings. None of his other pictures, including the heavy-handed *Faust* [1926] and all of his American efforts, comes anywhere within a measurable distance of that early masterpiece. *Tabu* is deliberate and forced in its playfulness, cheaply melodramatic in its tragedy, and unconscionably long-winded. It has neither the charm of Robert Flaherty's *Moana* [1926, doc.] nor the pictorial and dramatic force of *The Last Laugh*. (*The Nation*, April 15, 1931)

45. Children for the Grown-ups: *Skippy* (1931), dir. Norman Taurog; *Dirigible* (1931), dir. Frank Capra.

I have always had great admiration for writers of children's books. It is, of course, possible that their knowledge of child psychology consists only of a few tricks that, as they have learned from experience, never fail to impress their young audience. And yet much more than this seems to be present in a book or a play that is really popular with children. This is, I presume, mainly the ability to see and interpret the world with that freshness and innocence of outlook that give the quality of adventure to most of the child's experiences. It is here, too, that the mystery of the adult metempsychosis makes its entry. For an adult author to regain the innocence of childhood while thriving on the forbidden fruit of knowledge seems to be as marvelous a feat as that of the proverbial Russian virgin who knew how to combine innocence with the benefits of sin. Many a time, as I recalled my early delights with the little Brownies, I have regretfully had to admit to myself that I no longer found anything amusing about them. But it is scarcely possible that Miss Mulock [Dinah Maria Craik], their gifted authoress [*The Adventures of a Brownie*, 1918], felt similarly indifferent in describing their triumphs and tribulations, for she would have failed to convey them to her readers if she had not seen them herself through a child's eyes.

The conclusion to which I am impelled by this fact is rather disconcerting to me. It would appear that nothing short of a revelation from above could open my eyes and my heart to a masterpiece of art that sends into ecstasies my fellow humans of a less cynical age. This probably accounts for my utter failure to be amused by newspaper comic strips. I say "probably," because I am not at all sure that the strips are primarily intended for children. On the other hand, I have every reason to suspect that a book or a film dealing with children that appeals to me is most unlikely to make an equal impression on children.

Now, *Skippy* [1931], although based on a comic strip, is a thoroughly delightful film. Grown-up men like myself find it both droll and wistful. It has humor and pathos that make one feel like brooding over one's own memories of that blissful age. Moreover, its youthful actors bring to their parts a more than usual amount of convincing naturalness, and there is a similar absence of stage heroics in its simple plot. A reserve like this, which is so rarely encountered in the offerings from Hollywood, merits every praise and goes far to make the film a decidedly pleasant entertainment. But it is unmistakably an entertainment for the grown-ups. Most of its comedy is of the type in which the ingenuousness of the thing done or said is its only claim to being amusing. Its pathos, too, seems to be a little over-sentimentalized. And this brings me back to my initial problem: can the majority of us grown-up people ever see children as they really are? I am inclined to think that we cannot, although some of us may come perilously near to what is known as "juvenile mentality."

No particular subtlety of any sort will be found in *Dirigible* [1931], but the film has merits of a different kind, and these place it considerably above the Hollywood average. An aerial adventure involving the cracking up of a dirigible in mid-air, a flight in an airplane over the South Pole, and bloodcurdling incidents on land provide the spectacle and drama that lie in the grand tradition of the movies, and it is to the credit of Frank Capra, the director of the film, that he has made such an effective use of his material. The film cannot boast of the photographic excellence shown in some of the scenes in *Hell's Angels* [a.k.a. *For the Love of Mike*; 1927, Frank Capra], but its story is visualized with convincing vividness, and is told intelligently.

A more imaginative, if humorous, treatment of aerial thrills is presented in *Birds of a Feather* [1931, Burt Gillett], a Walt Disney animated cartoon (last seen at the Cameo) showing a striking advance in the application of rhythmic movement to linear design. By comparison, the Soviet picture *Cities and Years* [1930, Yevgeni Chervyakov], shown on the same program at the Cameo, is pretentious but unconvincing, despite some originality of treatment. (*The Nation*, April 29, 1931)

46. The Shrinking of Personality: *The Millionaire* (1931), dir. John G. Adolfi; *Svengali* (1931), dir. Archie Mayo.

It has been my experience this week to see, one after another, a number of films in which the principal part was played by a famous actor. The actors included George Arliss, John Barrymore, and, among the lesser lights, Constance Bennett and Jack Holt. As I now try to recall my main impressions, I am struck by a rather puzzling fact. None of the popular actors I saw stands out before me as a personality with whom I had a direct and all but physical contact.

Now I know that on the stage some of these actors and others of equal gifts were and are able to escape the shell of the characters they represent and to fill the entire theater with their own beings, so that one feels as if one has almost touched them. More phantom-like, but no less expansive and penetrating, were the personalities of the famous stars that radiated from the silent screen. Although the constant stressing of personal appeal was motivated by commercial aims and helped to cramp the progress of the silent film, there can be no question of the success of the producers in establishing their screen stars not merely as favorites with the public, but also as personalities that somehow (sometimes, no doubt, through mere inflation) transcended their screen characters and came into direct contact with the audience. The appeal of Charlie Chaplin, Douglas Fairbanks, Mary Pickford, Pola Negri, and Emil Jannings in the old days of silent cinema had that quality of expansion.

The situation with the talking pictures seems to be paradoxically different. The personal magnetism of the actor has lost its force. His entire personality has shrunk to something that is only a little more than the character he represents. This does not necessarily mean that his personality is completely submerged in the character. More often than not the reverse is actually the case, and the same George Arliss, for instance, will be seen in a number of characters that differ little from one another, being merely variations of Arliss's acting personality. This may be set against Arliss as an actor, for resourceful and accomplished as he is, emotionally he is always the same (*The Millionaire* [1931, dir. John G. Adolfi] is a case in point). But I doubt that his failure to loom as large from the speaking screen as he does from the stage, and as he probably did from the silent screen, is due to any lack of magnetism in his acting personality.

The reason for Arliss's failure, I am inclined to think, lies rather in the curious effect that the addition of mechanical speech has had on the relationship between the screen actor and the audience. The change in the actor's position has been made in two diametrically opposed directions. On the one hand, he has returned to the stage methods of acting and storytelling. On the other hand, he has stepped beyond conventional stage settings into the world of natural surroundings. The same world existed in the silent picture; yet the addition of speech has taken that world right out of the theater auditorium, away from immediate contact with the audience, and placed it in a space of its own. Bound to his surroundings, the actor, too, has become more remote, with the consequent loss in intimacy, in direct contact, and in the unobstructed flow of the magnetic force that conveys to the spectator the actor's power and stature.

The same shrinking of personality that was noticed in Arliss is also seen in John Barrymore. Excellent as he is in his flamboyant theatricalism in *Svengali* [1931, dir. Archie Mayo], he never succeeds in coming off the screen. And here, as an actor, he also suffers in another sense. Barrymore's acting has an unmistakable rhythmic quality, although not always quite precise and certain in its pattern. Gordon Craig, writing of Henry Irving, described this quality as "the dancing and singing of one's role" [see "The Face of Henry Irving" in Craig's *On the Art of the Theatre* (1912)]. But it is obvious that a rhythmic pattern built on the stage cannot be transferred bodily to the screen. In fact, it must be completely rebuilt in obedience to the entirely different principle of screen rhythm. No such attempt was made in the case of Barrymore in *Svengali*, and what emerges from the screen, striking as it is in individual scenes, lacks the swing and rhythmic unity of histrionic display that belong to this type of acting on the ordinary stage.

One cannot apply the same standard of acting to Constance Bennett, but able actress that she is, she seems to be constantly miscast. In *Born to Love* [1931, dir. Paul L. Stein], she is seen again in one of those maudlin parts that showcases a helpless, suffering beauty—suffering largely because of the stupidities of the plot. A little more character and strength would make Bennett into a more believable and interesting woman. But, then, Hollywood has its own standards of interest and credibility. *Subway Express* [1931, dir. Fred. C. Newmeyer], though it stars Jack Holt, is not remarkable for any individual acting, either, but it does deserve praise for excellent comedy and flowing direction. (*The Nation*, May 27, 1931)

47. Fantasy All the Way: *Le Million* (1931), dir. René Clair; *The Beggar's Opera*, a.k.a. *The Threepenny Opera* (1931), dir. G. W. Pabst.

René Clair's *Le Million* [1931], like his earlier *Sous les toits de Paris* [1930], is one of those rare pictures that make you their willing captive, immersed in their mood and letting yourself be carried away on the wings of their fancy. In *Le Million* the fancy is much more exuberant than it was in the previous picture, but it enforces submission upon you just as effectively, so that like everybody else around you, you inevitably exclaim: "What charm! What invention! What fun!" This spontaneous reaction, confirmed by the commendations you hear on all sides, is sufficient proof of the unique qualities of the film.

Le Million is the work or an artist who sees beyond the obvious, and who can view the comedy of life with a good-natured cynicism that proclaim its authentic sophistication. From under this gentle leg-pulling, there gradually emerges a fantastic world inhabited by not quite normal human beings who now and again burst into song and dance—the kind that reveals their hidden kinship with puppets. It is

Clair's great achievement as an artist that, though his characters' behavior here is at times grotesquely fantastic, it never appears incongruous with their surroundings or inconsistent with their normal actions.

Nonetheless, the achievement of *Le Million* is a *tour de force* that only disguises its fundamental weakness. The problem that René Clair sets himself to solve in this film is the old one of screen musical comedy. It has repeatedly been proved that the forms of singing and dancing seen in stage musical comedy are intolerably false and incongruous when transferred to the screen. The only successful treatment so far devised by Hollywood has been the use of plots in which song and dance are a natural part of the action. Stories of backstage life have been particularly in vogue in this connection. The field, however, is a small one, and it has been explored so thoroughly that, as the public has grown indifferent to such stories, Hollywood has practically stopped making musical pictures.

Now René Clair attempts to justify musical comedy by means that are directly opposite to those of Hollywood. Instead of making song and dance more natural, more in accord with the daily life of his characters, he makes the daily life of his characters more unnatural, more in accord with stage singing and dancing. Thus the story of a lost lottery ticket becomes a series of madcap adventures in which the everyday is hardly distinguishable from the eccentric. Clair's success in this daring experiment reveals the measure of his talent as an entirely convincing and vastly entertaining interpreter of human foibles. But his fantastic treatment is even more restricted in its application than the naturalistic one of Hollywood. Moreover, his approach to the problem of musical comedy is confined to the choice of subject, whereas the only way to solve the problem is to discover a cinematic form that would make dance and song spring as freely from the nature of screen entertainment as they spring from the nature of stage performance.

One had hoped that Ernst Lubitsch's *The Smiling Lieutenant* [1931] might come more effectively to grips with this artistic problem than did his *The Love Parade* [1929] or *Monte Carlo* [1930]. Such hope has not been fulfilled. With his interest centered on the comic minutiae of the princely fairyland that he so loves to depict, Lubitsch shows his concern with the formal problem of musical comedy only insofar as he tries to disguise singing and dancing in the conventional unreality of his fairy tale. In this he is not unlike René Clair, except that his somewhat less fantastic subject matter follows more closely in the footsteps of stage tradition.

Even in its particular medium of gay and polished naughtiness, however, *The Smiling Lieutenant* seems to be not nearly so subtle as its predecessors. Highly amusing as it often is, its persistent erotic emphasis, addressed all too clearly to frustrated wives and young couples, rather smacks of vulgarity. Nor does the movie show any great inventiveness in those quaint and twisted comic effects that are usually associated with the name of this director. In short, one is inclined to regard *The Smiling Lieutenant* as a routine "Lubitsch picture" with very little of Lubitsch that is of importance.

Two German films, *Liebeswalzer* [1930, dir. Wilhelm Thiele] and *The Beggar's Opera* [a.k.a. *The Threepenny Opera*; 1931, dir. G. W. Pabst], fall within the same category of musical pictures, but neither of them contributes anything to the solution of the problem here discussed. *Liebeswalzer* is a conventional musical comedy with a Graustarkian story that will please those who can admire royalty even when it is caricatured. *The Beggar's Opera*, though perhaps more artistically ambitious, also fails to produce a genuine thrill. The work of Georg Wilhelm Pabst, the film is characteristic of this director's extraordinary preference for discordance and distortion in his work. There is unrelieved morbidity in this movie, and it jars one's mind through its gruesome theme, its mixture of styles, and its persistent effort to appear "different" through pictorial as well as psychological attitudinizing. One leaves the theater utterly puzzled by the artistic impulse that found expression in this shrill and somber fantasy. (*The Nation*, June 10, 1931)

48. Hollywood "Entertains": *The Maltese Falcon* (1931), dir. Roy Del Ruth; *A Free Soul* (1931), dir. Clarence Brown.

The past fortnight having been singularly deficient in pictures of interest, my comments need go no farther than listing the films I have seen. These come under two heads: (1) stale junk rehashed without an atom of distinction, and (2) stale junk rehashed with just enough distinction to make it appear different. To the first category belong *White Shoulders* [1931, Melville W. Brown], *The Lady Who Dared* [1931, William Beaudine], *Lover Come Back* [1931, Erie C. Kenton], and *She-Wolf* [1931, James Flood]; to the second, *The Maltese Falcon* [1931] and *A Free Soul* [1931]. The only redeeming features about the last two films are that *The Maltese Falcon* treats its mystery-crime plot with an intelligence somewhat superior to that usually encountered in this type of film, and *A Free Soul* displays highly competent if artificial acting that lends its lurid story a certain superficial brilliance.

A picture that stands out against these second- and third-rate fabrications from Hollywood is *The Five-Year Plan* [1931], the Russian film at the Central. So momentous and so fascinating is the material of this extended newsreel that one refuses to cavil at the failure of the producers to convey as clearly as they could the actual mechanism of the Five-Year Plan. The film, it must be admitted, never shows us the dynamic force that relates the component parts of the plan to one another and has welded the industrial efforts of Soviet Russia into a drive of epic grandeur. But even with this important defect the film remains one of the most interesting on Broadway.

The main attractions on the list of feature films being what they are, this may be as good an occasion as any to dilate on the other, less prominent items of the movie programs. Here is a kind of picture that positively cries to heaven for some swift retribution. I refer to the one- and two-reel comedies. What sort of people make these films, and for what sort of audience are they intended? Most of them are so incredibly imbecilic that it is an agony to have to sit through them. During the past season the Cameo Theatre, the same that distinguished itself by a series of Soviet and travel pictures, was perhaps the worst offender. The Pathé and Columbia comedies with which it embellished its programs were the limit of ineptitude and incompetence. They made few if any people laugh. They made most gnash their teeth and cry for murder.

Unfortunately, this sadistic practice of subjecting innocent people to the torture of seeing and hearing these efforts in "entertainment" is not confined to one theater. There have been few programs during the fortnight under review that did not contain at least one comic short. At the Rialto the cannibal within us was roused by the tremulous bulk of Billy House, who in *The Headache* [1931, Billy House] kept winking at us as he does on the vaudeville stage. At the Strand a company of young people were busy smashing "effects and furniture" for twenty-five minutes in a criminal outburst called *Moving In* [1931, Albert Ray].

One could go on enumerating these outrages against all that goes under the name of art and entertainment. But that would be wasting time. The important thing is that the outrages should stop. The public should indicate to the exhibitors that, even in the matter of short subjects, it demands some consideration. As a rule it has no choice in submitting to the minor items of a program, for it is the feature picture that brings the short into the theater. All the more reason why the audience should be treated with at least the decency that is its due. (*The Nation*, June 24, 1931)

49. Love and Sex: *Transgression* (1931), dir. Herbert Brenon; *The Skin Game* (1931), dir. Alfred Hitchcock.

The change of seasons is not supposed to have any effect on the quality of the movies, so it is impossible to blame the summer weather for the fare that has been offered to the public during the past month. To discuss these films individually as embodiments of definite creative ideas would be futile, for the only idea they try to embody is that of box-office appeal, and their success or failure in embodying it is accordingly the only important thing that distinguishes one from another. It might be profitable, however, to consider them as a group rather than singly, for this procedure at least promises a few interesting sidelights on the psychology of the American audience.

Here, for instance, is a group of pictures dealing with that most popular of all subjects, "love." As a general rule, of course, nearly every film has some sort of love story, but three of those I saw during the past fortnight—*Transgression* [1931, dir. Herbert Brenon], *Men Call It Love* [1931, dir. Edgar Selwyn], and *Chances* [1931, dir. Alan Dwan]— had very little else. It is hardly necessary to add that they contributed little that was new to the lore on this subject. A conflict between a wife's loyalty to her husband and the temptations of a passionate Spanish admirer; a conflict between a wife's love for her unfaithful husband and the temptations of a polished and cynical admirer; a conflict between loyalty to one's loving brother and love for the girl he also loves—such is the amount of originality in the stories of the three movies mentioned.

Having seen hundreds of similar pictures, I am not surprised at that. What has always puzzled me is the mentality of the audience that accepts this sentimental "love" as readily as it does the most outspoken and lurid "sex." Is there any underlying unity between the two? Does not the extreme primitiveness of the emotional and intellectual content of this love reveal itself also in the ready acquiescence of the audience to sex *au naturel*, without the benefit of even a fig leaf? Ours is the age of naturalness, and boys and girls of today know more about birth control than their parents ever practiced. It is even possible to come across such scenes as I once encountered in an Automat, of all places, where an angelic-looking young thing was listening reverently to a boy of nineteen as he read out passages from a book on sex and accompanied them with detailed comments on the mechanics of contraception. After all, if love is only that, one may just as well be frank about it.

It is facts like this that seem to link the cheaply sentimental with the brazenly sensual, as both spring from the identical mental state of intellectual and emotional primitivism. Not only is it true that the same public that wallows in gushy sentiment delights in watching the graceful

May-poling around thinly disguised phallic symbols in a film like *The Smiling Lieutenant* [1931, dir. Ernst Lubitsch]. But, to go even further, it is also true that this public stands only one step removed from the supposedly more cerebral readers of books that attempt to give information on "the right understanding and enjoyment of the sex act . . . exactly how it should be performed." The disarming naïveté that characterizes the earnestness of such an appeal signifies, it seems to me, the same simplicity and crudeness of feeling that underlie the mawkish romantic rubbish of American movies.

The utter triteness of the Hollywood love formula is brought home by the unexpected impression of freshness and significance produced by such an ordinary and not over-profound film as *The Skin Game* [1931, dir. Alfred Hitchcock], based on John Galsworthy's 1920 play of the same name. If only for its freshness, this picture is worth seeing. (*The Nation*, July 8, 1931)

50. Lectures from the Screen: *Hell Below Zero* (1931, doc.), dir. Carveth Wells; *The Mystery of Life* (1930, doc.), dir. George Cochrane.

A spoken narrative illustrated by silent or sound pictures on the screen is a form of the talking picture that is quite distinct from the ordinary dialogue movie. The difference, and it is a very important one, lies in the fact that in the latter case the people and settings shown tell their own story, whereas in the former case the story is told by the lecturer, who arranges his film material with an almost unlimited freedom of treatment. It might have been expected that with this power over his material the movie lecturer would develop a flexible and dramatically effective technique making the utmost use of similarities and contrasts, of variations of tempo, of the many telling effects obtained from the camera, the film, and the screen. But it is extremely seldom that one encounters such originality of treatment. Not so long ago, at the Astor Theater, on the same program with *A Free Soul* [1931, Clarence Brown], a short sports newsreel showing a group of champion divers distinguished itself by some very ingenious stop-motion effects, the humor and charming narrative informality of which were much appreciated by the audience.

Hell Below Zero [1931], recently shown at the Cameo, is another entertaining as well as instructive example of the art of movie lecturing. It is true that, photographically, the picture does not rise to any great heights, but it is, at least, intelligently put together, so that the lecturer's talk becomes closely interwoven with the images on the screen. The honors of the film, however, go almost entirely to the lecturer, Carveth Wells, whose delightful wit and ease of manner enable him to carry and convey his knowledge with captivating charm.

For the benefit of those who are interested in such matters, I may mention that the title of the picture is rather misleading. The picture's record of the mysterious Mountains of the Moon in equatorial Africa contains nothing that can justly be described as "hellish," but, on the other hand it gives some extraordinary views of the vegetation of the region, which is probably the most fantastic thing seen on the earth. As an introduction to this, moreover, Wells treats us to some "inside information" on the African jungle, which does not appear to exist, and on the ferocious ways of lions, who, as Wells shows us on the screen, would do anything to run away from you if you would only let them go.

I do not know if the box-office value of *Hell Below Zero* had any relation to its qualities. But I do know that the picture that followed it at the Cameo, called *The Mystery of Life* [1930], is considered, and probably is, a great money-maker. Yet, aside from its subject, the story of evolution, which has acquired a kind of mystic significance in the eyes of the general public, and aside from the name of Clarence Darrow, who officiates at the ceremony of "explaining" evolution, I have seldom seen a picture so badly made and so dull.

The main trouble, of course, is that the film attempts too much. No intelligent story of evolution can be shown and explained on the screen in a film of ordinary length. Further, a subject that requires not only a display of data but a reasoned and telling demonstration can hardly be treated in the haphazard way of the motion picture in question. It is not enough to throw the facts onto the screen. They must be built up into syllogisms. In this case neither Darrow, slow, ponderous, and primitively theological in his evolutionism, nor his collaborator, Dr. Howard M. Parshley, who supplies the scientific data, has taken the trouble to tell his story in the clear and concise fashion demanded by the subject. But, then, neither of these two gentlemen can be expected to know much about filmmaking—and the company that made the film apparently never came to their rescue. (*The Nation*, July 22, 1931)

51. Out of Their Own Mouths: *The Common Law* (1931), dir. Paul L. Stein; *The Immortal Vagabond* (1930), dir. Gustav Ucicky & Joe May.

"Connie Bennett and Lew Cody are painting Paris pink. Lew keeps the joy joints working overtime. Connie gets tired waiting for Lew to keep a date with the preacher and leaves him flat. Joel McCrea is an artist. He's painting old Mother Eve and needs a good model bad. Connie, down to her last dime, asks for the job. Covered with blushes, she poses. P.S. She gets the job. Joel works fast on the painting. And faster on Connie. Two weeks later she's fixing his breakfasts for him."

Thus begins the account of *The Common Law* [1931], the recent "smash" at the Mayfair, in a full-page advertisement in *Variety*. The advertisement is prefaced with an apologetic "'Pardon my vernacular,' said the salesman to the exhibitor." But the apology is quite unnecessary: the vernacular fits the story like a glove; I wish I had space to let the reader taste the full flavor of this exciting narrative. That thrilling scene, however, when Connie, "covered with blushes" as she poses before the artist, deserves another quotation. As the advertisement informs us, "by the time she walks into that studio and proves that the French models have nothing on her, she owes the customers nothing. They really ought to pay another admission to see the rest of the picture."

"Sales talk," you will say. Precisely. But pictures are made to be sold, and what the salesman says out loud, the producer has previously thought out in the seclusion of his office. These confidences to the trade are a valuable testimony of what Hollywood sets out to achieve in its films. Another advertisement from the same firm, listing "sales angles on *The Common Law*," throws further light on the nature of attractions considered essential for the success of a film. Here are some of these "sales angles":

"Constance Bennett as an artist's model in gay Paree."

"Her philosophy of life and love are crystallized in the phrase: 'I don't care what people say,

as long as you say you love me !'"

"'Men called her the perfect woman' is a sales angle to interest both men and women." "Magnificent production. Exemplified by the gorgeous sequence of the Fine-Arts Ball in which over 500 players take part."

"Constance Bennett's reputation as the best-dressed woman on the screen, plus the gorgeous clothes designed for her in this production . . . are naturals for merchandise tie-ins, fashion shows, etc."

Poor Constance Bennett. An attractive woman and a capable actress, as she demonstrated in one of her early pictures, *Son of the Gods* [1930, Frank Lloyd], she has been turned into a characterless dummy wound up every time to go through the same set of flat and maudlin emotions. But what can one do, when business demands "glorification of love" as love and glorification are understood in Hollywood?

One more example of this profound understanding may be quoted from an advertisement of another production company: "*Morals for Women* [1931, Mort Blumenstock]. A startling insight into the code of a kept woman. A provocative theme to excite the curiosity of the movie-going public."

I am sorry to say that there is quite a quantity of such hokum, though of the Russian variety, in that otherwise superior picture *A*

Jew at War [1931, Grigori Roshal]. Its war scenes and its portrayal of life in a small Jewish town are impressive, if somewhat sketchy. The German picture *The Immortal Vagabond* [1930], with a skillfully grafted English dialogue, also deserves attention for its acting, Tyrolese background, and sensitive direction. (*The Nation*, August 19, 1931)

52. Emasculated Dreiser, Miraculous Capra: *An American Tragedy* (1931), dir. Josef von Sternberg; *The Miracle Woman* (1931), dir. Frank Capra.

If there is anything tragic about the film version of *An American Tragedy* [1931, dir. Josef von Sternberg], it is the pathetic spectacle of its producers' trying to crash the gate of artistic heaven with the yellow ticket of their profligate trade. I am no Saint Peter, but any person of moderate intelligence could have told these gentlemen that they were wasting their time in imagining that they could change the color of their ticket merely by protesting their fanatical concern for aesthetic virtue. Alas, this is about all they have done. They did not even have the foresight to disguise their cheap finery and loud manners under some borrowed cloak of academic respectability. This alone, of course, would not have placed their creative effort on the level of achievement represented by Theodore Dreiser's penetrating 1925 novel of the same name, but it would at least have proved their earnest desire to rise to the auspicious occasion.

And the occasion was an auspicious one. Whatever else can be said of Dreiser's opus, it does throb with the pulse of full-blooded reality, perhaps even a reality too raw for literary appraisal. An intelligent producer with enough imagination to translate life into cinematic terms would have dug into this mine of human material to unearth and mold into shape the elements that were most vital and meaningful. Not so the producers of *An American Tragedy*. All they could see in the story was some paste-board romance and the hackneyed dramatics of the courtroom. It is not even that they failed to note the social implications of the tragic murder, as the author himself has accused them of doing, that makes the film such a humdrum affair. More important is the producers' utter failure to infuse some genuine life into the characters that are paraded before us in all the familiar trappings of Hollywood puppets. Even the much touted courtroom scene contributes little to relieve the flatness and pointlessness of the picture. It leads nowhere, leaves the principal character as nebulous as in the preceding scenes, and merely tries to make up for the absence of dramatic climax by a much too liberal display of courtroom histrionics.

A superior motion picture, if only by virtue of its two magnificent scenes of evangelistic mummery in a tabernacle, is *The Miracle Woman* [1931, dir. Frank Capra]. Here, at least, is some excellent and genuine material from life, striking in its unfamiliarity and effectively presented. The director of the film, Frank Capra, can be congratulated on the skillful handling of these scenes; and there is also merit in the story insofar as it attempts to expose the fakery that goes under the name of evangelism. Its romantic motif, however, leaves much to be desired. With all its adumbrations of a blind boy (formerly an aviator) who falls in love with the evangelist and his rather theatrical penchant for revealing his mind through a ventriloquist's dummy, the movie never succeeds in ringing true and convincing. Nor, it must be added, is Barbara Stanwyck quite successful in conveying the magnetic glamor of personality that contributes so much to the evangelist's power for swaying the multitude. A Nora Bayes would have given an impressive portrait of the character. But then she was hardly the person to fit into the scenes of soft-pedalled romanticism.

To discuss *Bought* [1931, dir. Archie Mayo], with Constance Bennett in the leading role, would be to repeat my previous strictures. The only palliating thing to be said for the picture is that Bennett, though kittenish as ever, is a little more natural. Nothing need be said about the story. (*The Nation*, September 2, 1931)

53. Sidewalks of New York: *Street Scene* (1931), dir. King Vidor.

One has something to be grateful for when a Hollywood picture does more than pay lip service to artistic integrity. *Street Scene* [1931, dir. King Vidor] in its film version can scarcely be classed among the masterpieces of the screen, but it is a good picture that shows a conscientious effort to do justice to its theme, and that succeeds to a fair degree in conveying the authentic feel and color of human life.

In the circumstances the chief honors of the occasion go to Elmer Rice, both for his absorbing study of this little beehive of New York humanity and for the effective manner in which he condensed his 1929 play into a movie scenario. That some quality of the original was lost in the process of translation to a new medium was hardly his fault. The isolation of characters within the circumscribed limits of a self-contained world and their consequent loss of emotional impact on the spectator—these are the inevitable results of cinematic technique as understood and practiced in Hollywood. On the other hand, the lack of sustained unity of atmosphere and the deliberate stressing of individual character traits, as well as discrete episodes, must be charged largely to King Vidor's direction.

On the whole, it must be admitted, Vidor has treated his material with commendable reserve and quite adequate regard for the realities of life. His few concessions to Hollywood convention, as exemplified in his casting of Estelle Taylor, a strikingly handsome woman (though not too expert an actress), in the part of the rather humble wife of a stage electrician, are not obtrusive enough to affect the generally sober tone of the picture. Moreover, Vidor's handling of successive scenes has a flow and a swiftness of movement that are wholly admirable. All this, however, does not quite suffice to give the film that essential coherence and atmospheric unity that are the very substance of Rice's story.

Admittedly, the problem was not an easy one to solve. Constant change of setting is traditionally regarded as the most effective way of keeping a screen narrative continuously on the move, and here, in *Street Scene*, it has been willed by the author that all action should be confined to a single spot, the front of a house with its adjoining sidewalk. Nor is this choice of setting a mere stage device that can be ignored in the screen treatment. It happens to contain, as nothing else could, the knot of human relationships upon which we are invited by the writer to fix our gaze. To extend the action to other settings would be to destroy the main idea of the play.

It is to the credit of Vidor that he has refrained from any such pseudo-cinematic adventure and stuck resolutely to his exterior set. But he has failed to appreciate the dramatic significance of this house front and its symbolic focal point, the stoop. His photographic approach lacks the imaginative quality that would endow the house with a visual reality of its own, while Vidor's underscoring of separate characters, detached from their background, and his insufficiently contrasted treatment of single episodes reduce the dramatic pattern of the play to a brightly colored mosaic of a not particularly clear design.

No absolute demand for originality of cinematic conception is so far implied in this criticism. Vidor can be original when he chooses to be. But it is a great pity that, in *Street Scene*, he did not show more daring in tackling the fundamental problem of every talking picture: the link with the audience, the cinematic proscenium. To do this, however, mere originality is not enough. It requires a revolution in cinematic outlook. (*The Nation*, September 16, 1931)

54. Hollywood Tries "Ideas": *As You Desire Me* (1932), dir. George Fitzmaurice; *Two Seconds* (1932), dir. Mervyn LeRoy.

It is difficult *not* to sympathize with Hollywood. No matter what it does, in what direction it strikes out, it is always faced with the same problem: the problem of choosing between the devil of the theatrical stage and the deep sea of its own helplessness. Watch it launch its gaily painted film-craft, a thing of enormous size but shallow draft, on some daring adventure into the less familiar regions of art. Almost as soon as land is lost from sight, you see the ship's pilot indeed at sea and the ship itself as it founders in deep waters.

No wonder Hollywood is loath to undertake such adventures. But unless it keeps within a safe distance from the shore, what alternative has it? Obviously, there is only the devil of the theatrical stage, with his tempting offerings of polished dialogue and greater intellectual subtlety. To be sure, to accept stage dialogue is to sin against the inner truth of the movies, for on the stage dialogue is an artificially inflated thing that does duty, under the conditions of theatrical presentation, for a great deal of human conduct that is essentially wordless. But there is undeniable fascination in the glitter and stimulating impact of well-chosen words, and Hollywood would have been more than human if it had not yielded to the temptation.

Not so with the other offering held out by the stage, its relatively superior intellectual approach to the material of life. Ideas, it so happens, have no important box-office value unless they can be appreciated by the least intelligent. Mindful of this, Hollywood has been chary of adapting stage plays of any marked originality of thought. But times have changed. Even the easily pleased movie public seems to be turning away from the infantile hokum on which it has been fed for so many years. Hollywood has now discovered that it cannot quite do without ideas—ideas sufficiently safe, of course, to stand the test of the box office, but ideas all the same, no matter how slight, provided they can pass for novelty. Evidence of this awakening interest in ideas has been accumulating for some time. At present suffice it to cite a few pictures that are being shown this week on Broadway.

One of them is *As You Desire Me* [1932, dir. George Fitzmaurice], which is based on a 1930 play of the same name by Luigi Pirandello. The reputation of a profound thinker enjoyed by Pirandello has perhaps been too easily won. At least to this writer, his profundities have never seemed to amount to much more than conscientious, if rather dull and superficial, exercises in cerebral gymnastics. But meet

Signor Pirandello on the screen, and by contrast with other screen playwrights he appears almost an intellectual giant.

To be sure, Pirandello's drama contains no ideas of striking depth or originality. The problem of a woman's assuming the identity of another woman, dismissing her doubts as well as those of her supposed husband in order that she may satisfy his ardent love for his lost wife, is really only a variant on the old dictum that the wish is father to the thought, superimposed on the familiar Pirandellian quandary of whether we are what we and others think we are. But it is an idea after all, and a refreshing one at that, when compared with the endless variations on the love triangle in which the only "idea" is the animal attraction of the sexes. Apart from this consideration, *As You Desire Me* has little to distinguish it from the average product of the Hollywood studios. It is essentially a stage play, with its dialogue bearing the entire burden of dramatic development, and it is acted without much distinction—even by its principal star, Greta Garbo.

And now we may turn to Hollywood's own efforts to supply new ideas. Here is, for instance, *Forgotten Commandments* [1932, dir. Louis J. Gasnier & William Schorr]. Free love in Communist Russia, people who worship the state instead of God, all moral precepts reversed— "thou shalt covet thy neighbor's wife, thou shalt steal, and thou shalt kill, if it is for the good of the state." Ah, here is something decidedly different, original, new. And so it would be, but for the important fact that it is no more true of Soviet Russia than of the United States, and that, moreover, the picture shows neither Russia nor America but typical Hollywood, with all its cheap sentiment and lurid sex. As for the other novel idea of the movie—the contrast between the present and the past with the help of some excerpts from Cecil B. DeMille's *Ten Commandments* [1923]—the pasteboard dramatics of this screen ballet are enough to kill any moral it was supposed to suggest.

No more successful in the matter of new ideas is *Two Seconds* [1932, dir. Mervyn LeRoy], in which an attempt is made to add novelty to the familiar love triangle by telling the sordid story of a murder as it is supposed to have flashed through the mind of the murderer the moment before he met his death in the electric chair. This device, of course, is not new. It was tried on the screen in Paul Fejos's *The Last Moment* [1928]. But what makes it so pointless in *Two Seconds* is that no sooner is it introduced in the opening sequence than it is completely forgotten during the rest of the film, for we are shown incidents that could never have been seen by the man supposed to recollect them, and the whole story is told not as it might have flashed through the man's mind, but as it could be seen only by an outside observer. As to the story itself, it is hardly worth telling, so hackneyed are most of its ingredients. So much for ideas . . . (*The Nation*, June 22, 1932)

55. Morals, Facts, and Fiction: *Bring 'Em Back Alive* (1932), dir. Clyde E. Elliott; *The Doomed Battalion* (1932), dir. Cyril Gardner.

A Chinese mandarin may be an extremely cultured person. He will compose poems of superb refinement and keen delicacy of perception describing the beauty of a rose or a sunset, dilating on the pangs of love, or philosophizing on the vanity of life. He will show a connoisseur's appreciation of fine painting and will surround himself with exquisite furniture and porcelain. But he will not think twice before ordering the head chopped off of some poor beggar who has been found guilty of breaking the law. For their part, the pleasure-loving Romans who wrote poetry, copied Greek sculpture, and studied Greek philosophy were equally free from the Christian scruples about the taking of human life, and enjoyed nothing better than the spectacle of gladiators fighting one another to the death. Today we call this sort of thing barbarism and cruelty, but is it? Perhaps the difference lies only in the greater concern that our civilization shows for the individual, a concern that past civilizations did not share, and that future civilizations may not share, either.

All these profound meditations, however, are merely a preamble to the statement that fights-to-the-death between wild animals, of which fights there are a goodly number in *Bring 'Em Back Alive* [1932], are a fascinating sight, our enjoyment of which remains completely untainted by any feeling of sadistic lust. The day may or may not come when we shall set as much store by the life of an animal as we do by the life of a human being. But for the present, so far as animals are concerned, we still share the general attitude of the Chinese and the ancient Romans: their life simply does not count. And once we have dismissed moral considerations, we can freely admit that there are majesty and beauty in the combat of such opponents as a tiger and a python. There are other exciting fights in *Bring 'Em Back Alive*, but the tiger-python contest, which fortunately for both combatants results in a draw, is far and away the most interesting thing that has been shown on the screen for a long time.

It may be proper to inquire whether the fact that this film is essentially a record of actual life has not also contributed something to its appeal. Unhesitatingly we say that it has. Facts as such are not necessarily interesting. But unfamiliar facts are. And after the reels of stereotyped fiction that make up most films, it is a decided relief to see something that springs straight from life and has preserved its natural form and color.

Wild life in a jungle is not the only natural subject to have found its way to the screen this week. We have had some magnificent views of the Tyrolean Alps, with an exciting ski run through the mountains, in *The Doomed Battalion* [1932], a picture that in its fictional material and its treatment does not rise much above the mediocre, although, having been made in Germany, it is slightly less conventional than the war pictures of Hollywood.

We have also had a more intelligent picture than ordinarily comes out of Hollywood, *The Dark Horse* [1932, Alfred E. Green], whose claim to distinction is its good-natured but merciless lampooning of the cant and ballyhoo of American politics. Here again one is impressed not so much by the story, which is a little far-fetched and scarcely reveals an honest grappling with genuine facts, as by the general picture of the dishonesty and racketeering that rule election campaigns in the United States. The film is further marked by amusing and pointed dialogue, and on the whole is very competently acted: tender mercies by any other name. (*The Nation*, July 6, 1932)

56. Personality or Talent?: *Make Me a Star* (1932), dir. William Beaudine.

Merton of the Movies, the 1919 novel by Harry Leon Wilson, the great stage hit of a few years later [1922, adaptation by George S. Kaufmann and Marc Connelly], and the silent picture of 1924 [dir. James Cruze], has now been made into a sound film with the new name of *Make Me a Star* [1932, dir. William Beaudine].

One cannot say with certainty whether Wilson set out in his book deliberately to burlesque the movies. It is probable that all he was interested in doing was to tell the amusing story of a small-town simpleton whose naïve earnestness and weird notions of acting are adroitly used by a film company to turn him into a star comedian. The public, however, unquestionably regarded the work as a satire on the movies and on the absurd way in which ignorant and talentless nobodies rise to the dizzying heights of stardom.

Now it cannot be denied that an implication to this effect, whether intentional or not, is present in Wilson's story. The stage version certainly saw the cinema as if it were merely a vulgar copy of the stage. "Look," it seemed to be saying, "how ludicrous it all is. A fellow may be an utter fool and not know a thing about acting, but in this crazy movie world even his foolishness and ignorance can appear as a talent for acting." To which one can only reply, "And why not?"

For the ability to act and particularly to act intelligently, with the full realization of the effect of every movement, gesture, and vocal inflection—which is what good acting means on the stage—is not really an essential requirement for good film acting. In the days of the silent pictures, when *Merton of the Movies* was written, film acting neither resembled nor *could* resemble acting on the stage, although in the general treatment of their material the screen directors tried their hardest to imitate the stage play. So, at that time, *Merton*'s jibe was substantially beside the point. Today, in this era of talkies, it would have been more justified on general grounds, since the talking picture does imitate stage acting in its misguided attempt to reproduce stage dialogue and theatrical situations.

But, then, is *Merton*'s jibe quite true in fact? I do not think so. The majority of film actors today are recruited from the stage, and although there are quite enough incompetents among them, I doubt that the number is any greater than you would find in the theater. What is more important, the acting ability that shows itself off most successfully on the screen is decidedly of a lower degree of competence than that required on the stage. Unlike the stage actor, the film actor appears best when he acts least. All he needs is personality, character, for this is enough to make his acting both natural and convincing. For this reason an actor like James Cagney, who would probably cut no figure at all on the stage, makes one of the best screen actors; whereas Edward G. Robinson, who acts very effectively on the stage, seems forced and unconvincing when he does his very intelligent and expert "acting" on the screen.

Not without its own unconscious humor is the fact that *Make Me a Star*, which makes fun of unconscious humor in screen acting, belies its moral by demonstrating the superiority of natural character-acting over the more dexterous "impersonation" of a character. Stuart Erwin, who plays the small-town delivery boy who crashes the studio gate through his disarming artlessness, is perhaps too comic a character for his part, but his acting is natural and he succeeds in being telling without any display of histrionics. Joan Blondell, on the other hand, is much more of an actress, and her persistent efforts to play the part, emphasizing her points with facial expression, fall mostly flat precisely because of that emphasis. (*The Nation*, July 20, 1932)

57. Nonsense and Satire: *Million Dollar Legs* (1932), dir. Edward F. Cline; *What Price Hollywood?* (1932), dir. George Cukor.

Nonsense, like madness, has its queer logic, and the queerer the logic the more fascinating the nonsense. It needed a Lewis Carroll to think of such a perfectly convincing reply as the Mad Hatter's "It was the *best* butter," when his attempt to mend a watch by putting butter into it was questioned by Alice. But there have been few Lewis Carrolls in the world, and it would hardly be fair to measure all attempts at light-hearted and frankly nonsensical entertainment by applying to them the standard set up by the author of *Alice in Wonderland* [1865]. Who will measure up to it? Not even the Marx Brothers or Joe Cook, delightful as their brand of nonsense often is.

Joseph L. Mankiewicz, the author of the story providing the basis for *Million Dollar Legs* [1932], and his adaptors have clearly fallen far short of producing a masterpiece. But they did let their fancy run as far as it would carry them, and the result is a film that at times has a quality of delightful freshness and genuine imagination much too rare in Hollywood products. The best moments in the film are the episodes describing the crazy system of government that rules in the Republic of Klopstokia. What with the arm-pulling contests, which is the Klopstokian way of electing a president, and the constant popping up of mysterious spies, who include the inimitable Ben Turpin, cross-eyed, becloaked, and with a notebook in his hand, the story starts off in the true mood of reckless extravaganza. Unfortunately, this mood does not last.

While being thankful for small mercies, one cannot help regretting that the film fails to rise to its opportunities in two other respects, aside from its tame ending. Here was a story that seemed to cry for a fantastic treatment along the lines of René Clair's *Le Million* [1931]. Yet all we get in the film is a routine linking of scenes with not the slightest attempt to give them a crazy and sweeping rhythm that would reflect the mood of its story. The other missed opportunity one can hardly hope to see realized in Hollywood. There is implicit satire in the Klopstokian methods of government. But to bring it out and stress its points would have required courage and independence of mind, and when has Hollywood shown that it had any of these qualities or cared for them?

It would be equally idle to expect genuine satire in the pictures that are supposed to satirize Hollywood itself. Recently, we had *Make Me a Star* [1932, William Beaudine], a picture of life in Hollywood that made fun of imaginary evils while glossing over the real ones. The same formula is to be discovered in the latest picture of this cycle, bearing the eloquent name of *What Price Hollywood?* [1932]. If we are to believe the authors and producers of this film, the price of Hollywood is the social downfall and degradation of those unable to resist the temptation of drink, and the perpetual agony and thwarted home life of those who, thanks to their eminence, are constantly exposed to public gaze.

Well, well, we had better not ask what it is that drives the Hollywood geniuses to seek oblivion in drink, or who spends countless sums of money whipping up the morbid curiosity of the public in the private life of film luminaries. Let us be content to accept this gentle picture of amiable, warm-hearted, and unaffected people suffering through no fault of their own, thankful at least for the capable acting of Lowell Sherman and Gregory Ratoff, and for the less frequent glimpses of her ability that Constance Bennett has been allowed to reveal in this film. Have I made myself clear, boys and girls? (*The Nation*, August 3, 1932)

58. Madness from Hollywood: *Horse Feathers* (1932), dir. Norman Z. McLeod; *American Madness* (1932), dir. Frank Capra.

When the Marx brothers are in a picture, the picture is all in the Marx brothers. This means more than their own prominence. They could not, of course, be in a picture without making themselves its heart and soul, its center of interest. But this also means that the other people with whom they surround themselves, though in the picture, are not of it. Such a pity. As a result, the peculiar brand of lunacy that these gifted actors have made their own loses some of its point. Their antics appear as the mere antics of funny men, as pure clowning, whereas they could have been something far more interesting—a lunacy run riot and setting its entire little world on its head.

There is a suggestion of such lunacy in the opening scene of *Horse Feathers* [1932, dir. Norman Z. McLeod]. Groucho as the newly installed president of a college, after addressing the students on the benefits of education in his inimitable vein, breaks into a dance, and the entire faculty of solemn and bewhiskered professors follows suit in the mock style of the finale of a musical comedy. But the situation is not followed up. The students remain mere spectators in a show, and the professors are never given another chance to indulge in a few jolly capers of their own. Imagination staggers at the thought of what the campus life would have been like had Groucho conducted a course on love with the expert assistance of the college widow who figures in the story, creating perhaps a few more widows from among the professors' wives; had Harpo been appointed to the combined professorship of dog-catching and harp-playing; and had Chico been made the head of the college speakeasy and a professor of bootlegging. But the Marx family makes no attempt to put college education on a sound, or in any event satirical, basis. Instead it engages in a series of escapades that, mad and highly amusing as they are, do not amount to much more than just delightful fooling.

Harpo's gags come off perhaps best of all. His method of catching dogs with the help of a butterfly net and a variety of portable lampposts to suit dogs of different sizes, and his drive around the football field in a garbage man's cart looking for all the world like a chariot driver of ancient Rome, are two of his happiest conceits. But I wish for once that he had left out his solo number on the harp. It may be fine music, and it may be perfectly in its place in a vaudeville act, but it does not belong in a film like *Horse Feathers*. In fact, the main flaw in all Marx Brothers movies, if one can be so ungrateful as to pursue this subject, is the inability of these unique comedians to think of the cinema as being essentially different from the vaudeville stage.

American Madness [1932, dir. Frank Capra] also deals with madness, but of a different kind. The picture relates the story of a bank managed by an extremely able, honest, and likeable president, but brought to the very brink of ruin when exaggerated reports of its losses cause the panic-stricken public to make a run on its funds. The story is sheer propaganda for the banks and in some of its episodes falls short of the plausible, but it is skillfully told, capably acted—particularly by Walter Huston as the president—and directed with real distinction by Frank Capra. The scene of the run on the bank is film art at its best. (*The Nation*, August 31, 1932)

59. Premature Births: *Love Me Tonight* (1932), dir. Rouben Mamoulian; *Back Street* (1932), dir. John M. Stahl.

If the young ladies who go to the movies do not yet know all about the glory of romance and its frequent aftermath of disillusionment and misery, in one week recently they had an opportunity for completing their education in the space of a few hours. Starting at the Rivoli Theater, where a blissful prelude was being played out under the eloquent title of *Love Me Tonight* [1932], they might have gone next to the Hollywood Theater to learn of the painful consequences that follow such reckless conduct, as demonstrated in *Life Begins* [1932, James Flood], which begins, of course, in a maternity hospital. Finally, the young ladies in question should have retraced their steps to visit the Mayfair Theater and let *Back Street* [1932] open their eyes to the miserable lot of a woman who chooses to be the mistress of a married man. If, after taking this short course in the joys and sorrows of womanhood, they found it not too absorbing, I should probably agree with them. But then this is the best that Hollywood can do for them in a single day, and, as the French say, even the most beautiful girl cannot give more than she has.

As a mere male I must admit that I find but little in any of the three pictures mentioned that is not either flat and dull, or so overloaded with mawkish sentiment that it makes me feel distinctly uncomfortable. The dullness and flatness, I regret to say, are to be found in particularly irritating doses in *Love Me Tonight*. Maurice Chevalier, who used to charm us with the roguishness of a sprightly boy and the knowledgeable understanding of a man of the world that made him such a delightful screen lover, is revealed in this latest picture as a tired old chap who is trying his hardest to appear lively and irresistible. The lack of his usual verve and spontaneity is made particularly obvious in Chevalier's songs, one and all of which seem painfully forced.

Even more disappointing to me, because of the expectations aroused by his earlier work, is Rouben Mamoulian's performance as the director of the picture. In his first film, *Applause* [1929], made when the talkies were still in their infancy, Mamoulian was daring and original. Above all, he showed a quality of imagination that knew how to bring the unfamiliar and the significant out of the welter of photographic impressions. In *Love Me Tonight*, a musical comedy-romance with a touch of willful extravaganza, he either failed to find a subject after his own heart, or failed to discover in himself the power of imagination that would have made the movie's hackneyed story pointed and interesting.

Only once, and then merely by repeating himself, does Mamoulian succeed in striking a note of convincing inventiveness. This is in the opening scene, showing the sleepy Paris awakening to its daily labors in a swelling symphony of miscellaneous noises. In the rest of the picture he either attempts comedy in the style of Ernst Lubitsch, without the latter's flair for the bizarre, or follows the treatment of music in *Sous les toits de Paris* [1930, René Clair] through laborious repetition of the same song by various characters—quite regardless of its dramatic relevance to the story. After hearing about a dozen versions of "The Son of a Gun Is Nothing But a Tailor," at least one of the spectators was on the point of substituting a less printable language in the title.

Of the other two pictures, *Life Begins* has interesting material insofar as it describes the trials and tribulations of expectant mothers. It also has frequent flashes of genuine humor. But its dramatic theme is theatrically conceived, and its general sentiment is unbearably cloying. Flat, unconvincing, and mawkish are the only words that can be applied to *Back Street*, which should just go back where it came from. (*The Nation*, September 14, 1932)

60. Intermission: *Strange Interlude* (1932), dir. Robert Z. Leonard.

Eugene O'Neill is a tremendously earnest writer. He delves into the mysteries of human life and conduct with a passion and fearlessness that give his work a sort of incandescence. The very intensity of O'Neill's feeling invests his plays with a monumental quality that is rarely present in the work of other American playwrights. Yet underneath this impressive weightiness, which seems to be so solid and four-square, there is nearly always something that betrays an inner weakness. This is evident in his last play, *Mourning Becomes Electra* [1931], and to a still greater degree in his earlier *Strange Interlude* [1928].

In *Mourning Becomes Electra*, the fierce passions that drive its characters to destruction have the ring of reality (if one excepts, perhaps, the much too deliberate parade of Freudian complexes, particularly in the case of Orin Mannon). But behind this chain of seemingly inevitable calamities, one can see the author himself assuming the role of inexorable fate and blocking one possible detour after another, so that the play's characters may be forced to follow the course that he has laid out for them.

In *Strange Interlude*, O'Neill confronts his characters not so much with a situation of his own making as with a psychological theory, a concept of womanly love, which at his bidding they are compelled to enact in their various destinies. Nina Leeds's love is a compound of cravings for a child, a lover, a husband, and a father, and accordingly the play develops into a series of episodes in which all these cravings are finally gratified. The drama stands or falls by this concept of complementary loves. If we question its truth, then *Strange Interlude* becomes merely a brilliant exercise in dramatic make-believe.

Yet it is difficult not to question the play's truth. Without going into details, one may point out that the affectionate craving for a child and the sensual craving for a lover are not usually regarded as sojourning amicably in a woman's heart, one by the side of the other. Even if Otto Weininger's classification of women into two types, mothers and prostitutes, is unquestionably far-fetched, there is the penetrating analysis of feminine psychology in D. H. Lawrence's *Lady Chatterley's Lover* [1929]—dealing with a situation closely resembling that of *Strange Interlude*—which lends no support to O'Neill's view of the complementary nature of the erotic urge and the maternal instinct.

Nonetheless, Nina's sexual make-up as it is seen by O'Neill is the core of the play, which alone gives it unity and meaning. In the screen version of *Strange Interlude* [1932, dir. Robert Z. Leonard] now being shown in New York, this inner significance of Nina's relations with her four men is largely lost. The pentagon has been reduced to a triangle, with Nina's husband, Sam Evans, and her doctor-lover contending for her favors, instead of *Nina's* trying to hold all her strings in a balanced relationship that is completely satisfying to herself. The story is further conventionalized by the omission of two important episodes—Nina's resort to abortion in order that her husband's offspring may not inherit the taint of his family, and her frank proposal to Dr. Ned Darrell that he become her lover for the sole purpose of giving her and Sam a healthy child.

Yet even so bowdlerized and deprived of many of its subtler points, the film version of *Strange Interlude* is to be regarded as a notable achievement. For once Hollywood has dared to produce a picture that deals with life in terms of adult intelligence. But though the courage thus shown deserves every credit, the outgrowth of this courage, the picture itself, is hardly a feather in the producers' cap. It conforms faithfully to its Hollywood type of an uninspired crossbreed of the stage and the screen; and it is badly miscast in its two principal parts. The beautiful but cold Norma Shearer is not the actress for the role of Nina Leeds, nor is the uncouth Clark Gable the actor for the part of Ned Darrell. (*The Nation*, September 28, 1932)

61. School Days: *Mädchen in Uniform* (1931), dir. Leontine Sagan.

When you come to think of it, the movies are really one of the privileged arts. We ask so little of them, and are so greatly pleased when we get that little. A novel or a play giving no more than a true portrait of life would hardly rouse us to any fits of enthusiasm. But when a moving picture breaks away from the time-worn clichés of Hollywood, our hearts leap with joy and we feel we want to acclaim the courageous piece of work as a masterpiece of art. Such is our gratitude.

And well is this gratitude deserved in the case of *Mädchen in Uniform* [*Girls in Uniform*, 1931], the German-made picture now showing in New York. Leontine Sagan's film [from the 1930 play *Yesterday and Today*, by Christa Winsloe] does more than merely tell its story in an honest and straightforward way. It succeeds in permeating the story with an atmosphere of sensitive understanding that makes its characters supremely human.

The comedy of school life is familiar enough. It has been left to *Mädchen in Uniform* to show us something of its drama. It would have been easy in a subject of this kind to stress the obvious, and to appeal to the sympathy of the audience with scenes of heartless tyranny over children. Commendably, the film avoids this beaten path. It conveys the sense of drama merely by depicting the oppressive atmosphere of a girls' boarding school in Germany, a school ruled by a soulless discipline that stifles all natural human instincts and reduces the students to the condition of mere ciphers. Inevitably, now and again some sensitive youngster breaks down under this strain. Then enter hysterics, attempts at suicide, and scandal, as the situation is viewed by the guardians of school proprieties.

Perhaps the main charm of the movie is the naturalness with which the schoolgirls play their parts. The characterization of the mistresses is less happy, suggesting as it does the more deliberate emphasis on stage technique. An exception to this, however, is the acting of Dorothea Wieck—in the part of the idolized mistress, Fräulein von

Bernburg—who reveals remarkable reserve and delicacy of interpretation in a rather difficult role.

It may be ungracious to add that in its use of the cinematic medium, *Mädchen in Uniform* does not strike any note of originality, and in fact is quite conventional. But there is no need to be captious. The excellent taste, the thoroughgoing charm, and the abiding honesty of the film are enough these days to make us welcome it as far and away the most interesting picture of the season. (*The Nation*, October 12, 1932)

62. Class War: *Cabin in the Cotton* (1932), dir. Michael Curtiz; *A Bill of Divorcement* (1932), dir. George Cukor.

Hollywood has so often been criticized for pandering to the tastes of the least intelligent members of the moviegoing public that any attempt it may make to rise to the level of adult intelligence, however hesitant and timid such an attempt may be, deserves to be noted with a word of encouragement and praise. In regarding *Cabin in the Cotton* [1932, dir. Michael Curtiz] as such a praiseworthy effort, I am not unmindful of its failure to arouse anything approaching enthusiasm among the New York critics.

A story with only a modicum of sex appeal, a central figure that is neither particularly relevant to the main theme nor sufficiently interesting as a character study, and a plot that lacks dramatic suspense cannot be expected to stir the blood of the sentimental cynics who view the world from a Broadway window. Nevertheless, to those whose interest in drama extends beyond the conflicts of individual consciousness and the specious dramatics of contrived entanglements, *Cabin in the Cotton* will provide a welcome relief from the juvenile trivialities of the average Hollywood movie.

There is no need to dwell at length on the main theme of the picture—the fierce struggle between the tenants and the planters in the cotton-growing South. The general facts are familiar enough: ceaseless toil and squalor on the one side; ruthless exploitation, as well as a life of ease and luxury, on the other. But if the facts are not new, their presentation on the screen without any glossing over of their disturbing social significance is something to be decidedly grateful for. Here is a corner of human life simmering with passions and hatreds that now and again burst into flames of wholesale destruction; to have it brought home to one's mind and soul is to gain a valuable new experience.

It is not that the film is faultless even as a social document. It makes a feeble attempt to suggest that the conflicting interests of the tenants and planters might be reconciled by some amicable arrangement on the basis of cooperative enterprise. But this is obviously a concession that Paul Green, the author of *Cabin in the Cotton*'s scenario [from the 1931 novel of the same name by Harry Harrison Kroll], had to make to his producers to absolve them from taking sides in a social conflict.

One may wonder why a movie production company should feel constrained to disclaim any intention of approving or disapproving the implicit message of a story it produces, as Warner Brothers does in this case through a special introductory statement from the screen. After all, the public is not particularly interested in the opinions of the production companies. But such is the anomaly of the film industry. A film is not merely sponsored by a production company, as a play would be, but is actually written and directed under the constant supervision of its producers. Under the Hollywood system, then, it will be a long time before the author and the director are free to say just what they want to say and in the way they want to say it.

Only by bearing in mind such reservations as these can *A Bill of Divorcement* [1932, dir. George Cukor] be accepted as a picture of more than average merit. Clemence Dane's 1921 play has been transferred to the screen with a care and sensitiveness that have preserved all its essential qualities. The film is intelligent, moving, and capably acted. Its main defect, and it is the defect of the adaptation, is that the situation it depicts—the sudden return from an asylum of an insane husband when his wife is on the point of marrying another man—carries the hallmark of a stage conception designed to confront the spectator with a dramatic conflict that does not spring inevitably from the relationship of its characters. (*The Nation*, October 26, 1932)

63. Going into Politics: *Washington Merry-Go-Round* (1932), dir. James Cruze.

In the matter of politics the movies have so far been content to play the part of an unofficial apologist for the ruling classes, their interests and their policies. On occasion, the propagandist activities of the cinema have been directly and obviously inspired by those policies. But the organization and interests of the film industry have always been too closely bound up with those of the dominant class to make such direct inspiration necessary for the routine work of manufacturing popular entertainment.

Moreover, American motion pictures have done more than merely preach the comfortable gospel of earthly rewards awaiting the bold and enterprising in this land of opportunity. Owing to the peculiar quality of the film medium in its established form, which form incidentally has become established because of this very quality, the main appeal of the movies has been their power to conjure up a world of dreams, to supply the spectator with a sedative that would set free his pent-up longings for romance, adventure, and pleasures usually denied him. Thus, moving pictures have served as a disseminator of the approved social doctrine, on the one hand, and as a safety valve for public discontent, on the other.

In the light of this function of the movies, it is somewhat surprising to observe that, of late, they have been trying to deal with subjects that by their very nature refuse to stay confined in a world of dreams, but persist in awakening the spectator to the realities of his life. Such subjects are the social and economic conditions of America, which, in their present state, with all the suffering and injustice they involve, are too keenly felt by the masses of people to be sublimated into anything resembling the land of promise. Clearly, there must be special reasons to induce the film producers to depart from their established policy. It is a fairly safe guess that one of the reasons is the growth of a critical attitude among the moviegoing public, which is no longer so easily pleased with the tawdry glamor of conventional romancing, and demands something more clearly attuned to its present insurgent temper. But the leopard cannot change its spots, and the film producers, when obliged to adjust themselves to the new demand, cannot change their minds either—even if they succeed in changing their voices.

A case in point is *Washington Merry-Go-Round* [1932, dir. James Cruze], the Hollywood contribution to the election campaign, which sets out to expose the "malignant powers" ruling the United States behind the back and over the head of the official government. As an indication of the profound political thought that has inspired this piece of screen pamphleteering, it will be sufficient to say that the "malignant powers" referred to are represented in the person of a high-placed, tremendously wealthy racketeer who holds senators and congressmen in the palm of his hand, controls elections through his power over political bosses, and disposes of his opponents by means that, in an emergency, do not stop short of poisoning. This sinister personage naturally meets with condign punishment at the hands of a lion-hearted young man who comes to Washington to destroy the monster of privilege and corruption, and whose gospel of political faith is that honesty and justice would be reinstated in their seat of power if only the people would disregard the political machine and send honest men as their representatives to Washington.

It may be exaggerating the importance of this much too obvious melodrama to discuss it in terms of political intelligence. Nor is the picture so discussed here. *Washington Merry-Go-Round* is mentioned merely as a significant example of Hollywood's valiant efforts to catch up with the times. (*The Nation*, November 9, 1932)

64. Captive Comrades: *Kameradschaft* (1931), dir. G. W. Pabst; *I Am a Fugitive from a Chain Gang* (1932), dir. Mervyn LeRoy.

In Germany, Georg Wilhelm Pabst is regarded as one of the shining lights of the film world, a director who can always be relied upon to produce a masterpiece. I cannot claim familiarity with the entire body of Pabst's work, but the few silent pictures of his that I have seen and the two more recent talkies, *Westfront 1918* [1930] and *The Beggar's Opera* [1931], have not seemed to me to justify the claims made for them. My pleasure, therefore, is all the greater when I find in *Kameradschaft* [*Comradeship*, 1931] an example of Pabst's work that inspires genuine respect for his abilities as a director, and that unquestionably stands out as one of those rare events on the screen: a sincere, psychologically convincing, and powerful presentation of a vital theme.

It is possible to see the main distinction of *Kameradschaft* in its tempered yet eloquent appeal to the workers of France and Germany—and by implication to those of all other countries— to join hands in the defense of their common interests as a class. From this point of view, the story that the film tells, of German miners forcing their way across the border to assist in the rescue of their French comrades trapped in a coal mine by a disastrous fire, is an excellent parable glorifying the spirit of comradeship that rises triumphant over national prejudices and official obstacles.

Admirable, however, as this parable is, both in its message and in the restraint with which it is stated, I do not think that the didactic intent of *Kameradschaft* is the source of the movie's strength. What impressed me most was the extraordinary sense of reality conveyed by the film's consistent avoidance of specious dramatics. There was something particularly convincing in its plain, straightforward handling of its material, in the fine delicacy of its characterization—which went hand in hand with the perfect naturalness of the acting—in its sensitive appreciation of emotional values, and finally in the abundant and illuminating detail with which it set before our eyes the full significance of such a mine disaster. Many scenes in *Kameradschaft* etched themselves on my memory, but one of them is particularly haunting—the image of a young woman trudging with a child behind a truck as it takes her husband and other German volunteers to the scene of the disaster.

One blemish, though a small one, breaks the uniform excellence of the work. While G. W. Pabst is sternly realistic through most of the film, he inexplicably deserts the ground of observable facts to picture, in one of the episodes, the inner thoughts of a character. This is an unwarranted change of style and it strikes a jarring note. Aside from this, *Kameradschaft* is a notable contribution to the art of the screen.

I Am a Fugitive from a Chain Gang [1932, dir. Mervyn LeRoy] cannot compare with *Kameradschaft* in subtlety of treatment, but among Hollywood pictures it stands out as a conscientious piece of work that deals adequately, if not excitingly, with an important problem in American life. The film is based on the life story of one Robert Elliott Burns, who was condemned for a minor offense to serve in a chain gang in Georgia, succeeded in escaping, rose by honest work to the position of editor and publisher of a magazine in Chicago, was re-arrested after seven years of freedom, and, in spite of promises of pardon, was sent to complete his sentence in the chain gang—from which he at last again escaped. *I Am a Fugitive* exposes with telling effect the brutal cruelty of the chain-gang system, and should help to awaken the public conscience to the disgrace of its existence in a civilized country.

It was interesting to see the screen version of *Once in a Lifetime* [1932, dir. Russell Mack], which two years ago made history on the stage [1930 play by Moss Hart and George S. Kaufman]. It may have taken courage to broadcast to the world this satire on Hollywood, but the result need not disturb the sleep of the amiable Carl Laemmle [of Universal Pictures]. As a satire the film lacks fire. On the stage its buffoonery seemed willfully fantastic, but real enough because it made no pretense to being anything but extravaganza. On the screen the fantasy assumes an exaggeratedly realistic form, and therefore immediately becomes unbelievable as a story. Still, even regarded as a farce, the picture is good entertainment. (*The Nation*, November 23, 1932)

65. Gastronomy: *Trouble in Paradise* (1932), dir. Ernst Lubitsch; *The Most Dangerous Game* (1932), dir. Irving Pichel & Ernest B. Schoedsack.

One may wish there were more sting, more sarcasm, in Ernst Lubitsch's polished wit, but we must take the man as he is, and with all his limitations Lubitsch seems to be the only director in Hollywood who talks the language of adult people, and whose suave, subtle humor betrays a keen if cynical mind. His cynicism has earned him the title of the acknowledged master of "sophisticated" comedy. Yet in the last analysis it is probably the least important element in Lubitsch's make-up as an artist. It shines only by contrast with the primitive earnestness of Main Street. Regarded by itself, such sophisticated comedy suggests no more than the attitude of a good-natured gourmet who enjoys the oddities of the human smorgasbord. I have no quarrel with Lubitsch on this score. His intellectual mood has at least the grace of a certain refinement. I am more thrilled, however (if the word "thrilled" can be applied to the titillating sensation produced by his work), by the masterly skill with which he tells his after-dinner stories, the skill of a raconteur who makes his points without raising his voice.

Trouble in Paradise [1932] is one of the gossamer creations of Ernst Lubitsch's narrative art. The story, it goes without saying, is a trivial anecdote that deals with some adventures on the part of two society crooks. It is unnecessary to relate the plot in detail, and it would be impossible in this brief notice to describe the innumerable touches of wit and skill with which the narrative is unfolded. The opening scene gives the key to the treatment of the story. It shows us a man collecting garbage whom we presently discover to be a Venetian garbage man, carrying away his spoils in a gondola to the accompaniment of a raucous song. And so, throughout the picture, we see the adroit and impish Lubitsch turn his slightly crooked mirror now to one episode, now to another. It is all thoroughly delightful.

The difference between *Trouble in Paradise* and *The Kid from Spain* [1932, dir. Leo McCarey] is the difference between *soufflé* and spaghetti, but Eddie Cantor's spaghetti can be absorbed with considerable enjoyment, even when too filling and too highly seasoned. The picture, of course, is a star "vehicle." Those who, like myself, enjoy Cantor's playing the part of an innocent will find plenty of broad comedy in his adventures in Mexico, culminating in a hilarious bullfight.

Horror, like humor, can also be of two kinds. One hits you in the stomach, the other in the head. I cannot speak with certainty about the former variety, for clutching hands, screeching owls, or butlers made up to look like monsters never cause the slightest spasm in the lower part of my anatomy. But as films of this kind are made by the dozen, there must be enough people who enjoy abdominal horror. *Kongo* [1932, dir. William J. Cowen] comes near to being this type of picture, but its voodoo magic, with all its frenzy and human sacrifice, never stirred a hair on my head—or a muscle in my tummy. On the other hand, in *The Most Dangerous Game* [1932, dir. Irving Pichel & Ernest B. Schoedsack] I sensed something like incipient cerebral horror, although the movie had few of the usual trappings of its genre. In fact, the film's entire horror was contained in its Wellsian idea—the use of human beings as quarry in big-game hunting. No blood-curdling sensation was added to this horrible thought by the actual hunt.

The Conquerors [1932, dir. William A. Wellman] is another attempt to portray the rise of modern America on an epic scale. Made by the same company that produced *Cimarron* [1931, dir. Wesley Ruggles], the film follows the pattern of its predecessor without recapturing the latter's panoramic sweep or dramatic interest. I must also add that it is unbearably vulgar in its entire philosophy of the progress of the United States. (*The Nation*, December 7, 1932)

66. A Novel Idea: *If I Had a Million* (1932), dir. James Cruze & H. Bruce Humberstone; *The Sign of the Cross* (1932), dir. Cecil B. DeMille.

Sometimes it is art that copies nature, and sometimes, as we have learned from Oscar Wilde, it is nature that copies art. In the case of *If I Had a*

Million [1932] the situation is somewhat more complicated. The film itself is, with some allowance, a fairly creditable attempt at verisimilitude. It is safe to predict, however, that its effect upon life, if it has any, will be the reverse of Wilde's dictum. Instead of inducing people to copy its art, it will make them mend their ways and thus destroy the very "nature" that has provided it with its material and moral. I refer in particular to the refusal of some of the characters portrayed in the film to credit the genuineness of the million-dollar checks that have been presented to them by an eccentric millionaire. After the film has completed its round of the movie theaters of the country, there will be very few people, I am sure, incredulous enough to regard such gifts as worthless paper, and probably no keeper of a doss house will, in the future, light his cigarette with a genuine million-dollar check.

Of the other possible effects of *If I Had a Million* I can speak with much less confidence. Were Hollywood as capable of grasping the moral of this film as the public is likely to be, the production of *If I Had a Million* would mark an important advance toward a more intelligent conception of what constitutes an interesting film story. For the film is different from the usual run. Unfolding a series of independent episodes related to one another only through the general premise of what people are likely to do when they suddenly become rich, *If I Had a Million* proves conclusively that an interesting idea has as much power to cast a spell over the mind of the audience as any number of complications in the dramatic plot. In the case of the film under review, this power is demonstrated in spite of the mediocre quality of many of the individual stories that make up the narrative. If the film can only succeed in convincing Hollywood that intelligence adds value to its productions, it will have performed an important service in raising American movies from the mire of cheap sentiment and hokum.

That the latter two ingredients are much in evidence in Cecil B. DeMille's *The Sign of the Cross* [1932] is only what would be expected from the work of this stalwart of the Hollywood tradition. The film is frankly a "spectacle," with all the pyrotechnic display of the splendors and horrors of Rome during the days of Christian martyrdom to which we became accustomed in the silent examples of this type. Of its kind, the film is probably as good as any of its predecessors, and if one can believe in its Romans and Christians, one will find it sufficiently entertaining and at times perhaps even thrilling. I can only wish that somebody would give us a picture of Roman life that shows some genuine insight into the psychology and mode of living of those days. We have had a surfeit of cheap oleographs.

With Williamson Beneath the Sea [1932, J. E. Williamson], a picture of submarine fauna and flora, gives (in happy contrast to *The Sign of the Cross*) an interesting and vivid account of the unfamiliar life under water. Some of its episodes strike one as having been specially staged, but this takes away little from the informative value—and "nature"— of the picture. (*The Nation*, December 21, 1932)

67. Hemingway in Hollywood: *A Farewell to Arms* (1932), dir. Frank Borzage.

There is little in the past performance of Hollywood producers to encourage high hopes in a critic when he is preparing to see a new Hollywood picture. To be sure, a few films shown during this season, notably Ernst Lubitsch's *Trouble in Paradise* [1932], have made one think that the producers were awakening to the demands of the more intelligent section of the moviegoing public and were sincerely anxious to raise their standards. But apparently the occasional good things that come out of southern California are matters of accident, and the old ideas of what makes a good film still rule, even when an attempt is made to hitch the stars to a vehicle of recognized artistic merit. It is this disappointing fact that is glaringly evident in *A Farewell to Arms* [1932, dir. Frank Borzage], the latest bid for cinematic laurels, which in some usually discerning quarters has been hailed, unaccountably, as the greatest American picture ever made.

Though I too hoped to acclaim this new masterpiece, I am compelled to report that *A Farewell to Arms* not only falls short of being great in any sense of the word, but is actually merely another screen "romance," differing from its countless predecessors only in its more natural dialogue and better acting [by Helen Hayes and Gary Cooper in the leading roles]. Neither of these distinctions, however, is sufficiently strong to overcome the fundamental banality of the story as it is unfolded in this free adaptation of Ernest Hemingway's 1929 novel. To be sure, a film is not to be judged by its success or failure in giving dramatic form to the literary narrative that is its source. A cinematic work must be considered on its own merits. But in the case of *A Farewell to Arms*, it may be illuminating to point out how Hemingway's simple and charming romance has been vulgarized by the injection of cheap melodramatic or sentimental episodes, gratuitously introduced with the apparent object of making the story more dramatic.

At the outset it must be admitted that the story as told in the novel does not lend itself to successful dramatization. Except for the final, sad ending as the girl dies in childbirth, with the war in the background, there are no emotional developments and no dramatic situations in the entire course of the blissful love that unites the two characters of Hemingway's fiction. One might have expected the producers to let well enough alone and choose something more suitable to their ends. But the desire to present a bestseller must have been irresistible, and once the book was started on the course of screen adaptation, it inevitably came down to the level of the usual sloppy screen love.

If there is anything particularly striking in Hemingway's *Farewell to Arms*, it is the remarkable restraint in the conduct of his characters as well as in his account of the various episodes. In Frank Borzage's film there are tears and sad partings and prayers and painful complications, none of which exist in the novel. The heroine does not say good-bye almost cheerfully, as she does in the book, but must come to the train station by herself after the parting to watch her lover go away. She does not tell him that she is going to become a mother, but must go secretly to another country to bear her child. And all her letters to the man must be returned, so that she may collapse from shock. Nor do the two live in sin, happily, without much thought about proprieties. They must have a priest to throw a cloak of respectability over their union through a fervent prayer for their happiness.

One could go on enumerating the "happy" touches introduced by the adaptors [Benjamin Glazer & Oliver H.P. Garrett]. But they are all of the same kind and their effect is invariably to strike either a sentimental or melodramatic note, to make the situation conform more nearly to the traditional screen conception of the tragic course of true love. (*The Nation*, January 4, 1933)

68. More Celluloid: *Rasputin and the Empress* (1932), dir. Richard Boleslawski & Charles Brabin; *The Half-Naked Truth* (1932), dir. Gregory La Cava.

If you do not like the kind of literature that is published in the so-called pulp magazines, you just do not like it, and that is the end of it. You do not rush into print to expose the pathetic ineptitude of these weekly or monthly outpourings. With the cinema, unfortunately, the situation is different. Not only are there woefully few pictures that are worthy of serious consideration, but if you happen to be a critic, you are obliged to stop and analyze the incessant flow of bilge issuing from the film factories of Hollywood and elsewhere as if it were really to be measured by the standards of intellectual and artistic achievement. The whole procedure becomes unspeakably grotesque, resembling in a way what the Russians describe as shooting sparrows with cannon balls. Worse still, it becomes wearisomely repetitious, for in movies originality is found in virtues, not, as in real life, in sins.

Yet once more I have to devote this column to the exploration of motion-picture vices. The worst offender to come under review is *Rasputin and the Empress* [1932, dir. Richard Boleslawski & Charles Brabin]. Although one does not expect historical accuracy from Hollywood, the falsification of well-known facts as exemplified in this film goes far beyond the limits of tolerable license. In fact, it is nothing short of political partisanship to represent Czar Nicholas II, a shallow-minded weakling who paid with his life for his unfitness to occupy the throne of Russia, as a kindly ruler whose only thought was the well-being of his people.

Moreover, the portrait of Czarina Alexandra as drawn on screen is an extremely prettified version of her true character. In spite of the irrefutable evidence of scheming, ruthlessness, and neurotic megalomania supplied by the Czarina's own letters, the film shows her solely as an affectionate wife and mother whose only concern in life was the happiness of her family. In the attempt to whitewash her memory, the author of the screenplay—Charles MacArthur, of all people—represents the Czarina as abetting the murder of Grigori Rasputin, whereas her letters show that the death of the lecherous monk moved her to bitter cries for vengeance.

Aside from such historical inaccuracies, which are too numerous to be cited here in detail, *Rasputin and the Empress* does not even stand up as good melodrama. It neither grips one by dramatic suspense nor impresses by any display of histrionics. Lionel Barrymore, who plays Rasputin, never succeeds in suggesting the powerful, magnetic personality that Rasputin undoubtedly had, and which largely accounted for his rise to power. John and Ethel Barrymore are no more than colorless ciphers in their respective parts of Prince Paul Chegodieff and the Czarina.

Thankfully, there is little that can be said about *Cynara* [1932, dir. King Vidor]. Innocuous in its story and no more than slick in its acting and direction, this picture might have been fairly entertaining as comedy. As a romance with a touch of tragedy, it is merely nebulous. For its part, *The Half-Naked Truth* [1932, dir. Gregory La Cava], which relates with considerable gusto the adventures of a high-pressure publicity agent, has many loose ends in its own story. As it is only a farcical comedy, the movie goes merrily on without bothering to pick these up—which, in the end, perhaps does not really matter one way or the other. (*The Nation*, January 18, 1933)

Afterword

"Impressions in a Studio: Life Mirrored in Films" (1927), by Alexander Bakshy

At the Cosmopolitan Studios on 127th Street in New York, I was privileged to witness the birth of virtue under the magic incantations of three kind fairies in the squalid surroundings of a tenement house. Had art been of no concern, any tenement might have answered the purpose. But not so here. The director took great pains to secure a house that would best convey the atmosphere of the story. Wherever it was found, the producer took its details and, lo and behold, a few weeks later an exact replica of the façade of the house is found installed under the roof of Cosmopolitan Studios. The same may be said of the choice of other locations, as well as of the effects of lighting and acting.

The picture, which is being produced by Robert T. Kane for First National, will bear the obvious and highly expressive title of *Hell's Kitchen* [a.k.a. *For the Love of Mike*; 1927, dir. Frank Capra]. The fairies are represented by three old and grumpy bachelors, one of whom is a Jew, another an Irishman, and the third a Dutchman; and the prospective embodiment of virtue is, at this stage of the story, just about two months old, being a foundling whom the three disgruntled gentlemen, heretofore continuously at odds with one another, decide to bring up as a respectable member of the community.

During the hour I spent watching the shooting of the movie, the future hero, at his two months' stage played by one Baby Jackie, bore the trying experience of being amused by his three godfathers with extraordinarily good humor. Whether it was the music that accompanied the shooting, or the occasional rests in bed with his milk bottle at his service, Baby Jackie did not utter a single cry. And, like the rest of the company, he had to go through long shots and medium shots and close-ups—all these thrice repeated from different angles, so that the director may be able to pick out the best when the picture comes to the cutting room.

It is an amusing business, this present method of making movies. For the 300 feet that will represent the scene I finally watch in the finished film, as many as 3,000 feet were actually shot in the studio. It does seem a waste of resources. But such is the technique of the modern motion picture. Money is wasted and time is wasted. If only both could be used to greater purpose . . . (*New York Times*, May 29, 1927)

Bibliographical Record of Alexander Bakshy's Film Criticism

Film Reviews for the *Nation*

1. Realism au Naturel: *Chang: A Drama of the Wilderness* (1927), dir. Merian C. Cooper & Ernest B. Schoedsack.
   The Nation, May 18, 1927, p. 564.
2. Douglas Fairbanks: *The Gaucho* (1927), dir. F. Richard Jones.
   The Nation, January 25, 1928, p. 104.
3. Chaplin: *The Circus* (1928), dir. Charlie Chaplin.
   The Nation, February 29, 1928, pp. 247-248.
4. Character and Drama: *The Last Command* (1928), dir. Josef von Sternberg; *The Crowd* (1928), dir. King Vidor.
   The Nation, April 18, 1928, pp. 463-464.
5. The Russian Contribution: *Czar Ivan the Terrible*, a.k.a. *The Wings of a Serf* (1926), dir. Yuri Tarich; *The End of St. Petersburg* (1927), dir. Vsevolod Pudovkin.
   The Nation, July 25, 1928, pp. 94, 96.
6. The Language of Images: *Ten Days That Shook the World*, a.k.a. *October* (1927), dir. Sergei Eisenstein; *Shadows of Fear* (1928), dir. Jacques Feyder; *Four Devils* (1928), dir. F. W. Murnau; *Lonesome* (1928), dir. Paul Fejos; *The Wedding March* (1928), dir. Erich von Stroheim; *White Shadows in the South Seas* (1928), dir. W. S. Van Dyke; *Show People* (1928), dir. King Vidor
   The Nation, December 26, 1928, pp. 720-721.
7. A Year of Talkies: *Coquette* (1929), dir. Sam Taylor; *Broadway* (1929), Paul Fejos; *The Rainbow Man* (1929), dir. Fred C. Newmeyer; *Bulldog Drummond* (1929), dir. F. Richard Jones; *Madame X* (1929), dir. Lionel Barrymore; *The Trial of Mary Dugan* (1929), dir. Bayard Veiller.

The Nation, June 26, 1929, pp. 772-773.

8.   There *Are* Silent Pictures: *Four Feathers* (1929), dir. Merian C. Cooper, Ernest B. Schoedsack, & Lothar Mendes; *Evangeline* (1929), dir. Edward Carewe; *The Single Standard* (1929), dir. John S. Robertson; *Nana* (1926), dir. Jean Renoir; *The Constant Nymph* (1928), dir. Adrian Brunel; *Piccadilly* (1929), dir. E. A. Dupont; *The Fight for Matterhorn* (1928), dir. Mario Bonnard & Nunzio Malasomma; *In Old Siberia*, a.k.a. *Penal Servitude* (1928), dir. Yuli Raizman; *The Village of Sin*, a.k.a. *Women of Ryazan* (1927), dir. Olga Preobrazhenskaya & Ivan Pravov; *The Passion of Joan of Arc* (1928), dir. Carl-Theodor Dreyer.
       The Nation, August 21, 1929, pp. 203-204.

9.   The Talkies Advancing: *Applause* (1929), dir. Rouben Mamoulian; *Blackmail* (1929), dir. Alfred Hitchcock; *Sunny Side Up* (1929), dir. David Butler.
       The Nation, October 30, 1929, p. 503.

10.   Talkies and Dummies: *Disraeli* (1929), dir. Alfred E. Green; *Young Nowheres* (1929), dir. Frank Lloyd; *The Soul of France* (1928), dir. André Dugès & Alexandre Ryder; *Scandal* (1929), dir. Ivan Perestiani; *Rasputin* (1928), dir. Nikolai Larin & Boris Nevolin; *Sea Fever* (1928), dir. Alberto Cavalcanti.
       The Nation, November 13, 1929, pp. 562-563.

11.   A Miracle: *Arsenal* (1928), dir. Alexander Dovzhenko; *The Last Performance* (1929), dir. Paul Fejos.
       The Nation, November 27, 1929, p. 640.

12.   The Eye and the Heart: *The New Babylon* (1929), dir. Grigori Kozintsev & Leonid Trauberg; *Condemned* (1929), dir. Wesley Ruggles; *The Trespasser* (1929), dir. Edmund Goulding.
       The Nation, December 11, 1929, pp. 728-729.

13.   Mostly "For the Family": *The Taming of the Shrew* (1929), dir. Sam Taylor; *The Vagabond Lover* (1929), dir. Marshall Neilan; *Pandora's Box* (1929), dir. G. W. Pabst.
       The Nation, December 25, 1929, p. 784.

14. The Newsreel: *Devil-May-Care* (1929), dir. Sidney Franklin; *Lost Patrol* (1929), dir. Walter Summers.
     The Nation, January 8, 1930, p. 54.

15. As You Were: *The Virginian* (1929), dir. Victor Fleming; *The Mighty* (1929), dir. John Cromwell; *The Laughing Lady* (1929), dir. Victor Schertzinger; *Springtime* (1929), dir. Walt Disney.
     The Nation, January 22, 1930, pp. 106, 108.

16. Screen Musical Comedy I: *The Love Parade* (1929), dir. Ernst Lubitsch; *Sally* (1929), dir. John Francis Dillon.
     The Nation, February 5, 1930, pp. 159-160.

17. A Soviet Fantasy: *A Fragment of an Empire* (1929), dir. Fridrikh Ermler; *Demon of the Steppes* (1926), dir. Cheslav Sabinsky & Lev Sheffer; *The Last Night* (1928), dir. A. W. Sandberg; *Son of the Gods* (1930), dir. Frank Lloyd; *The Rogue Song* (1930), dir. Lionel Barrymore.
     The Nation, February 19, 1930, p. 226.

18. Inflated "Grandeur": *Happy Days* (1929), dir. Benjamin Stoloff; *Puttin' on the Ritz* (1930), dir. Edward Sloman; *The Green Goddess* (1930), dir. Alfred E. Green; *Not So Dumb* (1930), dir. King Vidor.
     The Nation, March 5, 1930, p. 280.

19. Color: *The Vagabond King* (1930), dir. Ludwig Berger; *Song of the West* (1930), dir. Ray Enright; *Men Without Women* (1930), dir. John Ford.
     The Nation, March 19, 1930, p. 337

20. Small Mercies: *China Express*, a.k.a. *The Blue Express* (1929), dir. Ilya Trauberg; *Sarah and Son* (1930), dir. Dorothy Arzner; *Anna Christie* (1930), dir. Clarence Brown.
     The Nation, April 2, 1930, pp. 404, 406.

21. Delightful Lunacy: *The Man from Blankley's* (1930), dir. Alfred E. Green; *Song o' My Heart* (1930), dir. Frank Borzage; *Mammy* (1930), dir. Michael Curtiz.
     The Nation, April 16, 1930, p. 465.

22. *Journey's End* (1930), dir. James Whale; *Under a Texas Moon* (1930), dir. Michael Curtiz.

The Nation, April 30, 1930, pp. 524-525.

23. Eisenstein's Latest: *Old and New*, a.k.a. *The General Line* (1929), dir. Sergei Eisenstein; *Paramount on Parade* (1930), dir. Dorothy Arzner, Orro Brower, Edmund Goulding, Victor Heerman, Edwin H. Knopf, Rowland V. Lee, Ernst Lubitsch, Lother Mendes, Victor Schertzinger, A. Edward Sutherland, & Frank Tuttle; *Hold Everything* (1930), dir. Roy Del Ruth.
The Nation, May 14, 1930, pp. 577-578.

24. American Natives and Nature: *The Silent Enemy* (1930), dir. H. P. Carver; *Asphalt* (1929), dir. Joe May; *King of Jazz* (1930), dir. John Murray Anderson; *The Song of the Flame* (1930), dir. Alan Crosland.
The Nation, May 28, 1930, p. 632.

25. Stark War: *All Quiet on the Western Front* (1930), dir. Lewis Milestone; *Turksib* (1929), dir. Viktor A. Turin.
The Nation, June 11, 1930, p. 688.

26. A Lesson from Moscow: *Cain and Artem* (1929), dir. Pavel Petrov-Bytov.
The Nation, June 25, 1930, p. 739.

27. At the South Pole: *With Byrd at the South Pole* (1930, doc.), dir. Julian Johnson; *The Big Pond* (1930), dir. Hobart Henley; *Caught Short* (1930), dir. Charles Reisner.
The Nation, July 9, 1930, pp. 49-50.

28. Enter Japan: *Slums of Tokyo*, a.k.a. *Crossroads* (1928), dir. Teinosuke Kinugasa; *Juno and the Paycock* (1930), dir. Alfred Hitchcock.
The Nation, July 23, 1930, p. 104.

29. Where Broadway Scores: *Holiday* (1930), dir. Edward H. Griffith; *The Big House* (1930), dir. George Hill; *Raffles* (1930), dir. George Fitzmaurice.
The Nation, August 6, 1930, pp. 160-161.

30. Ingredients: *The Dawn Patrol* (1930), dir. Howard Hawks; *Manslaughter* (1930), dir. George Abbott; *Grumpy* (1930), dir. George Cukor & Cyril Gardner.
The Nation, August 20, 1930, pp. 209-210.

31. Devil or Angel: *Hell's Angels* (1929), dir. Howard Hughes; *Moby Dick* (1930), dir. Lloyd Bacon.
    The Nation, September 3, 1930, p. 254.

32. Griffith's New Epic: *Abraham Lincoln* (1930), dir. D. W. Griffith; *Old English* (1930), dir. Alfred E. Green.
    The Nation, September 17, 1930, p. 305.

33. Screen Musical Comedy II: *Monte Carlo* (1930), dir. Ernst Lubitsch; *Animal Crackers* (1930), dir. Victor Heerman; *Storm over Asia* (1928), dir. Vsevolod Pudovkin.
    The Nation, October 1, 1930, pp. 356-357.

34. The Grafted Narrative: *The White Hell of Pitz Palu* (1929), dir. Arnold Fanck & G. W. Pabst; *Outward Bound* (1930), dir. Robert Milton; *Young Woodley* (1930), dir. Thomas Bentley.
    The Nation, October 15, 1930, p. 424.

35. Mother of Us All: *Earth* (1930), dir. Alexander Dovzhenko; *Swing You Sinners!* (1930), dir. Dave Fleischer; *What a Widow!* (1930), dir. Allan Dwan.
    The Nation, October 29, 1930, pp. 480, 482.

36. The Romantic Western: *Billy the Kid* (1930), dir. King Vidor; *The Big Trail* (1930), dir. Raoul Walsh; *The Girl of the Golden West* (1930), dir. John Francis Dillon; *Murder!* (1930), dir. Alfred Hitchcock; *Zwei Herzen im ¾ Takt* (1930), dir. Géza von Bolváry.
    The Nation, November 12, 1930, pp. 534, 536.

37. The Wages of Talent: *Kismet* (1930), dir. John Francis Dillon; *Playboy of Paris* (1930), dir. Ludwig Berger.
    The Nation, November 26, 1930, pp. 590-591.

38. The Travel Picture: *Wild Men of the Kalihari* (1930; doc), dir. C. Ernest Cadle; *Hunting Tigers in India* (1930, doc.), dir. George Dyott; *Mediterranean Cruise* (1930); *Morocco* (1930), dir. Josef von Sternberg; *Just Imagine* (1930), dir. David Butler.
    The Nation, December 10, 1930, pp. 657-658.

39. Selling Sophistication: *Fast and Loose* (1930), dir. Fred C. Newmeyer; *Laughter* (1930), dir. Harry d'Abbadie d'Arrast; *Igdenbu* (1930), dir.

Amo Bek-Nazaryan; *Razlom*, a.k.a. *The Break-Up* (1930), dir. Lev Zamkovoy.
The Nation, December 24, 1930, pp. 713-714.

40. One Notable Achievement: *Sous les toits de Paris* (1930), dir. René Clair; *The Blue Angel* (1930), dir. Josef von Sternberg; *The Royal Family of Broadway* (1930), dir. George Cukor & Cyril Gardner.
The Nation, January 7, 1931, pp. 25-26.

41. The Underworld: *The Criminal Code* (1931), dir. Howard Hawks; *Paid* (1930), dir. Sam Wood; *The Devil to Pay!* (1930), dir. George Fitzmaurice.
The Nation, January 21, 1931, pp. 80-81.

42. Shaw's First Movie: *How He Lied to Her Husband* (1931), dir. Cecil Lewis; *Al-Yemen* (1931), dir. Vladimir Shneyderov.
The Nation, February 4, 1931, p. 135.

43. Glories of the Epic: *Cimarron* (1931), dir. Wesley Ruggles; *The Fighting Caravans* (1931), dir. Otto Brower & David Burton.
The Nation, February 18, 1931, p. 199.

44. Chaplin Falters: *City Lights* (1931), dir. Charlie Chaplin; *Trader Horn* (1931), dir. W. S. Van Dyke.
The Nation, March 4, 1931, pp. 250-251.

45. Nature and Artifice: *Rango* (1931), dir. Ernest B. Schoedsack; *Westfront 1918* (1930), dir. G. W. Pabst; *The Easiest Way* (1931), dir. Jack Conway; *Pagliacci* (1931), dir. Joe W. Coffman.
The Nation, March 18, 1931, p. 305.

46. With Benefit of Music: *H₂O* (1929, doc. short), dir. Ralph Steiner; *Surf and Seaweed* (1931, doc. short), dir. Ralph Steiner; *Mechanical Principles* (1931, doc. short), dir. Ralph Steiner.
The Nation, April 1, 1931, p. 359.

47. Too Much Halo: *The Front Page* (1931), dir. Lewis Milestone; *Tabu* (1931), dir. F. W. Murnau.
The Nation, April 15, 1931, pp. 429-430.

48. Children for the Grown-ups: *Skippy* (1931), dir. Norman Taurog; *Dirigible* (1931), dir. Frank Capra; *Birds of a Feather* (1931, animated short), dir. Burt Gillett; *Cities and Years* (1930, Yevgeni Chervyakov).

The Nation, April 29, 1931, p. 485.

49. The German Invasion: *Zwei Herzen im ¾ Takt* (1930), dir. Géza von Bolváry; *Wien, du Stadt der Lieder* (1930), dir. Richard Oswald; *Skandal um Eva* (1930), dir. G. W. Pabst; *Das Mädel von der Reeperbahn* (1930), dir. Karl Anton; *Lumpenball* (1930), dir. Karl Heinz Wolff. *The Nation*, May 13, 1931, p. 538.

50. The Shrinking of Personality: *The Millionaire* (1931), dir. John G. Adolfi; *Svengali* (1931), dir. Archie Mayo; *Born to Love* (1931), dir. Paul L. Stein; *Subway Express* (1931), dir. Fred C. Newmeyer. *The Nation*, May 27, 1931, p. 590.

51. Fantasy All the Way: *Le Million* (1931), dir. René Clair; *The Smiling Lieutenant* (1931), dir. Ernst Lubitsch; *Liebeswalzer* (1930), dir. Wilhelm Thiele; *The Beggar's Opera* (1931), dir. G. W. Pabst. *The Nation*, June 10, 1931, pp. 645-646.

52. Hollywood "Entertains": *White Shoulders* (1931), dir. Melville W. Brown; *The Lady Who Dared* (1931), dir. William Beaudine; *Lover Come Back* (1931), dir. Erie C. Kenton; *The She-Wolf* (1931), dir. James Flood; *The Maltese Falcon* (1931), dir. Roy Del Ruth; *A Free Soul* (1931), dir. Clarence Brown; *The Five-Year Plan*, a.k.a. *Enthusiasm* (1931, newsreel); *The Headache* (1931, short), dir. Billy House; *Moving In* (1931, short), dir. Albert Ray. *The Nation*, June 24, 1931, p. 687.

53. Love and Sex: *Transgression* (1931), dir. Herbert Brenon; *Men Call It Love* (1931), dir. Edgar Selwyn; *Chances* (1931), dir. Allan Dwan; *The Skin Game* (1931), dir. Alfred Hitchcock. *The Nation*, July 8, 1931, p. 47.

54. Lectures from the Screen: *Hell Below Zero* (1931, doc.), dir. Carveth Wells; *The Mystery of Life* (1930, doc.), dir. George Cochrane. *The Nation*, July 22, 1931, pp. 94-95.

55. Out of Their Own Mouths: *The Common Law* (1931), dir. Paul L. Stein; *A Jew at War* (1931), dir. Grigori Roshal; *The Immortal Vagabond* (1930), dir. Gustav Ucicky & Joe May. *The Nation*, August 19, 1931, p. 192.

56. Emasculated Dreiser: *An American Tragedy* (1931), dir. Josef von Sternberg; *The Miracle Woman* (1931), dir. Frank Capra; *Bought!* (1931), dir. Archie Mayo.
The Nation, September 2, 1931, p. 237.

57. Sidewalks of New York: *Street Scene* (1931), dir. King Vidor.
The Nation, September 16, 1931, p. 290.

58. Hollywood Tries "Ideas": *As You Desire Me* (1932), dir. George Fitzmaurice; *Forgotten Commandments* (1932), dir. Louis J. Gasnier & William Schorr; *Two Seconds* (1932), dir. Mervyn LeRoy; *Monte Carlo Madness* (1932), dir. Hanns Schwarz.
The Nation, June 22, 1932, p. 708.

59. Morals, Facts, and Fiction: *Bring 'Em Back Alive* (1932), dir. Clyde E. Elliott; *The Doomed Battalion* (1932), dir. Cyril Gardner; *The Dark Horse* (1932), dir. Alfred E. Green.
The Nation, July 6, 1932, p. 18.

60. Personality or Talent?: *Make Me a Star* (1932), dir. William Beaudine.
The Nation, July 20, 1932, p. 63.

61. Nonsense and Satire: *Million Dollar Legs* (1932), dir. Edward F. Cline; *What Price Hollywood?* (1932), dir. George Cukor.
The Nation, August 3, 1932, p. 111.

62. Madness from Hollywood: *Horse Feathers* (1932), dir. Norman Z. McLeod; *American Madness* (1932), dir. Frank Capra.
The Nation, August 31, 1932, pp. 198-199.

63. Three Premature Births: *Love Me Tonight* (1932), dir. Rouben Mamoulian; *Life Begins* (1932), dir. James Flood; *Back Street* (1932), dir. John M. Stahl.
The Nation, September 14, 1932, p. 239.

64. Intermission: *Strange Interlude* (1932), dir. Robert Z. Leonard.
The Nation, September 28, 1932, p. 292.

65. School Days: *Mädchen in Uniform* (1931), dir. Leontine Sagan; *Goona-Goona* (1932), dir. Armand Denis & André Roosevelt; *The Night of June 13th* (1932), dir. Stephen Roberts; *Le Bal* (1931), dir. Wilhelm Thiele.

The Nation, October 12, 1932, p. 338.

66. Class War: *Cabin in the Cotton* (1932), dir. Michael Curtiz; *A Bill of Divorcement* (1932), dir. George Cukor.
The Nation, October 26, 1932, pp. 409-410.

67. Going into Politics: *Washington Merry-Go-Round* (1932), dir. James Cruze.
The Nation, November 9, 1932, p. 466.

68. Captive Comrades: *Kameradschaft* (1931), dir. G. W. Pabst; *I Am a Fugitive from a Chain Gang* (1932), dir. Mervyn LeRoy; *Once in a Lifetime* (1932), dir. Russell Mack.
The Nation, November 23, 1932, pp. 513-514.

69. Gastronomy: *Trouble in Paradise* (1932), dir. Ernst Lubitsch; *The Kid from Spain* (1932), dir. Leo McCarey; *Kongo* (1932), dir. William J. Cowen; *The Most Dangerous Game* (1932), dir. Irving Pichel & Ernest B. Schoedsack; *The Conquerors* (1932), dir. William A. Wellman.
The Nation, December 7, 1932, p. 576.

70. A Novel Idea: *If I Had a Million* (1932), dir. James Cruze & H. Bruce Humberstone; *The Sign of the Cross* (1932), dir. Cecil B. DeMille; *With Williamson Beneath the Sea* (1932, doc.), dir. J. E. Williamson.
The Nation, December 21, 1932, p. 624.

71. Hemingway in Hollywood: *A Farewell to Arms* (1932), dir. Frank Borzage.
The Nation, January 4, 1933, p. 28.

72. More Celluloid: *Rasputin and the Empress* (1932), dir. Richard Boleslawski & Charles Brabin; *Cynara* (1932), dir. King Vidor; *The Half-Naked Truth* (1932), dir. Gregory La Cava; *Silver Dollar* (1932), dir. Alfred E. Green.
The Nation, January 18, 1933, p. 76.

Essays & Articles in Various Publications

1. The Artistic Possibilities of the Cinema.
Kinematograph and Lantern Weekly (August 1913). Reprinted in *National Board of Review Magazine*, 3, no. 11 (November 1928): pp. 3-5.

2. The Cinema as Art.
    The Drama (Chicago), 6, no. 22 (May 1916): pp. 267-284.

3. The Problem of the Artistic Cinema.
    Proscenium, no. 1 (1919).

4. The New Art of the Moving Picture.
    Theatre Arts Monthly, 11, no. 4 (April 1927): pp. 277-282.

5. Impressions in a Studio: Life Mirrored in Films.
    New York Times, May 29, 1927, DRAMA (section 7): p. 4.

6. The Road to Art in the Motion Picture.
    Theatre Arts Monthly, 11, no. 6 (June 1927): pp. 455-462.

7. Drama and the Screen.
    New York Times, August 7, 1927, DRAMA (section 7): p. 5.

8. Vaudeville on Screen.
    New York Times, September 11, 1927, DRAMA (section 8): p. 4.

9. A Knight-Errant [on Chaplin].
    The Dial, 84, no. 5 (May 1928): pp. 413-414.

10. Hollywood Speaks.
    The Nation, September 26, 1928, pp. 285-286.

11. The Future of the Movies.
    The Nation, October 10, 1928, pp. 360, 362, 364.

12. Introducing the Dramatic Accent.
    Movie Makers, 3, no. 12 (December 1928): pp. 788-789.

13. The Movie Scene: Notes on Sound and Silence.
    Theatre Arts Monthly, 13, no. 2 (February 1929): pp. 97-107.

14. The Talkies.
    The Nation, February 20, 1929, pp. 236, 238.

15. Free-Lancers.
    The Nation, March 13, 1929, pp. 324, 326.

16. The Art of Directing.
    Movie Makers, 4, no. 4 (April 1929): pp. 234-235, 250.

17. New Dimensions in the Talkies.
    The Nation, December 24, 1930, pp. 702-703.

18. The Plastic Structure: Dynamic Composition.
    Experimental Cinema, no. 1 (February 1930): pp. 2-3.

19. S.O.S.
     The Nation, August 5, 1931, p. 142.
20. Concerning Dialogue.
     The Nation, August 17, 1932, pp. 151-152.
21. Acting and the Movies.
     New York Times, May 5, 1935, p. X4.
22. New Paths for the Musical Film.
     New York Times, June 9, 1935, DRAMA: p. 4.

Index